Contemporary Perspectives on
Serial Murder

D0862154

Ronald M. Holmes
Stephen T. Holmes
Editors

SAGE Publications
International Educational and Professional Publisher
Thousand Oaks   London   New Delhi

For information:

 SAGE Publications, Inc.
2455 Teller Road
Thousand Oaks, California 91320
E-mail: order@sagepub.com

SAGE Publications Ltd.
6 Bonhill Street
London EC2A 4PU
United Kingdom

SAGE Publications India Pvt. Ltd.
M-32 Market
Greater Kailash I
New Delhi 110 048 India

Printed in the United States of America

Library of Congress Cataloging-in-Publication Data

Main entry under title:

Contemporary perspectives on serial murder / edited by Ronald M. Holmes, Stephen T. Holmes.
 p. cm.
Includes bibliographical references and index.
ISBN 0-7619-1420-X (cloth: acid-free paper)
ISBN 0-7619-1421-8 (pbk.: acid-free paper)
 1. Serial murders—United States. 2. Serial murderers—United States—Psychology. 3. Serial murder investigation—United States.
I. Holmes, Ronald M. II. Holmes, Stephen T.
 HV6529 .C66 1998
 364.15'23'0973—ddc21   98-8948

This book is printed on acid-free paper.

05 06 07 08 10 9 8 7 6 5

Contemporary
Perspectives on
Serial
Murder

Contents

Preface

———————

Serial murder is a most baffling crime. Although it captures the attention of most citizens, it also repels the sensibilities of those who are susceptible to the suffering and victimization of several hundred people yearly.

The history of serial murder remains a mystery and an unknown quantity to those who are not interested in the study or investigation of serial murder. There are relatively few accurate academic treatises that deal with the subject matter of serial murder. Most writings are of the true-crime genre. These books deal with serial killers and their crimes and are often rife with errors and gross exaggerations. Some works of fiction, such as Thomas Harris's *The Red Dragon* and *The Silence of the Lambs,* are often more realistic—and more accurate—than the true-crime books. Many academics decry the themes in Harris's two books, but these are the same academics who have neither spoken to nor interviewed a murderer, much less a serial killer.

Serial murder became a major social concern only within the past 30 years. A new type of murderer emerged on the landscape of the United States and was first identified as a serial killer by Dr. Donald Lunde in his work, *Murder and Madness.* Since that time, knowledge, awareness, and a dedication to the eradication of the serial murder "problem" would become almost an addiction for those both inside and outside the criminal justice enterprise. The list of these early serial killers included such murderers as Jerry Brudos, David Berkowitz, Albert DeSalvo, and Edmund Kemper. Ted Bundy kept the mystique alive well into the late 1980s. New names have emerged since then as a litany of unholy saints: Robert Berdella, Westley Dodd, Douglas Clark, Donald Harvey, and many others. New names also become known in the academic study and investigation of the serial murderer. Names such as Eric Hickey, Steve Egger, Elliott Leyton, Jack Levin, Philip Jenkins, and others (please forgive us if we have failed to mention you) became the leading academics in the study of sequential homicide. Law enforcement professionals also made the news: Herb Swindler, Jerry Thompson, Mike Fisher, Don Patchen, Dr. Al C. Carlisle, and Ken Katsaris all became names connected with the Ted Bundy case. Other law enforcement professionals became attached to other cases, including killers such as John Gacy, Douglas Clark, Angelo Buono and Kenneth Bianchi, Wayne Williams, and many others. The study and the investigation of serial murder took on a life of its own, feeding the appetite of the interested public with both true stories and stories mixed with some facts and the ideas of true-crime authors such as Ann Rule, Darcy O'Brien, Stephen Michaud, and Hugh Aynesworth, among others. They estimated that almost one of four murders was the act of a serial killer! This was hardly the case, but it made some sense to the public, which had an appetite that was not easily satisfied.

The examination of the serial murder problem typically has been centered around either the theoretical issues of serial murder, including etiology, basis characteristics, and so on, or the investigation of serial murder cases. Academic books such as *Serial Murder* by Holmes and DeBurger, *Serial Killers and Their Victims* by Hickey, *Serial Murder: The Elusive Phenomenon* by Egger, *The Social Construction of Homicide* by Jenkins, Leyton's *Hunting Humans,* as well as Levin and Fox's *Mass Murder* were important works that examined the mind and the crimes of the serial killer.

The Federal Bureau of Investigation (FBI) wants us to rely upon their data, which are highly suspect. The FBI never made available their list of 36 serial killer subjects, nor did the Bureau permit social or behavioral scientists to examine the interviewing protocol. Society was so anxious to learn about the serial killer problem and the murderers themselves that we permitted their study to become the benchmark for all other research. Only recently has there been a movement to study serial killers by people other than federal law enforcement officials.

Other academics, such as Drs. Ronald and Stephen Holmes, Kim Rossmo, and Robert Keppel, have published books and articles about the investigation of the serial murder problem. Holmes and Holmes, for example, have written several books and articles on serial murder investigation. Keppel also wrote a book for law enforcement agents on the perils and pitfalls in the investigation of a serial murder case. Rossmo has emerged as the nation's authority on the impact of geography and serial murder. "Geoforensic analysis" has become an important tool, as has criminal investigation assessment (once called psychological profiling). There are new tools used, but old problems still exist.

As researchers in serial murder, we have kept abreast of the writings and advances in the understanding of serial murder. At the beginning of the 1980s, few articles existed concerning the serial murder problem. At mid-decade, however, articles were being published, and some became classics. For example, an article by Holmes and DeBurger in *Federal Probation*, titled "Profiles in Terror: The Serial Murderer," became a focal point for discussion among the academics, practitioners, and students of serial murder. Other articles soon followed. Early on, Egger discussed the problems of linkage blindness in his article, "A Working Definition of Serial Murder and the Reduction of Linkage Blindness"; Jenkins's work, "Serial Murder in England 1940-1985," made us aware of the fact that serial murder was not solely a North American problem. Serial killers existed in Europe—not to the same extent as in the United States, perhaps, but they did practice their deadly trade in England, Russia, Romania, Sweden, and other countries. Jenkins also made us consider the reality of African Americans being serial killers. Female serial killers were also examined by Hickey, Ronald and Stephen Holmes, and others.

For the past 10 years, Ronald Holmes has been teaching a class on murder in the United States. Obviously, he has used a variety of texts, including *Murder in America, Serial Murder,* and *Profiling Violent Crimes.* He has also adopted Eric Hickey's book on several occasions because he knows that Hickey needs the money for his Rogaine treatments. Holmes has also prepared handouts and made mandatory readings for the students from his own readings in serial murder. What he has found is that there is no single repository for readings on serial murder. The student must spend valuable time finding and then reading the articles.

Keeping this in mind, Steve and I decided that it was time for someone to prepare a reader for the serious students of serial murder. We have gathered selected readings; some are the classic articles on this emerging field of academic study, and the others have been deliberately written for this book. We thank the authors of both the new articles and those previously published.

Steve and I also thank the students and other professionals, both academic and professional, who may read this book. We sincerely believe it will fill a void that presently exists on the market and in the classroom.

PART I

WHAT IS SERIAL MURDER? THE CHARACTER AND THE EXTENT

Serial murder is relatively new in the United States, and the study of the serial killer is even newer. Not until the 1980s was there serious literature devoted to the topic. Certainly, true-crime stories were written about murders, but seldom was a connection made between the crimes and the possibility of a serial killer being the perpetrator. Actually, there was a formula used to ensure that the article or book would be accepted by the true-crime genre. One part of the formula included the apprehension and punishment of the killer or killers. Seldom mentioned were cases that depicted several victims fatally dispatched over a period of time; in other words, a case of serial murder or sequential homicide.

What is serial murder, and how does it differ from "traditional" homicide? Serial murder is the killing of three or more people over a period of more than 30 days, with a significant cooling-off period between the murders (Egger, 1993; Hickey, 1996; Holmes, 1997; Jenkins, 1994). The baseline number of three victims appears to be most common among those who are the academic authorities in the field. The time frame also appears to be an agreed-upon component of the definition. The time between the murders serves as a distinguishing factor and separates serial murder from mass murder and spree murder. Spree murder usually

1

involves the commission of a felony at the same time, whereas mass murder results when the victims are all killed at one time and in one place. Charles Starkweather serves as a good example of a spree murderer. James Oliver Huberty, who killed 21 people at a McDonald's restaurant in California, is an example of a mass murderer.

Multicide Classification

	Mass Murder	Spree Murder	Serial Murder
Victims	At least 3	At least 3	At least 3
Events	One event	At least 3 events	At least 3 events
Location	One location	At least 3 locations	At least 3 locations
Cooling-off period	No	No	Yes

In this section, the basic elements of serial murder will be examined. We take a controversial stand when we place early multiple killers such as Bonnie and Clyde, Billy the Kid, Ma Barrow, and, more recently, Richard Kuklinski as serial killers. In our latest book, the second edition of *Serial Murder*, we treat this type of serial killer as a comfort-type sequential predator. Not all academics agree with the position that those who kill for material gain are serial killers. Our position is that the number of victims, the motivation, and the anticipated gain (material or psychological) are all integral to the definition of a serial killer. In other words, we believe that one can kill serially for money or for sex and still be termed a serial killer.

The first chapter in this reader, Holmes and DeBurger's article "Profiles in Terror: The Serial Killer," first appeared in *Federal Probation* in 1985. This was one of the first endeavors to offer a typology of male serial killers. This typology—visionary, mission, hedonistic, and power/control—is now perhaps one of the best known and most often cited as a meaningful way to list the various types of serial killers, to understand their mindsets, and to aid in the investigation of serial homicides. The visionary serial killer is compelled to kill by visions or voices. The mission serial murderer kills "bad" or "undeserving" people; those who, in his own mind, are a detriment to the good people of society. This desire to eliminate those "undeserving" people comes not from voices or visions but from the killer's own moral or ethical structure. The hedonistic serialist has three subtypes: lust, thrill, and comfort. The first two kill for sex; the third kills for creature-comfort reasons, such as money, insurance benefits, or business interests. The fourth type is the power/control serial killer (the Ted Bundy type). This killer receives gratification from the absolute power he has over the destiny of another human being. Holmes and DeBurger's article was a forerunner of *Serial Murder*, which was published in 1988 and written by the same authors. Drs. Ronald and Stephen Holmes wrote the second edition of *Serial Murder*, which has just been published. Dr. James DeBurger has recently retired.

In the second chapter, Dr. Philip Jenkins, from Pennsylvania State University, gives the reader insight into the commission of serial murder by African Americans. His article, "African-Americans and Serial Homicide," quickly puts to rest the myth that serial killers are white males. Citing examples, explaining the role of race, and explaining basic etiological considerations, the author provides the reader with a wealth of information. This article has emerged as a leader in the understanding of the nonwhite serial killer. Are African-American serial killers fundamentally different from white serial killers? Is the stalking methodology different? Are the motivations and anticipated gains different? Jenkins discusses these and other issues.

The third chapter in this section deals with the female serial killer. Written by Dr. Robert Hale and Andrew Bolin of Southeastern Louisiana University, it gives the reader basic information concerning the history of female serial killers, and it is carefully illustrated by selected case histories. The fourth chapter, written by Drs. Stephen T. Holmes, Central Florida State University; Eric Hickey, University of California at Fresno; and Ronald M. Holmes, University of Louisville, was first to examine female serial killers, and it offered a typology similar to the one developed by Holmes and DeBurger in 1985. Disputing the FBI's claim that Aileen Wuornos was America's first female serial killer, this article offers a typology of female serialists in an attempt to better understand their mentality. The typology includes the disciple killer, the visionary killer, the comfort killer, and others. In examining the offered typology, the authors determined that not only are women serial killers, and of different types, but that their motives and anticipated gains are similar to their male counterparts.

The first part of this book will provide the reader with basic information concerning the history and types of serial killers. After reading this material, the student of serial murder will be in an intellectual position to move to the second section, The Mind of the Serial Killer.

1

Profiles in Terror

The Serial Murderer

———————

RONALD M. HOLMES
JAMES E. DeBURGER

Homicide is a crime which has historically galvanized public attention to the work of law enforcement personnel. In past decades, when the situational context of most homicides ensured or at least enhanced the probability of rapid solution, law enforcement personnel were lauded for their investigative skills. In recent years, however, both the public and those in law enforcement have expressed frustration and concern regarding the growing number of unsolved murders in this Nation. Since 1960, the solution rate for homicides has declined from over 90 percent to approximately 76 percent in 1983 (*Newsweek*, 1984). This dramatic decline in the solution rate coincides with a period of increasing sophisticated technology and an increase in the number of police officers per capita. Given the increased technology available for scientific investigation of these violent crimes, a fair conclusion is that the decrease in the solution rate can be attributed more reasonably to the character of many contemporary homicides than to the ability of the investigators. While about 20 percent of all homicides today have no apparent motive, in 1966 only 6 percent of all homicides were motiveless. Many of the currently unsolved homicides are believed to have been perpetrated by serial murderers.

———————

Authors' Note: This chapter first appeared in 1985 in *Federal Probation, 39,* 29-34. Reprinted with permission.

Serial murder, the focus of this article, is not a totally new kind of criminal behavior. Generally, however, this crime represents the emergence of a form of homicide which is very different from murders commonly investigated in earlier times. Stranger-perpetrated, this form of murder often reflects neither passion nor premeditation stemming from motives of personal gain.

More frequently, it tends to reflect non-rational or irrational motives or goals and its victims stand in a depersonalized relationship to the perpetrator. One alarming aspect of contemporary serial murder is the extent to which its perpetrators believe that violence against human beings is a normal and acceptable means of implementing their goals or motives. While the major purpose here is to describe a systematic typology of serial murders, an initial comment will be made on the significance of violence in the everyday social context as a possible contributory factor in the emergence of this form of violent crime.

Social-Cultural Context of Violence

There is growing evidence to support the view that social and cultural factors in postindustrial American society tend to enhance the probability of interpersonal causes and perpetration of criminal violence. And it also seems likely that serial murder represents an advanced form of, not an ultimate extension of, violence; for here is a form of homicide which by rational standards is pointless and unaccompanied by remorse or a sense of responsibility on the part of the perpetrator. Studies by Wolfgang and his associates on the subculture of violence (Wolfgang and Ferracuti, 1982; Wolfgang and Weiner, 1982) have clearly demonstrated the ways in which personal and contextual factors may interact to produce violent criminal behavior. It is difficult to establish the specific mechanisms by which a culture of violence may be translated into specific criminal acts such as serial murder. But it seems likely that the basic processes of socialization which affect individual behavior from childhood through adulthood are saturated with a potential for violence in interpersonal relations.

Both in terms of contemporary life in America and in terms of this society's European roots, there is a fertile cultural seedbed of violent examples for behavior. Currently, violence as a "normal" or appropriate response in many situations has explicit or implied approval in many facets of our American culture. This may stem largely from the recurrent, extensive, and essentially "pointless" violence that is commonly portrayed in mass media. There is a sensitivity-dulling exposure to it that reaches all age groups and pervades the waking hours of both children and adults. Television depicts violence in movies and in videos; rock stars, in their entertainment acts, make use of hammers, swords, clubs, etc. One study of children's TV programs by a Senate Committee found 16 violent incidents per broadcast hour. Such material connotes at least passive acceptance of violence. The news media provide further real-life examples of recourse to violence in politics, racial and ethic relations, labor relations, and the American family. The role of TV as an influence on personal acceptance of violence and as a precursor of violent behavior is still being researched and debated.

Historical and sociological study of American life has provided many examples of violence throughout our history. From very early days in this society, a passive acceptance of violence has existed. Our frontier was characterized by a poor system of law enforcement, little assurance that a judge would arrive in time for a hearing or trial, and a generally weak and uneven judicial system. In some areas, these conditions paved the way for initiation of a vigilante system. Vigilantism was a unique and often violent response to the conditions of frontier America. Often, vigilante leaders were social conservatives attempting to maintain what they perceived as necessary social order. Their victims, unfortunately, included a wide range of easily identified people—Blacks, Catholics, and others whose chief offenses lay in their unacceptable or unwelcome status. Even in contemporary America, political ideology of the powerful tends to legitimize the use of violence to protect the interests of the powerful. Our cultural norm which grants some acceptance to this use of violence probably stems largely from the frontier ideology.

Widespread individual acceptance of the perpetration of violence appears to be more predominant in the South and the West; however, it is suggested that there is a general increase in acceptance of violence throughout the Nation. Many urban minorities are arming themselves for protection against the new urban predators who seek to take their property or take their lives. The person growing up in American society tends to learn subtle lessons about violence which reinforce the positive aspects of interpersonal violence in certain situations.

Many people believe that violence is justifiable under certain circumstances; witness, for example, the growing acceptance of executions during the past decade. While many are repulsed by the idea of taking another person's life under any circumstances, others would justify this action in case of self-defense or other valid circumstances. In terms of criminal behavior, research clearly indicates that some have no reluctance whatever in resorting to violence in the course of crimes which are essentially property-related. Toward the polar end of the continuum of violence acceptance are those who see little or no intrinsic wrong in the murder of another human being. For example, serial killer Gerald Stano remarked that the killing of his victims was no different than stepping on a cockroach.

Aside from the contemporary social context and its possible contribution to violence, there exists a history of violence which includes commentary on an extreme form of violence—serial murder. A speaker recently introduced an address on this topic by saying that "serial murder is a product of the 1970s." But this is not accurate. The notoriety of the contemporary serial murderer has been widely covered by the printed media and also by television. Thus, a general impression exists that this type of homicidal predator has emerged only in the last few years. But this perception is not supported by a careful examination of literature on the topic, despite the fact that the names of contemporary serial murderers roll off the lips of criminal justice students like a litany of unholy saints—Gacy, Williams, Bundy, Lucas, Toole, Berkowitz, and others.

But historical study reveals other criminals who lived in much earlier times and committed atrocities of such magnitude that their names are not likely ever to be forgotten by serious students of homicide (Time, 1979; Science Digest; U.S. News). Gilles De Rais, a 15th century nobleman and confidante of Joan of Arc, is known to have tortured, raped, and killed more than 800 children. The gratification he received from his sadistic actions and necrophilia derived more from mutilation of the children than from traditional sexual relations. In the latter part of the 19th century, a man known as the "ogre of Hanover"—whose real name was Fritz Haarman—sodomized and murdered scores of young boys. Haarman reportedly obtained sexual pleasure by ripping out the throats of his young unfortunate victims (Holmes, 1983). But probably the most famous serial killer in all history was Jack the Ripper who lived in late 19th century England. His predilection for London prostitutes made his name a household word. According to learned estimates, however, his victims numbered not more than seven. The crimes of Jack the Ripper pale in comparison with the serial murders committed by contemporary killers such as Bundy, Lucas, and Toole.

Serial Killers: Geographically Stable and Transient

It should be apparent that there is a difference between mass murderers and serial murderers. Mass murderers kill a number of people in one place at one time. This type of killer usually exhibits a momentary frenzy and kills in his frenzy. He probably will not kill again. The serial killer murders a number of people over a long period of time.

There is a need to first identify serial killers in terms of their degree of spatial mobility. Two major forms can be noted. The *geographically stable* killer is one who typically lives in a particular area and kills his victims within the general region of his residence. John Wayne Gacy, for example, lived in Chicago. He was a well-known personality, a self-employed businessman, and an entertainer of children. Suspected of killing 33 young men and boys, he not only murdered his victims in or near his home, but buried them in such places as his crawl space in his home, in his attic, between the walls, under his patio and driveway, and other such unlikely places. Albert Fish, a resident of New York and self-confessed lust killer and cannibal of more than 200 young boys and girls, also was a geographically stable serial killer. One of the most famous serial killers is Wayne Williams. He was convicted of only two killings. However, his probable involvement in more than 30 killings of young black males in Atlanta qualifies him for classification as a geographically stable serial killer.

This type of homicidal predator is often employed in his own community, well-known and well-respected. His killings may occur over several years before his apprehension. The senselessness of his acts is a puzzle to law enforcement personnel since the usual motives for murder—spurned love, money, revenge—are missing. An additional source of great frustration is the lack of physical evidence usually accompanying homicide in these kinds of cases. The serial murderer kills for more exotic reasons—and these are reasons that are not immediately evident to the investigating officer. Very frequently, the motive is sexual in nature and the predator may slaughter a selected group of victims.

The other type who presents a different set of problems to law enforcement is the geographically transient serial killer. This type of serial murderer travels continually throughout his killing career. Typically he kills in one police jurisdiction and shrewdly moves to another. Consider Ted Bundy. Ted, a handsome former law student from Washington State, is suspected of killing more than a score of women in Washington, Utah, and Colorado. He eventually was apprehended and sentenced for the kidnapping of Carol DaRonch in Murray, Utah. Later taken to trial for the killing of Caryn Campbell, he escaped. His trail led to Chicago, East Lansing, Louisville, and finally to the campus of Florida State University in Tallahassee. Less than 2 weeks after his arrival, Bundy brutally attacked Lisa Levy, Margaret Bowman, Karen Chandler, and Kathy Kleiner at the Chi Omega Sorority House. Two blocks away, he broke into the home of Cheryl Thomas and assaulted her. Lisa and Margaret died as a result of this crime. Two weeks later, Ted killed his last victim, 12-year-old Kimberly Leach. When Don Patchen, supervisor of the Homicide and Assault Unit of the Tallahassee Police Department, interviewed Bundy regarding 36 cases of unsolved murder victims, Ted calmly told the veteran police officer that he could add one digit to that number. Patchen believes that Bundy has murdered more than 300 young women throughout the United States; many of these victims were from the great northwest. When Bundy was queried regarding the number of states in which he had killed, he admitted that his "entity" had killed in six different states (Michaud, Aynesworth, 1983; Patchen, 1984).

At this time, there is little known about Henry Lucas. But it can be safely said that his victims may be in the hundreds. At least 142 of his crimes have been verified. At times he has claimed responsibility for 365 killings and has led police officers to many grave sites.

Typology of Serial Murders

As is true of any specific type of human behavior, different people may have the same basic motive. This variation in behavior may stem from many factors. Social and behavioral scientists have developed a wide range of models for describing behavioral models. These models will not be reviewed here since our focus is on a specific type of a typical behavior-serial murder. Below, a typology is described which categorizes the major types of serial murderers. Within each type the motives which seem to predominate will be examined. In each type it will be apparent that the motives function to provide for the serial killer a personal justification for the violence he commits.

VISIONARY TYPE

Most serial murderers would not be considered psychotic. They are in touch with reality but have no feelings for others. By contrast, the "visionary type" is impelled to murder because he has heard voices or has seen visions which demand that he kill a certain person or a category of persons. For some the voice or vision that is perceived may be that of a demon; for others it may be from God. Consider the case of Harvey Carignan; he was convicted of killing six women. But it is believed he killed many, many more. All of his victims fell prey to Carignan because God told him to do it. He perceived the women as "bad" people and himself as God's instrument to do away with evil in the world. Another illustrative case is one in which a young male decapitated a 76-year-old woman and stabbed her lifeless body over 200 times. Within the next two weeks he assaulted three other elderly women, each time stabbing them in the neck and chest area. Upon apprehension, he related that he was possessed by a red demon who demanded this action and that he could find comfort only through killing.

Both killers heard voices that were only in their heads. Both operated because of a vision. One was god-mandated, the other was demon-mandated. These two subtypes give different justification for their actions even though the end product is the same, a homicide. The perpetration of violence is legitimized by the vision the serial killer "experienced." There is little doubt about the mental state of this type of serial killer. At times he is clearly out of touch with reality. He hears voices and sees visions. In psychiatric terms, this type of serial killer could be termed psychotic. A shrewd defense attorney could certainly make the case of an "insanity" plea.

MISSION-ORIENTED TYPE

The serial killer who has a mission to fulfill is one who consciously has a goal in his life to eliminate a certain identifiable group of people. He does not hear voices or see visions. However, he may decide on his own that it is his role to rid the world of a group of people who are "undesirable" or unworthy to live with other human beings. Recently, there was a case of four young women who were similarly murdered. All four victims frequented local night spots. One was a known prostitute, and the others had alleged reputations for casual sexual encounters. Their dress style appeared to advertise their personal availability and their willingness to participate in sex for money. The murderer of these women had a personal mission, a mission to rid his community of prostitutes. During the interrogation of the killer, not only was he aware of his killings but he verbalized a sense of pride because of rendering the community such a great service. The mission-oriented serial murderer is not psychotic; he does not hear voices or see visions. He has a self-imposed duty to rid the world of an unworthy group of people. The victims may be prostitutes, young women, Catholics, or any other group he defines as unworthy to live with decent people. He may be either an organized nonsocial or a disorganized asocial type (Hazelwood and Douglas, 1980; 2). He lives in the real world and interacts with it on a daily basis. Typically when this type of killer is arrested, his neighbors cannot believe that he is the person responsible for the deaths of so many people. Take the case of the above geographically stable, serial killer from Louisville. Neighbors described him as a nice young man who cared for the people in the neighborhood and was a social worker in a group home for convicted felons. No one had suspected him of murdering young women in his community.

HEDONISTIC TYPE

Physical evidence accompanying murders committed by the hedonistic type tend to be most striking and bizarre. Consider these examples.

The nude body of a young woman was discovered in an alley; her body had been mutilated, both breasts had been removed, and her vaginal vault had been crudely excised. In another case, in the summer of 1984, a street wino was found dead in a walkway in an urban area. The cause of death was internal bleeding. He was nude, and a crutch was found inserted seventeen inches into his rectum. As yet, no one has been arrested in either of these two cases.

Interview records with the hedonistic type reflect a perverted means of thrill-seeking. A young male presently awaiting sentencing in a multiple killing of young boys, described, with a gleam in his eyes, the great pleasure he received in killing the young men. He said that he felt a rush of excitation when he put the knife into the ribs of the young boys. Killing for him was a thrill, it was "pure" enjoyment. This is typical of the hedonistic serial murderer.

As difficult as it must be for most people to realize, there are some people who can kill simply for the thrill of it. These people kill not because of a goal in their life to rid the community of undesirables; neither do they kill because they hear voices or see visions. They kill because they enjoy it. They kill because the thrill becomes an end in itself. The lust murderer can be viewed as a subcategory of the hedonistic type because of the sexual enjoyment experienced in the homicidal act (Hazelwood and Douglas, 1980; 3). Anthropophagy, dismemberment, necrophilia or other forms of sexual aberration are prevalent in this form of serial killing. Often this type of serial killer is typically intelligent; less intelligent ones tend to be street smart. Apprehension of the hedonistic type is very difficult, especially if he is geographically transient. His method of killing, while sadistic and immeasurably pleasurable to him, makes investigation difficult for the law enforcement professional. He may be able to escape detection for years.

POWER/CONTROL-ORIENTED TYPE

The Power/Control-Oriented Type receives gratification from the complete control of the victim. Ted Bundy obviously experienced some great pleasure from exerting power and control in the killing of his victims. While one description of the killing of Kimberly Leach reports Bundy's sexual pleasure connected with the act, the fundamental source of pleasure is not sexual, it is the killer's ability to control and exert power over his helpless victim (Michaud and Aynesworth, 1983). In another case where there was indication of power-oriented behavior, the Red Demon Killer experienced orgasm while stabbing his victim (picquerism). Holding the power of life or death over a victim is symbolically the ultimate control that one person can exert over another.

By exerting complete control over the life of his victim, the murderer experiences pleasure and excitement, not from the sexual excitation or the rape, but from his belief that he does indeed have the power to do whatever he wishes to do to another human being who is completely helpless and within his total control. This type of serial murderer is not psychotic; he does not live in another world and is aware of the rules and regulations that he is expected to abide by. He chooses, however, to ignore them. He lives by his own code and typically fits the patterns of a psychopathic or sociopathic type of personality. His behavior indicates a character disorder, not a break from reality. While the power/control-oriented type and the hedonistic type are probably both psychopathic, they differ in that killing for the hedonist is simply pleasurable. The hedonist receives sexual gratification in the process of killing another person and may experience orgasm from knifing the victim (picquerism) or having sex with the corpse (necrophilia). The pleasure derived from the killing by the power/control-oriented type derives from his capture and control of his victim, rendering his victim powerless and helpless, while forcing the captive to obey his every command. The power/control-oriented type experiences a self-inflated sense of importance and power.

Serial Killers: General Characteristics

While it may be beneficial to cast serial murderers into various categories depending on their motives, it is just as necessary to indicate some of the general characteristics of the offender. These should be seen as characteristics, not causes of behavior. A fundamental difference exists between the two words; "characteristics" describe only what appear to be common variables whereas "causes" explain why certain behaviors occur. Rule (1984), an expert on serial murder, argues that it is impossible to speak in absolute terms when one is dealing with an aberrant personality. The majority of serial killers appear to share certain characteristics. First of all, most are white and are in the age group of 25 to 34 years of age. They are intelligent or at least "street smart." They are charming and charismatic; and many of them are psychopathic. Many, such as Edmund Kemper are "police groupies" and are fascinated by police work. Kemper frequently associated with off-duty police officers and questioned them about the progress which was being made on unsolved murders which he had committed. Serial killers often focus on one type of victim. Bundy selected young women, all with dark long hair parted in the middle. Williams chose young black males. It appears that the victim group shares two basic features: They are vulnerable and easy to control. Often serial murderers will use a ruse to gain access to their victims. Bundy, for example, frequently used a cast to simulate a broken arm to solicit sympathy and aid.

It is also interesting to note that serial killers appear to be highly mobile. Many will travel almost constantly, e.g., geographically transient type. They appear to be "night people." They appear to select, to stalk, and to kill their victims when most people are not as alert or aware of their personal vulnerability. They kill with "hands on" weapons such as knives, hands, fists; they have physical contact with their victims. In the beginning, their killings are elaborately planned. Toward the end of their killing careers, the plans disintegrate. They kill more in a "panic" and some kill more than one person at a time. Witness again the case of Bundy. He savagely attacked five women in the space of less than 2 hours; five were brutally beaten, and two killed. Normally, the serial killer waits, stalks, kills, waits, stalks, kills (Rule, 1980). Toward the end of his murderous career, there is little time between the waits and the kills.

Many of the known serial murderers were born out of wedlock. As children many were physically, sexually, or emotionally abused. These killers tend to abuse alcohol or drugs, and often this abuse exacerbates their sadistic fantasies. For example, their interest in media would lie more in the area of sadistic porn or other depictions of violence. Many are intimately involved with women who have no knowledge of their partner's homicidal activities. Sexual relationships with these women are often characterized by binding and other forms of sadistic behavior.

Serial Killers: A Problem
for the Criminal Justice System

The apprehension of serial killers by professionals in criminal justice appears to occur almost by accident. Due largely to the senselessness of their crimes, their mobility and intelligence, they may go on for years without being apprehended. Their killings are not of the "smoking gun" variety. One criminologist estimated that the number of serial murderers has tripled over the past two decades and that the overall murder-rate has more than doubled. Currently it is estimated that about 5,000 people each year are victims of serial killers. Contrary to the FBI's estimate of 30 serial killers roaming throughout the United States, this same criminologist believes that there are over 100. In a personal interview on death row in Florida, Ted Bundy suggested that the number is much higher (Rule, 1984; Newsweek, 1984; Bundy, 1985). Regardless of the number of serial murderers, the number of victims is significant. While other crimes such as robbery clearly affect more people, there should be no confusion when one speaks of the quality of an act versus the quantity of an act. In view of the mission of criminal justice, there can be no standard which uses numbers solely as a yardstick for action. The consideration of violence in the cultural context and comments here on the general characteristics of serial killers are intended solely to shed light on contemporary types of serial killers. But one compelling fact is apparent: There has appeared in contemporary times a class of homicidal predators who pose a clear and present danger to more than 5,000 Americans yearly. Certainly this is evidence enough that the criminal justice system take notice and develop a plan of action.

References

Bundy, Theodore. Personal Interview, 1985.

Darrach, Brad and Norris, Joel. "An American Tragedy," *Life* August 1984, p. 58.

Hazelwood, Robert R. and Douglas, John E. "The Lust Murder," *FBI Law Enforcement Bulletin*, April 1980, p. 1.

―――. "The Random Killers," *Newsweek*, November 26, 1984, p. 100.

Holmes, Ronald. *The Sex Offenders and the Criminal Justice System*. Springfield, Illinois, Thomas Publishing Co., 1983.

Michaud, Stephen and Aynesworth, Hugh. *The Only Living Witness*. New York, Linden Press, 1983.

Patchen, Donald. Personal Interview, 1984.

―――. "Profiling Serial Murders," *Science Digest*, October, 1984, p. 47.

―――. "Catching a New Breed of Killer," *Time*, November 14, 1983, p. 47.

―――. "The Mind of the Mass Murderer," *Time*, August, 1979.

Rule, Ann, *The Stranger Beside Me*. New York: W.W. Norton, 1980.

Rule, Ann, Personal Interview, 1984.

Wolfgang, Marvin E., and Ferracuti, Franco. *The Subculture of Violence*. Beverly Hills, CA. Sage Publications, 1982.

Wolfgang, Marvin E. and Weiner, Neil A. *Criminal Violence*, Beverly Hills, CA. Sage Publications, 1982.

2

African-Americans and Serial Homicide

PHILIP JENKINS

Introduction

The idea of serial murder has become well established in contemporary American culture, and it is difficult to avoid encountering celebrated names like Ted Bundy and Jeffrey Dahmer. However, there are other offenders who are quite as lethal, but who remain very obscure— names like Coral Watts, Milton Johnson, Calvin Jackson, or Alton Coleman. And often, these lesser-known offenders tend to be African-American individuals, customarily preying on Black victims. In other words, the popular stereotype of serial murder largely ignores the Black component of the phenomenon. This paper will try to assess the scale of African-American involvement in multiple homicide, and suggest why it has remained so relatively unexplored.

Creating a Stereotype

Popular interest in serial murder was awakened by celebrated cases of the late 1970s and early 1980s, such as the stories of Ted Bundy, David Berkowitz, Henry Lee Lucas and John Wayne Gacy. Public interest reached a new peak with the intense attention paid to the 1991 case of

Author's Note: This chapter first appeared in 1993 in the *American Journal of Criminal Justice*, 17(2), 47-60. Reprinted with permission.

Jeffrey Dahmer, in Milwaukee, Wisconsin, and the live coverage of his trial on national cable television over the following months. Numerous authorities on criminality and criminal psychology were interviewed in the media to provide insight into such cases, and these widely quoted opinions usually reflected a general consensus about the nature of the offense of serial murder, and the type of offender likely to be involved. This stereotype was reinforced by frequent repetition in fictional depictions in print or in movies such as *Silence of the Lambs.*

The serial killer, it was usually stated, was commonly a White male in his thirties or forties, who was primarily a sexually motivated murderer who preyed on either men or women depending on his sexual orientation. Dahmer, Bundy and Gacy would all fit this image perfectly (Egger 1990; Holmes and DeBurger 1988; Ressler et al 1988; Norris 1988; Levin and Fox 1985; U.S. Senate 1984; Sears 1991).

However, many criticisms are possible of the "Ripper" stereotype. For example, the question of sexual motivation is by no means as obvious as it may appear, and this pattern is not immediately apparent in cases of prolific "medical murderers" like Donald Harvey or Genene Jones. Also, there have been several attempts to list and quantify known serial murder cases, most impressively by Eric Hickey (1991); and such endeavors always tend to produce a surprisingly high proportion of female killers—at least fifteen percent of the whole. Moreover, it must never be forgotten that such lists will always be counting known cases, and will thus exaggerate the significance of crimes that are easily recognized as serial homicide. In particular, they will always include a disproportionate number of "Ripper"-type crimes, while perhaps understating crimes of less obvious violence, involving asphyxiation or poisoning.

Women serial killers—who generally employ such means of murder—are thus likely to be under-represented in any list of offenders (Jenkins, forthcoming).

But it is the racial question which is perhaps the most vexed. In the Dahmer case, a white male killed up to fifteen men and boys, who were predominantly drawn from African-Americans and other ethnic minorities, and this led to the case being portrayed in some accounts as a crime of racial bias and exploitation (Baumann 1991; Davis 1991; Dvorchak and Holewa 1991; Klein 1992).

This notion even appeared in popular culture, for instance in a video by the rap group X-clan ("Fire and Earth") which attacks negative stereotypes of Blacks. The singer refers to the time he has been called an animal; but meanwhile, "in Milwaukee, there's a cannibal." In the numerous media talk-shows and interviews in the months following the exposure of the case, both experts and members of the public repeatedly returned to the same themes; that serial murder appeared to be an offense committed by white men, and that one seldom heard of African-American or other minority offenders.

This point about racial disparity has been made by many scholars; Leyton, for example, writes that modern serial killers "were almost never drawn from the ranks of the truly oppressed; there are few women, Blacks or native Americans in our files" (Leyton 1986; 288).

When Black multiple killers are mentioned in the literature, it is usually in the context of politically motivated or terrorist activity, as in the "Zebra" murders of the early 1970s (Howard 1980; Newton 1990, 1992). It is ironic that the exception often cited was Wayne Williams, the alleged "Atlanta child-killer" of the early 1980s; but in fact, this case has been viewed as a possible miscarriage of justice, and it remains uncertain whether Williams was in fact guilty of any of the homicides with which he was so frequently connected (Keppel 1989; but see the critiques of this case in Fischer 1991, and Detlinger and Prugh, 1983).

For our present purposes, it is significant that the Atlanta incident became the subject of perhaps the most important and widely read literary work on Blacks and serial homicide, in James Baldwin's *The Evidence of Things Not Seen* (Baldwin 1985). This fully acknowledges the doubts about Williams' guilt, but the identity of the perpetrator is perhaps less important than the racial injustices which the cases illustrate; in fact, the murders are viewed as characteristic of the African-American experience within the White-dominated society of the United States, "the situation of the Black man in the American inferno" (Baldwin 1985; 20). The murders collectively become "the Terror," "racial terror," part of the ongoing assault upon Black communities committed successively (he argues) in the name of segregation, desegregation, and integration (27, 79, 120).

The crimes are explicitly compared to the lynchings and other racial persecutions of the early twentieth century, the memory of which forms so potent an element in modern American political culture. Baldwin draws parallels between the murder of Clifford Jones, which brought the Atlanta attacks to public attention, and the 1955 lynching of Emmett Till, a notorious atrocity which did much to galvanize the Civil Rights movement: this is "a comparison I wish neither to force nor avoid" (40). The Atlanta murders are thus mapped together with perceived racial injustices through history, including the anti-Semitic policies of Tsarist Russia or Nazi Germany, until the child murders become "this latest program" (79). Even Williams himself becomes a victim of systematic oppression, and "must be added to the list of Atlanta's slaughtered Black children" (125). Once again, serial murder is seen as something alien to the African-American community.

If the view of limited African-American involvement is correct, there are many implications. For example, it might suggest that serial murder is explicitly a crime of hatred and intimidation committed by one group (White males), and directed against other groups which they hate and fear, such as women or ethnic minorities. This would naturally fit in with feminist theories proposed by authors like Phyllis Chesler (Chesler 1992).

At the least, the racial disparities indicate that serial homicide is of its nature very different from "regular" homicide, where minorities represent a high proportion of alleged perpetrators (Lynch and Patterson, 1992; Rose and McLain 1990). For example, African-Americans make up some ten percent of the US population, but generally account for forty to forty-five percent of homicide arrests (Riedel and Zahn 1985; Block 1987; Daly and Wilson 1988). In contrast, African-Americans appear seriously under-represented among serial killers.

It will be argued here that the stereotype of the serial killer that became so common following the Dahmer case is incorrect in many aspects, and the racial element is very misleading. In reality, African-Americans make up a significant number of recorded serial killers, far above what might be expected from public perceptions and recollections. In addition, it may be that factors such as victim selection and racial bias in law enforcement lead to significant disparities in the recognition and apprehension of African-American multiple homicide offenders. Ironically, racial factors may here lead to criminality by minority offenders being underestimated rather than (as so often) exaggerated.

This finding is significant for law enforcement agencies, in terms of investigation and crime prevention policy. From a theoretical and political perspective, reassessing minority involvement in serial homicide seriously undermines the notion that the offense is in any meaningful sense a "hate crime."

Methodology

Ideally, we require a comprehensive listing of serial murder cases in a particular period (say, in the last decade or quarter-century), with cases broken down by the race and gender of both offender and victim. Such a complete resource remains a distant dream, but it is possible to make some general statements about the proportion of minority offenders.

We must begin by defining "serial murder," a procedure that is by no means as obvious as may initially appear. For the purposes of this study, serial murder will be defined as any case occurring in the United States where an offender was associated with the killing of at least four victims, over a period greater than 72 hours. The "association" is derived either from law enforcement sources, or from reputable media accounts. It is obvious that the criterion of "association" involves a number of problems of subjective interpretation, but such a reputational approach is perhaps the only means of proceeding in such a contentious area. This definition further excludes cases where the offender acted primarily out of political motives, or in quest of financial profit. Organized and professional criminal activity is thus excluded, a limitation that would not be accepted by all researchers. Of course, the list cannot include cases that did not come to the attention of law enforcement, or where neither police nor media recognized a linkage in a series of homicides. Also, the exact number of cases in a particular series is highly controversial.

Once defined, the next step is to assess the number of serial murder cases in a particular period. There are many difficulties involved in compiling such a list that has any claims to be called comprehensive; and any worthwhile study of the topic will admit to these problems at an early stage. There are killings which are not recognized as homicide, or which are seen as murder, but not attributed to a series linked to a single offender. There might be cases misattributed to a serial killer, and even the crimes associated with particular offenders might exaggerate or understate the actual extent of his or her career. Even confessions cannot be taken as an infallible standard of proof, as there are many motives, rational or otherwise, which might lead an accused offender to portray his crimes as either more or less numerous than they actually were.

Cases were listed from three major sources. The first involved three well-indexed and authoritative newspapers, the *New York Times, Los Angeles Times* and *Chicago Tribune*. This material was supplemented from a variety of secondary sources on serial murder, which have been fully listed in several earlier articles (Jenkins 1988a-b, 1989, 1990, 1992; see especially Nash 1990). Finally, a number of references were acquired from Michael Newton's recent "encyclopedias" of serial murder, *Hunting Humans* and *Serial Slaughter* (Newton 1990, 1992; and see the discussion in Jenkins 1992). *Hunting Humans* in particular is by far the most comprehensive available listing of serial murder cases, including the vast majority of references which had been found in the search of media and secondary sources.

Serial murder can thus be defined, and it is possible to make general statements about the frequency of the offense and the number of killers active at any particular time. However, there is one additional problem in examining the racial factors central to the present study, and that is the issue of defining "race." Race and ethnicity play a major role in American debates over crime and justice, but these factors are rarely defined; this country has no official classifications of race equivalent to those found in nations like South Africa. Racial identification is often easy, but there are cases where media accounts leave considerable room for doubt about whether a given individual should properly be classified as (for example) Black or Hispanic. Where possible, classifications used here follow the consensus of media and law enforcement accounts, but there are likely to be cases where serial killers will have been improperly categorized as to race.

There will also be controversial cases like that which occurred in Gary, Indiana, during 1991, when an African-American man named Christopher Peterson was arrested as the "Shotgun Killer" in the random murders of seven local citizens. This became highly controversial, because police had initially suggested that a White offender was implicated, and many in the local African-American community felt that Peterson had been unjustly charged. It is still difficult to discuss this case with any confidence, or to assess whether the culprit was in reality Black or White. Similarly, doubts have been raised about the identification of Jerome Dennis as the culprit in the recent (April 1992) series of murders of women in East Orange and Newark, New Jersey.

On the positive side, it should be noted that this account does not seek to provide a comprehensive or exhaustive account of the phenomenon of serial homicide among African-Americans and minorities, so that the failure to include a number of cases is not of critical importance. The first priority is to demonstrate that this offense does occur with some frequency, and more precise tabulation can be the goal of future research.

A Historical Perspective

African-Americans have been well-represented in the history of serial murder in the United States, and in the mid-twentieth century, Black offenders were among those claiming the largest number of victims. This group included Jarvis Catoe, Jake Bird and Clarence Hill, all of whom can be described as fitting the classic stereotypes of serial murder. They were also among the very few American cases who could plausibly be compared with the then better-known German "lust-murderers" of the 1920s and 1930s (Jenkins 1989).

Jake Bird, for example, was arrested in 1947 for two ax-murders in Washington state, whereupon he began confessing to a string of over forty homicides committed over the past two decades. There are obvious resemblances to the 1980s case of Henry Lee Lucas, and it is equally difficult to confirm his claims. However, the case created considerable sensation.

Jarvis Catoe was implicated in some eight sex-murders mainly committed in New York City and Washington, D.C. between 1935 and 1941, while Clarence Hill killed several victims in a New Jersey "Lovers' Lane" area around the same time (Newton 1990).

It will be apparent that none of these cases have left much trace in popular memory, in contrast to better-known White figures of these years, like Albert Fish, Ed Gein, William Heirens, and even Caryl Chessman (and it will be noted that of these four, only Albert Fish was beyond doubt a serial killer). There are no mid-century movies depicting African-American multiple killers, and nothing to compare with major fictional studies like *Sniper*. Moreover, none of the African-American cases feature in the extensive criminological literature of these years, in contrast to the abundant attention paid to Fish and Heirens.

This lacuna can partly be explained by the general neglect of Blacks and Black themes in popular fiction of this era. African-Americans were not portrayed as serial killers in mainstream movies, but equally they rarely received serious treatment in any role whatever.

This neglect has changed in recent decades; but it is notable that Blacks have not been featured as villains in the "slasher" or "psycho" films of the last few years. Presumably, there are two reasons for this: film-makers do not wish to have their work categorized as exclusively of "Black interest," while they are also anxious to avoid being accused of depicting crude or controversial racial stereotypes.

This last element may also help to explain why criminal case-studies during the mid-century did not include the stories of figures like Bird or Catoe. In the context of these years, it might well have been thought inappropriate or tasteless to focus on the acts of Black offenders. If unduly sensationalized, these events could have given ammunition to racists and segregationists anxious to justify their opinions about Black violence and criminality. Whatever the reason, the consequence was to limit the attention paid to African-American offenders, and thus to shape the stereotype of the multiple killer in a racially selective manner (Jenkins 1989).

African-American Serial Killers 1971-1990

African-American serial killers may have left little impression in the collective memory, but they undoubtedly exist. In his study of American serial murder from the 1790s to the 1980s, Eric Hickey has suggested that about 13 percent of known cases can be associated with African-Americans (Hickey 1991; 133-134, 169-70). This is closely comparable to the findings of Michael Newton, who suggests that 16 percent of American cases during the present century involved Blacks (Newton 1992; 49).

From the late 1960s, the scale and frequency of serial homicide activity in this country accelerated dramatically, and the number of African-American cases grew proportionately. Accurate figures are difficult to come by, but one method of proceeding is to focus on "extreme" serial cases, those offenders claiming eight or more victims during their careers. Such spectacular cases are likely to be widely reported, and will therefore be found in national media.

Between 1971 and 1990, there were approximately a hundred such cases in the United States. Of these, about thirteen involved African-American offenders, again confirming the estimates of Hickey and Newton.

TABLE 2.1. Cases of Alleged Extreme Serial Homicide (Eight or more victims), 1971-1990

Offender	Where active	Dates
Nathaniel R. Code	LA	1984-87
Alton Coleman & Debra Brown	OH/MI/IN/IL	1984
Carlton Gary	GA	1970-78
Kevin Haley & Reginald Haley	S. CA.	1979-84
Calvin Jackson	NY	1973-74
Milton Johnson	IL	1983
Devernon LeGrand	NY	1968-75
M. Player		
N. ("Marcus Nisby")	S. CA.	1986
Coral E. Watts	MI/TX	1979-83
Wayne Williams	GA	1979-81
"Freeway Phantom"	Washington DC	1971-72
"Southside Slayer"	S. CA.	1983-87
Unsolved series?	MD/Washington DC	1986-87

NOTE: It will be noted that this list includes several cases which remain unsolved, and it is naturally difficult to assert the racial origins of an individual not yet apprehended. It is also possible that some of these cases might not in fact represent true "series": both the Atlanta and "Southside Slayer" cases have been subjected to this criticism. Given this caveat, it should be emphasized that police in both the Washington and the "Southside Slayer" cases consistently describe an African-American suspect or suspects.

Doubts may be raised about the exact number of African-American-offenders in this category, but there can be no doubt that such serial killers do exist. Coral Watts remains perhaps the most notorious of the African-American serial killers, a sexually motivated offender whose crimes make him quite comparable to Ted Bundy. Born in 1953, Watts' known record of homicide began while he was enrolled at Western Michigan University in 1974. After brief periods of incarceration and mental treatment, he resumed his attacks against women in 1979, first in the Detroit area (where he became known as the "Sunday Morning Slasher") and subsequently in Houston, Texas (Linedecker 1988). His "career" reached its height in Texas between 1980 and 1982, and he confessed to ten murders in the Houston area, though he has been plausibly linked to over twenty killings (Newton 1990). This figure falls short of the crimes linked to Bundy or Gacy, but it is in excess of the far-better publicized cases of Jeffrey Dahmer, David Berkowitz, or Joseph Kallinger.

Comparably obscure is Milton Johnson, believed to be responsible for the "weekend murders" of some seventeen individuals in Joliet, IL, during 1983. This case attracted intense local publicity, as it involved several separate incidents of what has been described as "random whole-sale slaughter" (Newton 1990). Four people died in one incident, five in another. Alton Coleman was an equally dangerous offender, a multiple sex offender who launched a two month crime spree through the Mid-west in 1984, leaving some ten people dead (Linedecker 1988).

Carlton Gary was identified as the "Stocking Strangler" who murdered six elderly women in Columbus, GA, during 1977 and 1978. However, he has also been associated with a number of similar crimes in New York state during the early 1970s (Newton 1990; Linedecker 1990; Crockett 1991). Gary's crimes were also significant in that they were viewed in the community as racially motivated assaults on White people, and the murders touched off a local controversy as intense as that in Atlanta in 1980-81 or Milwaukee in 1990-91, when it initially appeared that Blacks were being targeted on ethnic grounds.

It appears that the notoriety of a particular case depends on neither the savagery of the attacks, nor the absolute number of the victims. This suggestion seems confirmed by other cases of extreme multiple homicide involving African-American offenders, none of whom have achieved the celebrity status of some of the White killers; and it is significant that there are no in-depth "true crime" studies of Alton Coleman, Milton Johnson, Carlton Gary, or Coral Watts to compare with the proliferating genre that focuses on killers like Dahmer and Bundy (although there are brief chapter-length studies of some Black cases in collections like Linedecker 1988, 1990; Crockett 1990, 1991). Within the last few years, there have been book-length case-studies of numerous killers, often of only local celebrity, murderers of White origin such as Robert Hansen, Arthur Shaw-cross, Larry Eyler. However, it is worth reiterating that in terms of the number of victims, none was as serious an offender as Coral Watts or Milton Johnson.

Almost certainly, the determining factor here is the attitude of publishers toward what constitutes newsworthy or saleable material, and the assumption that cases of African-American offenders are less likely to appeal to a mass audience. Books of this sort are likely to be relegated to the "Black Studies" sections of major stores, and even to be marketed only in urban centers. This was, for example, the case with Detlinger and Prugh's excellent study of the Atlanta child-murders, which was published by a small Atlanta concern: the few stores which stocked it confined it to the "Black Interest" shelves.

In this context, it is interesting to compare two superficially similar (though unrelated) cases which occurred in Philadelphia, PA, during the mid-1980s. Gary Heidnik and Harrison "Marty" Graham both imprisoned and murdered a number of people in their respective houses in poor sections of the city; and the media widely reported the horrific scenes that were uncovered by police. Heidnik became the center of national attention, and is the subject of a book-length study (Englade 1988); in 1991, he was the subject of an interview on the network television show *60 Minutes.* Part of Heidnik's story was popularized in the book and film of *Silence of the Lambs,* where the fictional killer "Buffalo Bill" similarly imprisons young women in a basement. In contrast, Graham's case received little attention outside the Philadelphia area, although he was convicted of no less than seven murders, in contrast to Heidnik's three. There appears to be no reason for the disparity in treatment, except that Heidnik is White, and therefore fits accepted stereotypes of the multiple killer; while Graham is Black.

The Role of Victim Choice

African-American serial murder emphatically does exist in the United States, and it is clearly not a new phenomenon. However, it remains to be asked whether the cases of which we have record are an accurate reflection of the total phenomenon. Many serial murder cases remain unknown to police; but it might be argued that cases involving Black offenders and victims are especially likely to escape official attention. African-American serial homicide might therefore be a seriously underrecognized phenomenon.

This phenomenon can be explained in terms of the likelihood of a particular crime being recognized, first, as an act of homicide; and second, as part of a linked series of crimes. There are a number of factors at work here, but the victimological element is central. These victim-oriented factors are complex, but in general they tend to benefit criminals who operate in certain regions, and against victims of particular racial and social groups (Jenkins, forthcoming).

For a number of reasons, law enforcement agencies are less likely to seek or find evidence of serial murder activity where the victims are African-American. Partly, this may result from overt racism on the part of police agencies, and this factor has certainly played a part in many periods of American history. Between about 1910 and 1935, one of the most prolific serial killers in the U.S. was Albert Fish, a White man who chiefly preyed on Black children in big cities like Washington DC and New York (Schechter 1990; Jenkins 1989). Fish remained at large for a quarter of a century, which was remarkable in view of his flagrant record of perversion and child molestation. However, he made clear that he survived through a deliberate policy of victim choice. As he remarked in his final confession, the police simply did not care about "colored" children, and paid far less attention when they died mysteriously or disappeared suddenly. Significantly, Fish's downfall came when he murdered the daughter of his White middle-class neighbors (Jenkins, 1989).

Discriminatory police attitudes go some way toward explaining the low priority attached to African-American murder victims, and this benefits any offender who chooses to pursue minority victims. As homicide is primarily an intra-racial crime, this would then mean that African-American serial killers would be far more likely to escape detection. Racial attitudes here are profoundly linked to social stereotypes: it is not so much that Blacks as such attract lower police priorities, but that poor people living in certain high-crime neighborhoods appear to inspire less concern when they die or vanish (Jenkins, forthcoming).

The case of Calvin Jackson is suggestive here (Godwin 1978). When Jackson was arrested in 1974 for a murder committed in a New York apartment building, he confessed with little prompting to a series of other homicides committed in the same building over a six month period. Before this confession, there had been no suggestion that any of the crimes were linked, or indeed that most of the deaths were caused by anything other than natural causes. In retrospect, it seems that this lack of police concern was in large part a consequence of the nature of the victims and of the environment in which they died. The building in question was a single-occupancy hotel, where most of the guests were poor, isolated, and often elderly.

It was commonplace for police to be called to the hotel to deal with cases of sudden death or injury, often arising from problems associated with drugs, alcoholism, or old age. In the case of Jackson's victims, foul play was only recorded in cases where victims were killed with conspicuous signs of violence; and autopsies appear to have been rare. Deaths resulting from smothering were customarily dismissed as the result of natural causes. Where foul play was noted, the police saw no reason to suspect a serial killer, and naturally viewed the crime as part of the interpersonal violence that was endemic in such a transient community. As there was no apparent evidence of grotesque sexual abuse, police saw no need to fit the crimes into the context of "sex-killings"; and thus linkages were ignored (Newton 1990).

In other words, police naturally approach a suspicious death with certain preconceptions that depend both on the nature of the victim and the social environment in which the incident occurs. In some contexts, a sudden death can be explained in many ways without the need to assume the existence of a random or repeat killer; and serial murder activity is thus less likely to be noted. This is particularly true of urban environments characterized by poverty, isolation, transience, and frequent violence. In Jackson's case, by no means all the victims were Black; but the same factors apply with particular relevance to urban African-American communities (Jenkins, forthcoming).

Moreover, the police attitudes which allowed Jackson to continue unchecked for so long have not changed fundamentally since the mid-1970s. In fact, contemporary police agencies have even more preconceptions about the likely causes of sudden death in the inner cities, to the possible benefit of repeat killers. To illustrate this, let us imagine a Black serial killer living in a major city, who chose as his victims young African-American men or women. If the killer possessed moderate intelligence or ingenuity, it would be easy for him to disguise these crimes by means of planting money, drugs, or even gang insignia at the scene of the crime, in order to suggest that a particular murder was the result of gang- or drug-related conflict. The deaths would thus be interpreted as falling into what is currently a well-known category of urban homicide, and serial murder would probably not be suspected. By such means, it would be possible for such a murderer to continue to operate for years.

Conclusion

For centuries, the lives of African-Americans have often been blighted by stereotypes, usually negative, and frequently associating them with crime and violence (Lynch and Patterson, 1992; Rose and McLain 1990). This paper has considered an area where stereotypes imply a diametrically opposite image, and Blacks appear disproportionately free of involvement in the most serious of violent crimes. However, this image is false; and this apparently favorable stereotype is both as inaccurate and as pernicious as any of the more familiar racial slurs. Significantly, the very failure to draw attention to Black serial killers might in itself arise from a form of bias within the media and law enforcement.

African-Americans make up a sizeable proportion of serial killers, and this has practical consequences for the fate of those Blacks and other minorities who are most likely to fall victim to this type of predator. Underestimating minority involvement in serial homicide can thus lead to neglecting the protection of minority individuals and communities who stand in greatest peril of victimization.

References

Baldwin, James (1985), The Evidence of Things Not Seen, New York; Holt, Rinehart and Winston.

Baumann, Ed (1991), Step Into My Parlor, Chicago: Bonus Books.

Block, Carolyn R., (1987) Homicide in Chicago. Loyola University of Chicago: Center for Urban Policy.

Chesler, Phyllis (1992), 'A Double Standard for Murder?', New York Times, January 8.

Crockett, Art, ed., (1990), Serial Murderers. New York: Pinnacle.

——— (1991), Spree Killers. New York: Pinnacle.

Daly, Martin and Margo Wilson, eds., (1988), Homicide. Kawthorne, NY: Aldine de Gruyter.

Davis, Don (1991), The Milwaukee Murders New York: St. Martin's Paperbacks.

Detlinger, Chet and Jeff Prugh (1983) The List. Atlanta, GA: Philmay Enterprises.

Dietz, Mary Lorenz (1983) Killing for Profit. Chicago: Nelson Hall.

Dvorchak, Robert J., and Lisa Holewa (1991), Milwaukee Massacre. New York: Dell.

Egger, Steven A., Ed., (1990). Serial Murder: An Elusive Phenomenon. New York: Praeger.

Englade, Ken (1988), Cellar of Horror, New York: St. Martin's Press.

Fischer, Mary A. (1991). 'Was Wayne Williams Frames?', GO April : 228 ff.

Godwin, John (1978), Murder USA. New York: Ballantine.

Hickey, Eric W. (1991) Serial Murderers and their Victims. Monterey, CA,. Brooks-Cole/Wadsworth.

Holmes, Ronald M. and James DeBurger (1988), Serial Murder. Beverly Hills CA: Sage.

Howard, Clark (1980) Zebra. New York: Berkley.

Jenkins, Philip (1988a) 'Myth and Murder: the Serial Murder Panic of 1983-1985', Criminal Justice Research Bulletin. 3(11) 1-7.

—— (1988b) 'Serial Murder in England 1940-1985', Journal of Criminal Justice 16:1-15.

—— (1989)'Serial Murder in the USA 1900-1940: A Historical Perspective' Journal of Criminal Justice 17: 377-392.

—— (1990) 'Sharing Murder: Understanding Group Serial Homicide', Journal of Crime and Justice 13(2): 125-147.

—— (1992) 'A Murder Wave? Serial Homicide in the United States 1940-1990', Criminal Justice Review.

—— (forthcoming) 'Chance or Choice', in Anna V. Wilson ed., Homicide: Dynamics of the Victim-Offender Interaction, Cincinnati: Anderson.

Keppel, Robert (1989) Serial Murder, Cincinnati: Anderson.

Klein, Lloyd (1992) 'The Milwaukee Chainsaw Massacre: Serial Murder as Deviant Social Behavior', Paper presented to the Academy of Criminal Justice Sciences, Pittsburgh, PA., March.

Levin, Jack and James A. Fox (1985) Mass Murder: America's Growing Menace. New York: Plenum.

Leyton, Elliott (1986) Compulsive Killers. New York University Press.

Linedecker, Clifford (1988) Thrill Killers. Toronto: Paper jacks.

—— (1990) Serial Thrill Killers. New York: Knightsbridge.

Lynch, Michael J., and E. Britt Patterson, eds., (1992) Race and Criminal Justice, Fairfax, VA: Harrow and Heston.

Nash, Jay Robert (1990). Encyclopedia of World Crime, Six volumes. Wilmette, IL: Crime Books, Inc.

Newton, Michael (1990), Hunting Humans. Port Townsend, WA: Loompanics.

—— (1992), Serial Slaughter. Port Townsend, WA: Loompanics.

Norris, Joel (1988) Serial Killers. New York: Dolphin.

Ressler, Robert K., Ann W. Burgess, John E. Douglas (1988). Sexual Homicide Patterns and Motives. Lexington, MA: Lexington-Heath.

Riedel, Marc and Margaret Zahn (1985). The Nature and Patterns of American Homicide. Washington: Justice Department, NIJ.

Rose, Harold M., and Paula D. McClain (1990). Race, Place and Risk: Black Homicide in Urban America. SUNY Press

Schechter, Harold (1990), Deranged, New York: Pocket Books.

Sears, Donald J. (1991), To Kill Again: the Motivation and Development of Serial Murder, Wilmington DE: Scholarly Resources.

U. S. Senate (1984), Committee of the Judiciary Committee on Juvenile Justice. Serial Murders: Hearings before the subcommittee on juvenile justice of the committee on the judiciary, US Senate, 98th Congress, 1st Session, on patterns of murders committed by one person in large numbers with no apparent rhyme, reason or motivation, July 12, 1983. Washington DC: US Government Printing Office.

3

The Female Serial Killer

ROBERT HALE
ANTHONY BOLIN

When thinking of serial murder, it is often presumed that the offender will be male. There are several reasons for this perception. First of all, the typical violent offender is male, and this is true for murder. In addition, because of a constant focus on male criminality, women have not been thought of as committing murder. Only since the 1970s, and as a result of an expanding women's movement, have women been the focus of research into violent behavior. Finally, publicity of serial murder, whether it be through the news media, movies, or books, has sensationalized and publicized the acts of males.

Although it is correct to attribute the majority of violent acts, including murder and serial murder, to men, doing so overlooks the significant number of women who commit serial murder. It should be pointed out that some are unaware of the number of females who commit multicide (Reynolds, 1993). But in fact, throughout history, women have been responsible for mass and serial murders, the same as men. To ignore the work of women would overlook the murders committed by Elizabeth Bathory, the "Countess Dracula" of Hungary, who tortured more than 80 female victims before bathing in their blood; she began her crimes in 1580 and continued until 1610. An estimated 183 other women have committed multicide.

The Case Studies presented in this chapter are excerpted and adapted from *Women Serial and Mass Murderers: A Worldwide Reference, 1580 through 1990,* by Kerry Segrave. Used with permission.

This chapter will examine the female who commits serial murder in an attempt to better understand her motives and methods. Female serial killers, although small in number, are not a recent phenomenon, although most have begun killing since the 1970s. The methods used by women serial killers will be discussed, as well as the victims they select.

Explanations for Sex-Based Differences in Aggression

Several explanations have been developed to explain gender difference in committing homicide. These explanations tend to fall under either the biological or social-learning perspectives.

SOCIAL-LEARNING PERSPECTIVE

A number of researchers believe that differences in rates of aggression, including homicide, are caused primarily by the social roles that have been traditionally assigned to men and women. Within the culture of the United States, there are many ways in which children are taught that aggression is more appropriate for men than for women. Popular literature and the mass media consistently show men, rather than women, fighting. Parents buy toy weapons for their sons and dolls for their daughters. Aggression in boys is more likely to be approved and rewarded. Directly and indirectly, and from a number of varied role models, youngsters learn that males are aggressive and females are not; that aggression is acceptable for males as a means to defend rights and correct perceived wrongs. This pattern continues as boys grow into men, leading more men than women to approve of force and aggression as a means of control, to enforce power, and to manage interpersonal relationships.

Women are also more aware of the consequences of aggressive behavior for themselves and others. Eagly and Steffen (1986) report that women are quicker than men to think of the possible outcomes of using violence. Women are more likely to consider the suffering of the victim, the possibility of the loss of the relationship, and the effect on their reputation. It is assumed that with these possible negative outcomes in mind, women are more likely to hold back their aggression.

BIOLOGICAL PERSPECTIVES

Biological research into the causes of aggression has followed a variety of paths. These paths have included studies into the autonomic nervous system, neurophysical responses, and genetic studies; for a comprehensive review, see Wolfgang and Weiner (1982). However, only a few of these studies provide any insight into differences in aggression between men and women.

Recent research into gender differences in the biology of aggression have focused on hormonal influences. There are actually several male and female sex hormones, but the most important to the study of aggression is testosterone. Testosterone is the hormone that stimulates the development of masculine characteristics when it begins to circulate at puberty. Hormones such as testosterone are thought to influence behavior in two ways: (a) by organizing the developing human brain in such a way that particular responses become more likely, and (b) by activating the physiological mechanisms that help govern certain behaviors.

Although the sex of any animal, including humans, is set at birth, the gender is not entirely fixed at conception. The growing fetus is thought to be inclined in one direction or another (either masculine or feminine), but development can be affected by the concentration of male or female hormones circulating within it; culture also influences the formation of gender identity. A relatively high concentration of testosterone can push the central nervous system in a masculine direction, and the individual develops masculine physical characteristics and tends to act in a "male" manner at times.

Research has shown that young girls who had been exposed to relatively high levels of male hormones before birth because of a malfunctioning adrenal gland engaged in more masculine behaviors and tended to initiate more fighting than their sisters (Maccoby & Jackin, 1974; Meyer-Bahlburg & Erhardt, 1982; Money & Erhardt, 1972). Similar results were found among children who were exposed to the hormone progestin, which can also have a masculizing effect on developing fetuses. Reinisch (1981) found that both boys and girls who had been exposed to progestin during prenatal development were more likely to choose aggressive physical and verbal responses to situations of conflict than were nonexposed children. Reinisch concluded that the progestin had influenced the developing brain in some way toward aggressive reactions.

TABLE 3.1. Percentage and Rate of Murder, by Sex (per 100,000 people)

	Percentage		Rate	
Year	Male	Female	Male	Female
1983	85.6	14.4	11.7	2.2
1984	86.4	13.6	11.1	1.9
1985	86.9	13.1	11.4	1.9
1986	87.3	12.7	12.2	1.8
1987	87.2	12.8	11.5	1.6
1988	88.2	11.8	11.9	1.6
1989	88.5	11.5	12.2	1.6
1990	89.7	10.3	13.6	1.8
1991	90.3	9.7	13.8	1.7
1992	90.3	9.7	14.5	1.6
1993	90.8	9.2	13.3	1.5

Research has also found hormones to have the opposite effect on behavior. For instance, children who had been exposed before birth to the chemical MPA, which suppresses the production of male sex hormones, tended to be comparatively nonaggressive than did nonexposed children (Meyer-Bahlburg & Erhardt, 1982).

Although there seems to be increasing evidence that sex hormones have a brain-organizing influence, there is less consensus about whether hormones can activate aggression. Ethical constraints limit the type of research that can be done, but there have been some studies that indicate that men who have high testosterone levels are also prone to aggressive modes of behavior (Dabbs & Morris, 1990; Olweus, 1986; Rubin, 1987).

Females and Murder

According to arrest statistics provided by the Bureau of Justice Statistics, an overwhelming number of killers are male. In 1993, 9.4% of all murders were committed by women. This number reflects a slight decrease in the percentage of murders committed by women over previous years, but women have committed roughly 10% to 13% of all

TABLE 3.2. Rate of Female Offenders, by Age and Race (per 100,000 people)

	Age					
	14 to 17 years		*18 to 24 years*		*25 years and older*	
Year	*Black*	*White*	*Black*	*White*	*Black*	*White*
1990	5.2	1.1	14.4	2.1	7.8	0.9
1991	7.9	0.9	15.3	1.9	7.3	0.8
1992	7.6	1.1	13.0	1.7	6.5	0.7
1993	6.6	0.9	14.1	1.6	5.9	0.8

murders over the past 15 years. During this same period, the rate of female offenders has steadily decreased from 2.3 to 1.5 per 100,000 people; for males, the rate has fluctuated between 12.8 and 13.3 per 100,000 people. Table 3.1 reveals the trends for the past decade.

Bureau of Justice Statistics data also reveal that, relative to white women, black women are overrepresented in arrests for murder in all age categories. Table 3.2 provides a look at female offending by age and racial category.

An Overview of Females and Multicide

Women who commit multicide tend to share a number of common characteristics. The average female mass or serial murderer kills for the first time when she is just over 31 years of age. The vast majority are in their 20s or 30s when they commit their first murder: Thirty-four percent are in their 20s and 39% are in their 30s. Seven percent are less than 20 years of age, 13% are in their forties, and 5% are in their 50s when they committed their first murder. On average, the female serial killer continues to kill for 5 years until she is apprehended by police. She has killed an average of 17 victims before she is discovered. Most of the murders take place inside the killer's residence; murders that occur inside the victim's residence are a distant second. Often, the murderer and her victim share a residence. The most common weapon for murder is arsenic.

TABLE 3.3. Preferred Murder Methods Among 184 Female Serial Killers

Method	Number Who Preferred It	Method	Number Who Preferred It
Poison	59	Firearm	24
Knife	11	Strangulation	10
Suffocation	9	Drug overdose	8
Asphyxiation by gas	7	Bludgeoning	3
Starvation	3	Arson	3
Drowning	2	Torture	1
Hatchet	1	Automobile	1
Throwing from tall building	1	Pushing from a bridge	1
Hanging	1	Various (Two or more of the above methods)	39

The majority of her victims are family members, either immediate or extended family. Other victims have close ties to the woman, either as friends, potential lovers, or employers. The victims of women tend to come from the powerless groups: the very young, the old, or the infirm. The more defenseless the victim, the more direct and aggressive the female killer tends to act. Finally, a variety of motives tend to drive women who kill. Like males who commit serial murder, a motive for the murder can usually be found if enough attention is paid to the circumstances of the event.

METHODS OF FEMALE SERIAL KILLERS

Among the 184 female serial killers researched for this study, there were a number of weapons used to commit murder. Some shot their victims, whereas others beat their victims to death; strangulation was used, as was drowning. Table 3.3 lists the weapons of choice for the women in this study.

Obviously, poison has been the popular method of murder, and arsenic was a particular favorite. To appreciate the choice of arsenic requires an understanding of the history of arsenic.

Many females who committed multicide operated before the 1900s. During this period, arsenic was readily available as an over-the-counter product. Arsenic was known to be poisonous and was often used to kill rats and other animals. However, Hickey (1991) includes a testament from the period regarding the positive effect of a small amount of arsenic; apparently, arsenic in small amounts was thought to improve the complexion and increase one's "sexual desire" (p. 114). However, it is deadly and nearly undetectable when mixed with hot food or drinks like cocoa or coffee. Depending on the size of the dose, death can occur within hours or can be prolonged for weeks or even months.

Biographical texts of female serial killers are full of stories of women who used arsenic to kill their victims. The story of Helene Jegado provides a look at one of these women.

Helene Jegado

Victims: More than 27

Preferred Murder Method: Arsenic Poisoning

Other than the fact that she simply did not like the victims, there seems to be no logical motive to the killings by Helene Jegado. The fact that she was unable to read and write is thought to have prompted her to fantasize often, imagining that people were constantly doing her wrong in various ways. These thoughts typically led her to kill. If an employer accused her of stealing some petty item (which was a common charge: besides being a killer, Helene had a reputation as a kleptomaniac), or if someone disagreed with her in an argument, it was almost certain that death would soon follow. In a bizarre twist, however, it was also common for Jegado to nurse her victims after they became sick, and when the inevitable end came, she mourned openly alongside the family members.

Helene Jegado was born around 1803 in Brittany, France. By the age of 7, both of her parents had passed away; she was sent to live at the local pastor's house, where two of her aunts were working as domestic servants. She ended up working as a servant for the pastor for about 17 years. After her employment ended, she went out on her own to start a violent career as a poisoner.

Working as a cook/housekeeper in 12 different towns in the local area gave Jegado access to the food of the houses in which she worked, food that she laced with arsenic. She apparently did not discriminate: She poisoned men, women, and children alike.

Jegado had earned a poor reputation as early as 1831. A Mademoiselle Kearly was warned many times that Jegado had a "fatal influence" but hired her despite these warnings. The woman was repaid for her kindness by the death of her father and another one of her servants. Dismissed for the theft of a petty item, Jegado moved to the village of Guern. While in a house in Guern, she poisoned seven more, including her own sister! Soon after, still working as a servant, she would poison three more in the house.

After the death of her sister and the others, suspicion fell on Helene, but she adamantly denied being involved. When the judge questioned her about being the cook and the nurse at the house where several had died, Jegado replied, "Yes. I always nursed the sick—that has been my misfortune. That is the cause of my troubles today." After being cleared in this case, Jegado went to work in Locmine. While at a house where the mother died and the child became ill, she reportedly told the daughter (before the mother's death) that she fully expected the mother to die, saying, "I carry death with me." Because of the number of deaths associated with Jegado, the people of Locmine regularly chastised her in the streets, calling her "the white-livered woman." She fled Locmine because of the harassment and, ironically, entered a convent. However, she was quickly dismissed after being accused of cutting all the bed linen into pieces. Helene always denied this, claiming that she was asked to leave because she was too old to be taught how to read and write.

Mrs. Hippolyte Roussel was the next to hire Jegado, and she would be the next to suffer for it. After Roussel had questioned Jegado about stealing an umbrella from one of the other servants, she was stricken with severe vomiting after she had eaten soup prepared by Jegado. When a judge asked about this, Jegado replied that Roussel would have become sick whether or not she had taken the soup. When Jegado was asked if it was true that Roussel became worse to the point she could barely walk, she replied, "She could scarcely walk before."

Soon after, Roussel's youngest daughter died suddenly, and the entire family became severely sick. Although no other family members actually died, years later, two of the family suffered from body numbness, recurrent pain, and partial paralysis. Once again, the finger was pointed at Jegado, and she was fired. She quickly moved on to nearby Port Louis, again as a servant, where she was fired for stealing a sheet.

From 1841 to 1848, Jegado seemed to have simply stopped poisoning. This abrupt stop is extremely uncharacteristic of serial killers and adds to the peculiarity of the case. One report claims that Jegado felt that she had received some sort of divine intervention. She claimed that God had forgiven her sins, and she had turned over a new leaf. These religious beliefs were scattered, for she still stole and drank heavily, and they would soon be pushed by the wayside, because in 1848 she did resume her career.

In 1848, five members of the Rabot family died after they had publicly accused Jegado of stealing and drinking their wine. A similar case occurred in

nearby Rennes, when the young child living in the house where Jegado was employed died the day after Jegado had been accused of stealing some brandy. Jegado decided to stay in Rennes, where she found employment at an inn called The World's End. It was an eery title for a place where another servant, named Perrotte Mace, would find her own world coming to an end. Helene Jegado resented Mace's beauty and youth, and soon Mace was bedridden. Her symptoms were the usual: vomiting, pain in the stomach and extremities, distention in the abdomen, and swollen feet. Mace complained that Jegado, whom she had also grown to dislike, had given her food and drink that "burned her." The doctor did not feel her illness was serious, but Helene knew otherwise. She announced that Mace was sure to die, and when Mace died on September 1, 1850, suspicion fell on Jegado. Jegado was fired shortly thereafter, again for stealing liquor.

Still in Rennes, she was hired by a university professor named Theophile Bidard. Bidard found that his new servant was a hard worker but said she had a "malicious sense of humor." Helene developed an instant dislike for another servant, named Rose, who became violently ill after a noon meal prepared by Jegado. After Rose's death, Jegado pleaded to no avail that no other servants be hired; but there were others, and one would die. When the police came to investigate this death, Jegado immediately cried, "I am innocent!" to which the police replied, "Of what? No one has accused you of anything!" Jegado was taken away after autopsies of three recent victims showed they had been poisoned. Proclaiming innocence until the end, Jegado was sentenced to death and climbed the guillotine in 1851.

Susanna Fazekas remains the last known female serial killer who exclusively used arsenic to kill. She is alleged to be responsible for more than 100 deaths in her Hungarian community during the 1920s. Restrictions limiting the availability of arsenic have not ended the trend of murder by poison; other poisons of choice have emerged in its place.

Today, potassium chloride is a common choice, especially among women who kill within a medical setting, because it is difficult to detect once the body is prepared for burial. Another favorite poison is succinylcholine, which is used to relax muscles during surgery. As a murder weapon, this drug inhibits the chest muscles from functioning, and the victim simply stops breathing. Genene Jones serves as a modern-day example of a woman who used poison to kill.

In 1984, Genene Jones was sentenced to prison in Texas for 99 years for causing the death of a 15-month-old patient where Jones worked as a nurse. The young victim had been given a lethal dose of succinylcholine. Jones was implicated in harming six other children through the doctor's office where she had worked for 3 weeks. In an ironic twist, Jones claimed an altruistic motive for her actions: She was attempting to show the need for a pediatric intensive care unit in the town of Kerrville, where she worked. She was also suspected of causing as many as 46 other deaths using succinylcholine and up to 21 deaths by administering an overdose of digoxin, a drug that affects the heart muscle.

Although Jones has offered no explanation for any of the poisonings other than the seven at the physician's office, the altruistic motive she expressed is not rare among women who commit serial murder. In another case involving a nurse who injected potassium chloride into her patients, Terri Rachals was convicted of murder and suspected of up to 24 additional attacks. During her trial, a court-appointed psychologist provided testimony that Rachals "believed she was relieving them [the patients] of their pain and misery" through the injections. Resnick (1970) also found that women convicted of felicide (the killing of a child over 24 months old) commonly believed that their children were better off dead.

The idea that the female serial killer would express sympathy toward the victim is easier to understand once the typical victim is described. Women who commit multicide tend to target victims who have been described as "latent victims." Latent victims are those who are unable to defend themselves, or have limited abilities to defend themselves, because of their general condition. These victims, who are usually children, old or sick people, or sleeping people, make themselves defenseless and are thus easy targets for the killer. According to Rasko (1976), two thirds of the victims were found to be unable, or had limited ability, to defend themselves. Although some say that this shows that female offenders are more treacherous than their male counterparts, it may be more an issue of tact by the offender. A female who plans to kill her husband or lover by a means other than poison understands that she may be less powerful than her intended victim. Therefore, to gain an advantage, she may wait until the victim is asleep, or is in a drunken state, before she attacks.

Women who select their children as victims tend to use more violent methods to kill. Annie Jones murdered her own children by luring them into nearby woods, where she shot them to death.

Annie Jones

Victims: 4

Preferred Murder Method: Firearm

Thirty-two-year-old Annie Jones lived just over the Canadian border, a few miles from the town of Madison, Maine. In 1936, she lived with her husband, Erwin, and their five children. The eldest was 14-year-old Charles; Shirley, their eldest daughter, was 12; the twins, Robert and Edward, were 4 years old; and Norman was 2 years old.

There were never any problems reported among the family, besides the fact that Annie had been under the care of a doctor for about 2 years, presumably for a mental illness. Friends described her as depressed. Annie had made previous threats on several occasions to kill herself along with her children, but she had never made any attempts and therefore was thought to be harmless. In June of 1936, Annie threatened to kill husband Erwin when he learned that she had purchased bullets for the family rifle.

On June 21, Annie lured the younger children into the woods behind their house by showing them a bag of cookies and promising them a picnic. Using rags and a rope that she had packed along with the picnic items, she tied the twins up and blindfolded them. Norman was tied to the others' waists, but he was not blindfolded. Annie shot and killed the three children before killing herself with the rifle she had previously hidden in the woods. Erwin Jones, who owned an auto repair shop across the street from the family home, found the four after Shirley had reported that they had not returned from the picnic. The bodies of the children had been neatly arranged, face up and laid next to Annie Jones.

Segrave (1992) theorizes that women hold the most power over their children, and the children exhibit a level of trust that allows their mother to get close enough to use more physical and powerful methods of murder. At least 25 women can be identified who fit this description. More than half chose suffocation as the method of death for their children. One woman hung her children in the house cellar, whereas another woman threw her children from the top of a building to their death on the street below. Charlotte Juenemann stood by and allowed her children to starve to death; their deaths took more than a week to complete. Many of these 25 women then attempted or completed suicide after the deaths of their children.

Lillian Edwards

Victims: 3

Preferred Murder Method: Strangulation

Lillian Ralston was a minister's daughter. She grew up in San Jose, California, and her childhood seemed quite normal. She graduated from San Jose State College, and with her degree, she chose to teach school in Monterey County for 3 years. She gave up her career when she married former San Jose High student body president and star athlete, Kenneth Edwards. The couple resided for a time in San Francisco, where their first child was born. In 1933, the three moved to Fresno, where two more children were born, the youngest being born in January of 1940. The life of Lillian Edwards seemed to be perfect, but this happy story would have a tragic end.

Just after the birth of their third child, Lillian began to develop problems with her mental health. She was first admitted to a private hospital in San Francisco for the treatment of what doctors called a nervous disorder. After several months at the hospital, a judge committed her to the Stockton State Hospital for the insane. That staff diagnosed Lillian as suffering from manic-depressive psychosis. Oddly, this was Lillian's first bout with her mental health. After being admitted to Stockton, Lillian was viewed as severely depressed, but she also seemed to make a rapid recovery. As her condition seemed to improve, her constant request was for the doctors to let her return home so that she could care for her children.

On December 5, 1940, Lillian was given a trial release period of 1 month. Dr. Margaret Smyth said later of the release, "She always talked quite rationally. . . . There was never any indication of any violent element in her nature." Dr. Smyth's observations could not have been more wrong. Lillian Edwards did have a tendency for violence, and it was displayed during her release.

While Lillian was in the institution, Kenneth Edwards had employed Fay Reuter as a housekeeper to take care of the children. Ms. Reuter stayed overnight with the children when Kenneth, who was a salesman, was on the road. On December 11, Kenneth left on a business trip, leaving Reuter at home with Lillian and the children. Reuter, who apparently misunderstood the directions of Kenneth, left later that evening. (Kenneth later stated that he was under the impression that Reuter knew that she was to stay with the children and Lillian at all times, whereas Reuter claimed to have had an agreement where she did not have to stay overnight at any time.) After Fay Reuter left, Lillian Edwards washed and put the kids to bed. She then strangled 9-year-old Veryl Ann, 6-year-old Donald, and 11-month-old Susan to death with bed sheets.

When Reuter reported to work the next day, she was met by Lillian, who was wearing only a blood-spattered slip. Lillian had inflicted minor abrasions to her wrists and neck with a knife. She then chased Reuter from the house, and, in turn, Reuter called the police. Lillian Edwards was taken into custody, and the three children were found with pieces of sheets tied around their neck.

Lillian claimed that she had no recollection of the murders. Her statement was this:

> Then they came, the man and the woman, in white and unlocked the front door. They had lots of keys and a big black car. I don't care about myself, but I love my babies and they took them away to operate on them just like they did me. Why wasn't Kenny there—he loved us and didn't want us to go away forever.

Lillian was found to be insane, and the doctors said she may never know what happened that night. She was admitted back into Stockton State Hospital, from which she had been released less than 1 month ago.

Whereas most women limit the number of serial killings they commit, there are a few extreme examples of women who murdered hundreds of victims. Elizabeth Bathory, Mariam Soulakiotis, and "Madame" Popova (who will be presented later) are examples of this type of female serial killer. Operating independently, they were responsible for hundreds of murders that were committed through heinous torture. Again, though, these women are rare examples of female serial killers.

MOTIVES OF FEMALE SERIAL KILLERS

A close personal relationship between the female murderer and her victim is common, regardless of whether it is a single case or multicide. In the examples above of Genene Jones and Terri Rachals, a nurse-caregiver killed her patients. Otherwise, almost 40% of the victims were the husband, common-law husband, or lover of the offender, and 20% were children of the female killer. (Victims of infanticide are excluded; if they were included, they would constitute the largest class of victims.) Thus, about two thirds of the victims are linked to the female killer by some type of familial or close personal relationship, and most often, the victim is living with the offender.

Because women are likely to kill those with whom they enjoy a close relationship, this might imply that female serial killers routinely commit lust murder. Among males, lust as a motive for murder has been thoroughly documented, both in this text and in other sources. However, lust is simply not a strong motive for murder among female serial killers. There are some females who have killed for this reason, with Vera Renczi and Anna Zwanziger as examples. Lust was a motive for Marie Becker, who killed to obtain the money that would make her attractive to younger men. Martha Beck used sex as a part of her murders, as did Mary Ann Cotton. However, lust was but one motive for Mary Ann Cotton.

Mary Ann Cotton

Number of victims: At least 21

Preferred Murder Method: Arsenic Poisoning

Mary Ann Robson was born in October of 1832 in County Durham, in the English mining town of Low Moorsly, as the result of a teenage marriage. Mary Ann was described as an outgoing child, very pretty (a trait that would draw men to her for her entire life), and was faithful in her church attendance by the age of 14. With these characteristics, few would believe that such a charming little girl would grow up to be one of the most prolific serial killers from Great Britain.

At the age of 16, she took a job as a domestic servant, and she married for the first time in July of 1852. Her husband, William Mowbray, worked as a miner and was 6 years older than Mary Ann. Mary Ann's father was a miner as well, so she was familiar with life in the mining camps. It was nothing new to her when she had to travel extensively with her husband during the first 5 years of their marriage while he searched for work. They finally returned to Mary Ann's hometown of Durham in 1857, this time with the addition of a 1-year-old daughter, who was also named Mary Ann. Mother Mary Ann told friends that she had four children prior to her newest, but that all had died soon after birth. More infants would follow. Later, in 1857, Mary Ann bore a child that died suddenly just a few days after birth. Two more daughters were to follow: Isabella, in September of 1858, and Margaret, in October of 1861. Oddly, in the midst of the joys of childbirth, 4-year-old Mary Ann died on June 24, 1860. The cause of death was listed as "gastric fever," a trend that would follow many of Mary Ann's immediate family members. A son, John Robert, was born in November of 1863. After the death of the younger Mary Ann, William Mowbray was prompted to make what may have been a fatal mistake. He took out life insurance on himself and the rest of his children.

John Robert was the next to die, in September of 1864. The cause was listed as "diarrhea." Four months later, in January of 1865, William Mowbray was home from work with an injured foot. "Diarrhea" struck him so hard that he died that very same day. Margaret June was the next to die from "gastric fever," after being sick for only 2 days. By April of 1865, Mary Ann Mowbray was left as a widow with only one child, Isabella. Mary Ann then left Isabella with her mother. If the insurance money was the motivation for these murders, the reward was surprisingly small. Her total collection on William and the children paid only 30 pounds sterling.

After the rash of deaths, Mary moved to Sea View Harbor. While there, she acquired a lover by the name of Joseph Nattrass. Nattrass was married, and he refused to leave his wife, so Mary simply moved on. She found a job working in a Sunderland infirmary. It was in the 20-bed fever ward that she found her next husband; she married ex-patient George Ward in August of 1865. Ward did not last long; he died from "fever" just 14 months after their marriage and left everything to Mary Ann.

Just 1 month later, James Robinson, a recent widower himself, was left with five children to care for, and he advertised for a housekeeper. Mary Ann applied for the position and was granted the job. She moved in shortly before Christmas. Mary Ann was in the house for only 1 week before the youngest child, just 10 months old, was stricken with sickness and died. Once again, "gastric fever" was listed as the cause of death.

In March of 1867, Mary Ann's mother, a Mrs. Stott, became sick and asked that Mary Ann come and nurse her back to health. How very misguided that request turned out to be! Doctors said that the illness was minor and should not be of any serious risk, but Mary Ann adamantly disagreed. She told neighbors and friends that she predicted that her patient had very little time in which to live. While Mrs. Stott was sick, Mary Ann all but looted the house. She took linen, clothes, and other household items for herself, keeping them at friends' houses, with the explanation that her mother had presented them to her as a present on her death bed. As Mary Ann had predicted, Mrs. Stott did not live much longer. She died at the age of 54, nine days after she had become sick. It was said that neighbors and friends were suspicious of Mary Ann's actions surrounding the death of Mrs. Stott.

Mary Ann then took Isabella, who was 9 years old at the time, and returned to the Robinson house. She brought sickness with her, and soon, 6-year-old James Robinson, Jr., and 8-year-old Eliza were stricken. Mary Ann, who had told neighbors that she was dedicating herself to the care of the children, also stated that she feared for the welfare of her daughter, Isabella. Again, her prophesy came true, and all three were dead by April of 1867. All reportedly had the same symptoms: rolling around in bed, foaming at the mouth, and vomiting. "Gastric fever" was again attributed as the cause of death for the three children. She received a small amount of insurance money for the death of Isabella. Mary Ann openly grieved for the children and scolded herself for not taking better care of them. Robinson, who was clearly in love with Mary Ann by this time, seemed to see no connection in all of the deaths. It was a common practice for physicians of that time to list "gastric fever" or "diarrhea" as the cause of death. Both terms were broad and were usually used if a doctor was unsure of the cause. Robinson's sisters, however, grew wary of the housekeeper and were the first to accuse Mary Ann of being a poisoner. Nevertheless, Robinson married Mary Ann on August 11, 1867; she signed the marriage certificate as Mary Ann Mowbray, and it is likely she never told Robinson about her second marriage to Ward. Mary Ann Robinson gave birth to a daughter in November of 1867; the baby died of "gastric fever" in February of 1868. Mary Ann bore another of Robinson's children in 1869.

From the first day of marriage, Mary Ann urged Robinson to take out insurance policies on their children, but he refused. When Mary Ann went against his will and tried to have his own life insured, he quickly put a stop to it. Robinson did give to Mary Ann the small amount of money he was given by the community for the deaths of his children, as well as the books for his financial affairs. Mary Ann abused this trust by doctoring the entries and stealing his money. Robinson was infuriated when he found out; he demanded that she repay the money and leave. She agreed but soon skipped out on Robinson, taking the baby with her. Later, she left the baby at the home of a friend, who then returned the child to Robinson.

After living with several different men, Mary Ann was introduced to Frederick Cotton by his sister Margaret. Margaret had been a long-time acquaintance of Mary Ann's, a friendship that would ultimately cost her her life. Within a couple of weeks after Mary Ann moved in as Frederick's housekeeper, his youngest child had died. Two months later, Margaret died; the motive may have been the fact that Margaret was too familiar with Mary Ann's past, and Mary Ann may have feared that she would be exposed. By April, Mary Ann was pregnant once again, and she married Frederick; because Robinson was still alive, the marriage was bigamous. Mary Ann had another child in January of 1871.

The neighbors gossiped about Mary Ann, and about how she had been pregnant before the wedding. The stories became so heated that the family was forced to move. Later, the village pigs were all killed by a mass poisoning, which was attributed to Mary Ann. Ironically, Mary Ann and Frederick lived on the same street as her ex-lover, Joseph Nattrass. Rumors flew that the relationship was rekindled. Once again, gastric fever struck the household, and Frederick died suddenly in 1871. Joseph Nattrass moved in soon after as a "lodger." Mary Ann and Joseph had intended to be married when she took a job as nurse to a Mr. Quick-Manning, but she soon became the lover of her new employer. At this point, Nattrass and his children were simply in the way. Between March 10 and April 1, 1872, Mary Ann poisoned Joseph Nattrass, Cotton's oldest surviving child, and the child Mary Ann had with Cotton. Once again, "gastric fever" was listed as the cause of death. Nattrass left what little money he had to Mary Ann. Within 2 weeks of the new wave of deaths, Mary Ann became pregnant with Quick-Manning's child. She was still living alone except for the baggage of the 7-year-old Charles Cotton. Mary Ann tried to give the boy to an uncle to get him out of the way, and she complained openly that it was "hard for her to care for the boy since he was not her own." Mary Ann's fatal mistake would be another such inconsiderate comment. She told a storekeeper that "perhaps it will not matter as I won't be troubled long. He'll go out just like the rest of the Cotton family."

Just a few days later, on July 12, 1872, Charles died. The storekeeper found Mary Ann's comments too coincidental and reported what he knew to the police. An autopsy showed traces of arsenic in Charles Cotton's body. Other victims were exhumed, and traces of arsenic were also found in all of these bodies. Mary Ann was brought to trial for murder in March of 1873. She claimed that the Cottons had died due to exposure to wallpaper, which was colored with arsenic. Prosecutors quickly quelled this myth by pointing out the rest of her victims had not been exposed to this room. Mary Ann was convicted on all counts and was hung at Durham County jail on March 24, 1873.

In addition to lust, other emotions such as greed, fear, and desperation drove Florence Ransom and Sophie Ursinus to murder. Ransom became jealously obsessed with her husband's ex-wife, and Ursinus used murder to dispose of an ex-husband and to keep her current husband from leaving her.

Although these examples indicate that female serial killers select their victims from close relations, the opposite is true. An intimate is more likely to be the victim of a single-incident female killer rather than a female serial killer. In the case of serial murder, 25% of female serial killers kill only people with whom they have a close relationship; more than 70% of the victims of a single-incident female killer are intimates of the perpetrator.

This indicates that the motives of a female serial killer differ from the motives of a single-incident female killer. Single-incident female killers will usually kill in response to a long-standing conflict situation, or because they have been hurt emotionally by males; it is unlikely that these offenders will become serial killers. This may be because these women are acting violent in response to another's aggression, and when that aggressor is eliminated, the offender no longer feels the motivation to kill.

Writing in the 1940s, Hans Von Hentig may have best described the link between the female who kills in a single episode and her victim when he described the victim as an active element, an interacting agent, of the murder. Interacting victims are those victims who contributed to their fate by creating conflict situations between themselves and the offender. In a study by Rasko (2976), 40% of the victims were classified as interacting victims. This type of provocation took many forms, such as an alcoholic mate who is violent when drunk, or simply an abusive mate; the violence could have been directed to either the female or her children. In these cases, the female sees no way out of the unhealthy situation other than the elimination of the violent partner.

Alcohol abuse has been found to be a contributing factor in many of these murders: About half of the victims were alcoholics. The result is that alcohol abuse leads to other forms of conflict, thus provoking aggression. In other situations where the conflict is long-standing, a build-up of aggression over time is blamed for the subsequent act of violence.

Females who commit serial murder, on the other hand, become aggressive for strikingly different reasons. Looking at victim selection, one third of female serial killers reported killing only strangers, and more than half have killed at least one stranger. One fourth of all female serial killers target exclusively family members, and one half have killed at least one family member. From 1900 through 1975, female serial killers killed strangers and family members in an equal number; since 1976, there has been an increase in female serial killers killing strangers. From 1900 to 1975, 52% of all victims of female serial killers were related to the killer, whereas 48% were strangers to the killer. Since 1976, 68% of the victims were strangers to their female killer. Although the cause of this increase in stranger victims cannot be wholly determined, it is noteworthy.

Overall, 53% of females who commit multicide were at least partially motivated by money, whereas 41% killed for money only. Patty Cannon and Kate Bender independently operated motel-inns and would rob and kill motorists who checked in for an overnight stop. Residents at a nursing home operated by Amy Archer-Gilligan would pay a set fee for life care; it was more lucrative for Archer-Gilligan to hasten the resident's death once the fee was paid. Sarah Malcolm was a robber who became a serial killer by taking three lives in the course of a single robbery. The Gonzales sisters managed to murder close to 100 victims as a side business to their prostitution ranch.

Delfina Gonzales and Maria Gonzales

Victims: 91 or more
Preferred Murder Method: Torture and Beatings

In the late 1950s and early 1960s, the Mexican sisters Delfina and Maria Gonzales managed to operate a white slavery business. During this time, no less than 91, and maybe more than 100, people were killed by the sisters. Operating from a small ranch in a remote section of Mexico, the two would often recruit girls into prostitution by placing help-wanted ads in the newspaper. The ads claimed that the girls responding to it would be maids for the two sisters. If they were physically attractive enough, the girls would be promised good pay and a "home away from home."

After being hired, the girls were shipped off to San Juan de Lagos, the site of a second house of prostitution owned by the sisters. Most of the girls recruited by the sisters staffed their brothels, but others were sold to other madams for anywhere from $40 to $80. As might be expected, many of the girls rebelled once they found out the requirements of the job, but those who did would pay dearly. Those who resisted were sometimes beaten, made to hold heavy bricks, clubbed, or thrown into freezing water. These various tortures were administered until the girl either agreed to work or died. Many of the girls were forced into cocaine or heroin addiction, making resistance less likely. All of these girls were considered prisoners at the houses. Most of the girls lost their attractiveness after about 5 years, and at that point, they were usually killed. If one happened to get sick (which was likely, because the girls were fed only a daily diet of tortillas and beans), she was clubbed to death. If one of the prisoners became pregnant, she was hung by her hands and beaten until she lost the baby. Each of the houses had private cemeteries. It was reported that bribes were paid to police and local politicians to look the other way.

Early in 1964, three inmates of the brothel escaped to nearby Leon. There, the girls told their horrifying story. An investigation followed, but the sisters had been alerted of the raid and had escaped. In excavating the site, the remains of 80 women, along with the remains of an unknown number of infants, were found; also, 11 male bodies were discovered. It was later discovered that the sisters gave knock-out drops to some migrant workers who returned over the border with their checks. The migrants were then robbed and killed.

Delfina and Maria Gonzales were finally captured trying to sell their possessions and use the money to flee the country. Neither sister would admit guilt in the trial, and Delfina proclaimed, "The little dead ones died all by themselves. . . . Maybe the food didn't agree with them." They were both found guilty of murder and sentenced to the maximum of 40 years under Mexican law. The money that the sisters made was divided among the surviving victims and the families of those killed.

While the Gonzales sisters worked in tandem, it should also be noted that more than half of the female serial murderers had male accomplices, which raises the possibility that some women are coerced into committing multicide. Some female offenders, such as the women of the Manson family, serve as examples where the female may be coerced or stressed to the point that she is manipulated into participating in other crimes because of a "disciple" relationship with her male accomplice.

Only recently has the connection between stress and female-perpetrated multicide been explored. In an unscientific survey, the *New York Times* found that nearly every female serial killer had witnessed violence as part of her upbringing, typically in the form of watching her mother being physically abused by her father. In addition, many of the women had themselves been the victim of either physical or sexual abuse.

The same study also found that more than half of the women had experienced the loss of someone close during childhood. The loss was caused by death in many instances, but divorce, abandonment, and foster care were the cause in other cases. This loss typically brought on further stresses, such as the loss of companionship from a role model, the physical and mental uprooting of an established home life, and related questions that accompany any loss. In many cases, these early losses were later manifested in the female's adult life, when she experienced her own divorce or other dysfunction.

Of course, everyone experiences life stressors, and females who commit multiple murders do not appear to have experienced more trauma than what is considered typical. Thus, as Hickey (1991) has already suggested, the association between stress and mass murder must be closely considered. What may be the case with these women, and others who appear to "snap" under stress, is that they are unable to deal effectively with the stress; they remain victims throughout much of their lives. Later interactions are affected, placing certain women at risk for violent behavior. By this model, the dysfunction becomes a predisposing, rather than a precipitating, factor in murder.

As mentioned earlier, some women commit their murders in conjunction with a partner. Bonnie Parker (with Clyde Barrow) and Caril Fugate (with Charles Starkweather) are two examples familiar to the general public. Less renowned, but equally as deadly, were Myra Hindley and Martha Beck. Regardless, there remains one question: Would these women have murdered on their own, or were they coerced or encouraged to murder by their partners?

Bonnie Parker
(working in conjunction with Clyde Barrow and gang)

Victims: at least 13
Preferred Murder Method: Firearms

Many times, the film industry can make heroes out of social protesters. People see the images on the silver screen and are somehow drawn to he romantic traits that they take on. This was the case of the film *Bonnie and Clyde*. In real life, however, the couple were a far cry from their on-screen image. Bonnie Parker was born in 1911 in Rowena, Texas. Her father died when she was only 4 years old. The rest of the family moved to Cement City, Texas. At a young 16, Bonnie married Roy Thorton. Thorton was constantly running from the law, and problems with the in-laws forced the two to separate. It is said that by this time, Bonnie had a strong sex drive and slept with many different men, even as she was living with Thorton. This sex drive would follow her the rest of her life.

In January of 1930, Bonnie met Clyde Barrow. Bonnie would later say that she was "bored crapless" and ready for excitement. By this time, Thorton was definitely out of the way, serving 99 years for murder. No one is exactly sure how Bonnie and Clyde met, but a story accepted by most is that they met while visiting a mutual friend, who was ill. Clyde went home with Bonnie that night and ended up staying so late that Bonnie's mother let him sleep on the couch.

He must have slept well, because he was still asleep the next morning when police came to arrest him on seven counts of burglary and car theft. It has also been said that Bonnie was more upset that her new romance was taken away so quickly than by the fact that Clyde had criminal tendencies. Bonnie started visiting him immediately, and within a month, she helped him escape by using a gun that she had taped to her thigh. Clyde was quickly recaptured and sentenced to 14 years, but he was released later on a general parole granted by the governor of Texas.

In March of 1932, Bonnie left home with Clyde to team up and start a campaign of robbery and murder. The gang that was formed would become one of the most feared, and most infamous, groups in the southwestern United States.

In her first month with the gang, Bonnie was arrested for stealing a car. While she was in jail, the gang committed the first of what was to be many murders, killing a jeweler during what turned out to be a $40 robbery. Soon after Bonnie's release, the gang held up a gas station and got away with $3,500. In the career of these petty thieves, this was the largest sum they ever stole. Bonnie and Clyde toured in the fall of 1932, spending their money, eating at fine restaurants, and staying at fancy hotels. It was also said that Bonnie picked exclusive clothing and frequented beauty parlors.

When the pair began running out of money, they returned to robbing. Bonnie fired three shots into a 67-year-old butcher after robbing him. In November of 1932, the two kidnapped a gas station attendant named William David Jones. Jones romanticized the idea of riding with the infamous Bonnie and Clyde and joined the gang. He later stated that the time he spent with the pair was "18 months of hell." It is thought that Clyde needed help satisfying Bonnie's constant sexual urges, and that Clyde needed help himself satisfying his own homosexual needs.

The three traveled around robbing stores and banks, usually for petty amounts of money, earning between $50 and $1,000 for each hold-up. They also continued to murder. While stealing a car, they shot and killed the owner's son, and they later shot and killed a policeman who was setting a trap for another set of bank robbers. In March of 1933, the gang once again expanded, this time picking up Buck Barrow, who had just been paroled, and his wife Blanche.

Many of the killings committed by Bonnie and Clyde seemed to have no motive other than the cold-blooded desire to kill. For example, on one occasion, Bonnie asked directions from a traffic cop. After receiving the information, she pulled out a shotgun and shot him dead. It is because of this style of impulsive killing that the total number of deaths is unknown, although it is thought to be at least 13. Among those killed were six policemen, all of whom were killed on separate occasions. The gang had a knack for escaping capture, something that added to their mystique up until their gruesome deaths. In late 1933, the gang was ambushed by a group of 200 policemen. Buck Barrow was shot and killed, and his wife was captured, but again, the other three managed to escape unscathed.

Still on the loose, their murderous adventure continued. They helped a former friend and partner, Roy Hamilton, break out of jail, killing a correctional officer in the process. On April Fool's Day of 1934, Bonnie and Clyde sprayed a pursuing police car with machine gun fire, killing the two policemen inside. One week later, another cop was also gunned down in cold blood. Finally, on May 23, 1934, Bonnie and Clyde's luck ran out. Six police officers set up a trap in Gibsland, Louisiana, and the now-famous pair drove straight into it. The police officers did not wait for a surrender. They fired 167 rounds into the car. Clyde was hit 25 times, Bonnie 23. One of the policemen later stated, "We just shot the hell out of them, that's all. . . . They were just a smear of wet rags."

Oddly, the public mourned the deaths of the menacing duo. Instead of rejecting the havoc the pair had wreaked on society, the American public embraced the romanticized legacy that the media had created. Ironically, the top gangsters of that day felt exactly the opposite. John Dillinger, for one, was quoted as having said, "They were kill-crazy punks and clodhoppers, bad news to decent bank robbers. They gave us a bad name."

However, these women are the exception rather than the rule. The majority of female serial killers act alone, a feature shared with male serial killers. More than 93% of the female serial killers examined in this study operated alone. Those who do act alone tend to use less violent means to commit murder; they are more likely to use poisons or suffocation. Females who have male partners are more likely to beat their victims to death or to shoot them.

Overall, female serial killers will kill more victims than do their male counterparts. Most sources place the total number of victims by male serial killers at 10 to 12, with the typical career extending 8 to 10 years. On the other hand, as mentioned earlier, the average female serial killer averages 17 murders over a span of 5 years. Although most of the general public is familiar with the exaggerated claims of Henry Lee Lucas, who alleged to have killed hundreds during his career, there are females who boast of equally grand numbers. "Madame" Popva was responsible for a reign of terror on Samara, Russia that matched the atrocities of Henry Lee Lucas.

Popova

Victims: 300
Preferred Murder Method: Poisoning

Little is known about this Russian female serial killer, other than the fact that she is one of the most prolific killers ever known, regardless of gender. Brief articles were published about her career in both the *New York Times* and the *Chicago Tribune.* Unfortunately, no follow-up articles or other stories were ever published.

Known only as Popova, this killer worked for 30 years, dealing with women who wanted to rid themselves of their husbands; it seems that Popova was an advocate of "women's liberation" long before the term took on its present-day meaning. Popova charged very little, sometimes nothing at all, and seemed to enjoy her work. Killing provided her relief from the distress she felt from her perception that the peasant women of her area were being held "captive" by their abusive and aggressive husbands.

After 30 years of "service," she was arrested after a client, who was feeling guilty, turned her in. She was arrested in her hometown when an angry mob tried to take their own justice by burning her at the stake, but they were restrained by police. As her defense, Popova confessed to the murders, with the boast that she "did excellent work freeing unhappy wives from their tyrants."

Again, our lack of familiarity with these cases may be due to a reluctance on society's part to believe that women can be so vicious.

An indication of the perception of female serial killers can be found in the nicknames given to some of these women. Whereas males have been given monikers such as the "Monster of Dusseldorf," the "Hillside Strangler," and "The Killer Clown," females are given softer, even more complimentary nicknames. Consider "Grandma," the "Giggling Grandma," and the "Beautiful Blonde Killer," who collectively killed an estimated 33 victims. "Old Shoebox Annie" and "Mrs. Bluebeard" were killers from the early 1900s, and the "Belle of Indiana" killed between 16 and 20 victims during this period as well.

Finally, when sentenced for their crimes, female serial killers seem to benefit from society's reluctance to believe that women are capable of mass killings. In his limited study of the disposition of cases involving these killers, Hickey (1991) notes that only 3% have been sentenced to death row. An estimated 12% of all female serial killers have been executed throughout history. The vast majority of cases are sentenced to either life in prison (40%) or to some prison time (18%). Interestingly, Hickey estimates that 12% of all female serial killers are never apprehended.

Conclusion

Female serial killers are a curious group. Many operated before the turn of the 20th century, murdering the very people they should be closest to: family members. From the stories above, however, it is obvious that these women lacked the bond of familial attachment. Recently, the female serial killer has developed a different look. She now kills strangers and uses more violent methods to murder. Whether or not the number of female serial killers has increased in the past years is debatable. But one thing is without doubt: The final result is as deadly as any act committed by her male counterpart.

References

Dabbs, J. M., & Morris, R. (1990). Testosterone, social class, and antisocial behavior in a sample of 4,462 men. *Psychological Science, 1*, 209-211.

Eagly, A. H.. & Steffen, V. J. (1986). Gender and aggressive behavior: A meta-analytic review of the social psychological literature. *Psychological Bulletin, 100*, 309-330.

Maccoby, E. E., & Jackin, C. N. (1974). *The psychology of sex differences.* Stanford, CA: Stanford University Press.

Meyer-Bahlburg, H. F. L., & Erhardt, A. A. (1982). Prenatal sex hormones and human aggression: A review and new data on progesterone effects. *Aggressive Behavior, 8*, 39-62.

Money, J., & Erhardt, J. J. (1972). *Man and woman, boy and girl.* Baltimore, MD: Johns Hopkins Unversity Press.

Reinisch, J. M. (1981). Prenatal exposure to synthetic progestin increases potential for aggression in humans. *Science, 211*, 1171-1173.

Reynolds, B. (1993). The neuroendocrinology and neurochemistry of antisocial behavior. In S. A. Mednick, T. E. Moffitt, & S. A. Stack (Eds.), *The causes of crime* (pp. 239-262). Cambridge, UK: Cambridge University Press.

Segrave, K. (1992). *Women serial and mass murderers: A worldwide reference, 1580 through 1990.* Jefferson, NC: McFarland.

Wolfgang, M. E., & Weiner, N. A. (1982). *Criminal violence.* Beverly IIills, CA: Sage.

4

Female Serial Murderesses
The Unnoticed Terror

STEPHEN T. HOLMES
ERIC HICKEY
RONALD M. HOLMES

Introduction

Serial murder is probably the most disturbing crime of the 1990s (Holmes and DeBurger, 1988). Research on the subject appears both on an academic level (Hickey, 1991; Holmes and DeBurger, 1985, 1988; Jenkins, 1987; Levin and Fox, 1985; Leyton, 1985; Ressler et al, 1988) and other more narrative formats which tend to be deficient in documentation. Both types of research and writings, however, indicate that the overwhelming number of serial killers are men. For example, in a listing of forty-seven serial killers by Holmes and DeBurger (1988: 22-23), only three were females. Of the three female serialists, two killed family members and the other murdered with her male lovers. None is examined by any of the previously cited researchers. Given the apparent scarcity of females involved as multiple homicide offenders, sources are few which address their incidence and etiology. By contrast, homicide is one of the most carefully monitored crimes in American society.

Authors' Note: This chapter first appeared in *The Contemporary Journal of Criminal Justice* (1991). Vol 7(4): pp. 245-256. Reprinted with permission.

Data on "Traditional" Homicide

The rate of homicide has decreased in the last decade. The Bureau of Justice Statistics reports:

> ... the most recent decade of homicide data from the National Center for Health Statistics shows rates rising from 1976, peaking in 1980, and declining to levels below the 1976 rate (15).

Studies now, however, indicate an increase in homicide rates, at least in many urbanized areas. Statistics in 1990, from more than a dozen large cities in America, report that homicide rates are higher now than ever. New York City, for example, recorded over 2,000 violent deaths by the end of 1990. The record number of homicides within the city limits of Washington, D.C. solidifies its reputation as "Murder Capital of the United States." Throughout the 1980s the yearly toll of murder victims hovered near the 20,000 figure. In 1990 this figure rose to approximately 23,600. This represents not only a marked increase in the total number of murders but also a significant increase in the rate of killings (FBI, 1991).

The Uniform Crime Report, compiled by the FBI, noted that most victims of homicide during the 1980s were killed by family, friends, and acquaintances. Most of these murders were a result of impulsive violence (Block, 1985) often fueled by alcohol or illegal drugs (Goodman et al., 1986). Increasingly, several large U.S. cities have seen persons die as a result of victim-offender disputes involving the sale, distribution, or use of illicit drugs (Zimring and Zuehl,1986).

There are, however, few studies which empirically measure the number of those victimized by serial killers. Since most serial murders are considered to be "stranger to stranger," homicide detection and apprehension is considerably more difficult. In turn, collecting accurate data becomes problematic. One source reported as many as 5,000 victims a year who fall prey to serial killers (Bernick and Spangler, 1985). Their data were gathered from interviewing "experts in the field." While there is no precise method to confirm this number, there is growing concern by law enforcement officials over the increase in the incidences of new cases each year. Similar to homicides in general most of these serial killings are victims who fall prey to men.

Rationale for Serial Murder

Persons who murder serially kill for different reasons. Men kill typically for a psychological gain and are intrinsically motivated. The anticipated gain is normally one which is psychological: sexual pleasure, the ultimate power over another human being, or aberrant hedonism (Holmes and DeBurger, 1985; Holmes, DeBurger and Holmes, 1988). Under normal conditions these types of offenders kill because of an inner need or compulsion to murder. There are indeed some males who kill serially because of visions or voices, but they are rare in comparisons to most serial murderers (Holmes, 1988; Hickey, 1991).

By distinguishing the different types of men who murder serially and utilizing an analysis of motivation, victim selection, anticipated gain, methods of murder, and based upon an analysis of 400 cases, a taxonomy was developed of four different types of serial killers: Vision, Mission, Hedonistic and Power/Control (Holmes and DeBurger, 1985). But these classifications were based solely upon an examination of male offenders. Now, by expanding serial murder research, a similar typology is needed for consideration of female offenders.

The Female Serial Murderess

Despite the claim of Egger (1985) or Rule (Reynolds, 1990), there is clear evidence that some women are serial killers. One reason for the reluctance to accept women as serial killers, perhaps, has been an aversion to perceive women as being capable of fatal violence. Women tend not to kill for sexual reasons, nor does God or the devil typically impel them to homicide (Holmes, 1990; Hickey, 1991). Women have been stereotypically viewed as nurturing and vulnerable, not physically or psychologically capable of murder, unless provoked in an abusive situation. Such notions are being challenged as more research focuses upon women and their propensity for violent behavior.

The preponderance of women who kill do so because of ill-fated personal relationships. The typical female murderer not only kills someone she knows, but often inside her own home. For example, sometimes in a marriage where physical violence is commonplace, the perceived manner in which to escape may be through fatal violence. In other cases, women having been spurned in love may kill as a perceived just response. In one highly publicized case, Jane Harris killed her lover, Dr. Townover, because of love gone awry. While these types of domestic homicides are common, serial murder involving females as offenders is relatively rare.

Hickey (1991) examined thirty-four serial killers. He noted among his findings that 82% of the cases of serial murder had occurred since 1900 and that almost one in two killers had a male accomplice. Perhaps one of the most interesting finding in Hickey's work was that more than one third of the women began their killing career since 1970. He offered several explanations for this apparent occurrence; improved police investigation, population increase and increased media attention. The average woman killed for 9.2 years before her killing stopped, for whatever reason. Most were homemakers (32%), nurses (18%), or involved in other types of criminal careers (15%). One in five killers reported no occupational title whatsoever. Ninety-seven percent were white and the average age was 33 when they began their killing careers.

Regarding women who stalked victims, Hickey found that in contrast to male serial offenders only one third of female serial killers reported having killed strangers. And almost without exception, the females did not travel to more than one state in their quest for victims. Their motives and methods also differ from their male counterparts; these women murder for material gain using poisons or pills (Ibid., 107-118). Some women who kill serially may do so because of their involvement in cults or "disciple" relationships. This type is illustrated by the women associated with the Charlie Manson family. Charlene Gallego, the common-law wife of serial killer Gerald Gallego, willfully aided in the selection, abduction and murders of at least ten young people (van Hoffman, 1990).

There appears to be an increasing number of women who murder multiple victims. By simply using the parameters of three or more victims killed in a span of thirty days or more (Holmes and DeBurger, 1985), several cases involving female offenders can be identified. Belle Gunness murdered an estimated 14 to 49 husbands and suitors in LaPorte, Indiana. Nannie Doss murdered 11 husbands and family members in Tulsa. Martha Beck and her lover, Ray Fernandez, stalked and murdered as many as 20 women. In the early 1980s, Carol Bundy (no relation to Ted Bundy) became an excellent example of the lust serial murderess. Decapitating a former lover along with several other young female runaways, she and Douglas Clark are believed to have carried out numerous homicides in the Los Angeles area. She currently is serving time in prison for the murder of only one male victim while Douglas is on death row in California for the murders of 6 young women.

Often women serialists kill for purchases of comfort: money, insurance benefits or business interests. Dorothea Puente of Sacramento County, California, was charged with 9 murders of elderly roomers who rented rooms in her boarding home. She allegedly signed and cashed her victims' Social Security checks after their deaths. For some offenders, targeting the elderly may be financially attractive. Since 1975, there has been an apparent increase in multiple homicides involving the elderly (Hickey, 1991).

There are, however, often female serialists who do not kill for comfort considerations. Sex, revenge, spurned love, all emerge as intrinsic motivations for homicide. The anticipated gains and loci of motivations may often vary from one female offender to another. Consequently, we will first examine some primary characteristics central to female serial killers including those of spatial mobility, gain, motivation, and method of murder.

Primary Characters and Typologies
Of Female Serial Murderers

Utilizing the previously discussed parameters to identify female serial offenders: those who have killed more than three victims in a time span of at least thirty days, there emerge distinctions on several ways in which to examine female serialists. Initially, distinctions were made among groups of female serial killers which included nurses, black widows, and other categories (Hickey, 1986). However, further differences among categories may facilitate identification of definitive traits. Hopefully, these traits will aid law enforcement in the understanding and apprehension of these female offenders.

Spatial Mobility and Serial Murder

Initially, serial killers can be distinguished according to their geographic mobility. They tend to be either *geographically stable* or *geographically transient.* The first type is offenders who reside in one location and seek out their victims in that same or nearby area. Carol Bundy and Pricilla Ford are two examples. Carol lived in Los Angeles and selected victims usually from the Hollywood and Vine area. Priscilla Ford killed victims in her hometown of Reno, Nevada. Her unfortunate victims were randomly selected pedestrians whom God commanded she kill.

Unlike the male serialist who appears to be almost equally divided between the stable and transient types, the female serial offender almost exclusively falls into the geographically stable category. This may occur as a result of traditional female roles which have centered most activities around the home and family. Additionally, women have not been as occupationally mobile as their male counterparts. Consequently, spatial mobility is limited, which in turn narrows the victim selection process.

The geographically transient are those few females who travel continually throughout their killing careers (Holmes and DeBurger, 1985: 30-31). Christine Gallego is an example. She and her common-law husband killed in California and Nevada. The geographically transient female serial killer presents problems similar to men of the same genre. Jurisdictional issues, lack of communication among law enforcement agencies, as well as the mobility of the killer, all add to the complexity of apprehending offenders.

In contrast, geographically stable female offenders, because of their lack of mobility, increase the likelihood of detection and apprehension. These offenders often maintain personal, occupational and social ties to the community. In addition, most of these cases involve only one law enforcement jurisdiction, which eliminates most interagency "turf" issues and facilitates communications. In Table 4.1, factors including spatial locations, method of killings, and victims were paired with the five types of serial murderesses identified in this paper.

The Visionary Serial Killer

Most serial killers are not considered psychotic and understand legally, if not morally, that murder is wrong (Hickey, 1991). They have no apparent feelings about the concern and welfare of others; most, perhaps, could be classified as character defects such as possessing antisocial personalities. By contrast, there are some who commit the acts of

TABLE 4.1. Homicidal Behavior Patterns of Female Serial Killers

Factors	Visionary	Comfort	Hedonistic	Disciple	Power
Victims					
Specific		x	x		x
Nonspecific	x			x	
Random	x		x		
Non-random		x		x	x
Affiliative		x			
Strangers	x		x	x	x
Methods					
Act-focused	x			x	x
Processsed		x	x		
Planned		x	x	x	x
Spontaneous	x				
Organized		x	x	x	x
Disorganized	x				
Spatial Locations					
Concentrated	x	x			
Nomadic			x	x	x

homicides because they are extrinsically compelled to do so. A few see visions demanding that they kill everyone in the world or at least in their neighborhood. This was the case of Joseph Kallinger, profiled by Flora Schriebner in her book, *The Shoemaker.* "Charley," a floating head, periodically would speak to Kallinger with a command that he destroy all humans in the world, then his family, and finally commit suicide. In a correctional hospital setting, Kallinger still admits that he sees Charley and would kill again if he were released from the secure facility where is presently is serving his sentence (Schiebner, 1984).

In this type of homicide, the perpetrator has a severe break with reality. This break can be demonstrated by the person's admission that she has spoken to God, an angel, a spirit or Satan himself. The motivation is extrinsic to the personality and comes from an apparition or an auditory hallucination. In such a case, the attack tends to be spontaneous, with the killer selecting a victim predicated upon a description given by the message-giver.

Priscilla Ford is an example of a Visionary serial killer who heard the voice of God as she walked down the streets of Reno, Nevada. This voice demanded that she kill people she crossed on the street because they were 'bad people' and deserved to die. The insanity defense was insufficient to keep her from Nevada's death row.

Another Visionary serial murderess was Martha Wise. A forty year old widow living in Medina, Ohio, she killed her family members simply for revenge. She used arsenic to poison her mother after she had been ridiculed for being involved romantically with a man younger than herself. She later fed arsenic to her aunt and uncle but bungled an attempt in using the poison to kill the rest of her family. Wise claimed the devil had followed her everywhere and forced her to do the killings.

The Comfort Serial Killer

In contrast to the visionary type, the comfort serial killer is motivated to murder for material reasons, not for psychological gain. They tend to be the most prevalent of all female serialists. There are no voices or visions from God or the devil demanding that everyone must die. The offender will usually kill persons with whom she is acquainted. The material gain is typically money or the promise of money such as insurance benefits, acquisition of business interests or real estate.

In 1901, Amy Archer-Gilligan opened a rest home in Connecticut. During the next fourteen years she disposed of at least twenty-seven men and women by poisoning them. Of the men she nursed, she married five, insured each for substantial amounts of money and then poisoned each one. In other instances she killed elderly women after she helped them rewrite their wills. Similarly in Cincinnati, Anna Hahn, self-proclaimed "angel of mercy," provided "constant care" for several elderly men, only to see them each die suddenly.

During the mid 1970s, Janice Gibbs of Georgia killed her husband, three sons, and an infant grandson for $31,000 in insurance money. Mary Eleanor Smith trained her son in the "art of killing" to rob men and then dump the bodies in muriatic acid beneath their home in Montana. Dorothea Puente in Sacramento County, California, was charged in 1988 with nine counts of murder after the authorities found bodies in the side yard of her rooming house. She allegedly killed her roomers for their Social Security checks. Earlier in her criminal career, she had been convicted of forging checks belonging to her tenants. If guilty of the charges brought against her, she would join the ranks of geographically stable, comfort serial murderesses.

Hedonistic Serial Murder

Perhaps the least understood and the one least represented of all female serial killers is the hedonistic type. Hedonism is the striving for pleasure. In this sense, the hedonistic serial killer is one which has made the critical connection between fatal violence and personal, sexual gratification. Carol Bundy of California was allegedly involved not only in the killing of a male victim but several young women who were runaways and prostitutes. She is believed to have helped her male accomplice, Douglas Clark, abduct and decapitate victims and then place the heads in her refrigerator. Later, the heads were retrieved and used in aberrant sex acts (Personal interview, Douglas Clark). The motivation for the killings appears to be intrinsic to her personality: personal and sexual pleasure. To murder was pleasurable; Bundy did not rob the victims; no money, jewelry or personal articles were taken. The anticipated gain appears to be purely psychological. Bundy continues to maintain her innocence.

Power Seekers

Power is the ability to influence the behavior of others in accordance to one's own desires. Power may also be defined in this context as the ultimate domination of one person by another. For example, Jane Toppan, a nurse, is believed to have killed between seventy and one hundred victims. She proudly exclaimed that she had fooled the authorities, " . . . the stupid doctors and the ignorant relatives . . . This is my ambition—to have killed more helpless people—than any man or woman has ever killed" (authors' files). Some killers will repeatedly poison their victims and then nurse them back to health. Finally, the patient is killed and the offender, usually a private nurse, moves on to another victim.

Genene Jones, a pediatric nurse in San Antonio was arrested for the murder of young children in hospitals often for very minor medical problems. Thought to be responsible for as many as sixteen deaths of infants

(Elkind, 392), Jones felt a sense of importance working in a hospital setting as a primary medical caretaker. Recently, the Munchausen Syndrome by Proxy has been applied to individuals who fabricate and induce medical problems in children under their care. Some individuals temporarily boost their feelings of self-esteem and worthiness through their involvement in life and death situations, such as those found in an emergency room, operating room or critical care unit. Jones was such a personality. Her behavior is akin " . . . to the volunteer fireman who sets a blaze, then appears first at the scene in hope of becoming a hero" (Ibid). Offenders usually receive some form of psychological satisfaction such as praise from superiors or gratitude from the patient and family.

Disciple Killer

Finally, some women kill when they are under the influence of a charismatic leader. One of the most infamous cases involved the female followers of Charles Manson: Lynette Fromme, Leslie Van Hooten, and others who willingly butchered victims at Manson's command. The gain is psychological; the personal acceptance of the women by her "idol." Victim selection is usually decided upon by the male leader and reflects more of the leader's wants than those actually committing the murders.

In 1982, Judy Neeley and her husband, Alvin, were involved in forgeries, burglaries and robberies. Eventually, they began to seek greater thrill by abducting, abusing, raping and murdering their victims. Judy claimed that her husband forced her to commit tortures and murders because she was completely dominated by him. While in Alabama, they abducted a 13 year old girl and held her captive. Judy watched while Alvin raped, tortured and abused the child. Finally, Judy injected Drano into the girl's veins, but when that failed to kill, she shot her victim in the back and pushed her over a cliff. They later abducted a married couple, took them into a wooded area and shot them both. The man survived the shooting and later testified against the couple. The final number of their victims was never determined.

In another case, Charlene Gallego married her husband, Gerald, not knowing he was still legally married to another woman. She quickly accepted his lifestyle including his bizarre sexual fantasies. Involved in at least the killings of nine young women and one young man, Charlene eventually was apprehended and testified against her husband. She is presently in a Nevada prison serving two 16 year concurrent sentences.

Martha Beck and her love Ray Fernandez advertised in lonely hearts magazines for female companionship. Approximately twenty women answered these ads and they were strangled, battered, drowned, poisoned or shot to death. To demonstrate her loyalty for her lover, she eagerly drowned a two year old child, she summoned Fernandez to the bathtub, her hands still holding the dead girl under water and gleefully exclaimed, "Oh, come and look what I've done, Sweetheart."

Personal relationships appear to facilitate violence in certain cases. Some individuals, in all likelihood, would never kill without the involvement of another person(s). Mutually shared fantasies involving violence and sexual experimentation appear to stimulate some relationships to actualize their fantasies. This observation has been documented among all sexual orientations.

This chemistry is never more evident than in the case of Alton Coleman and Debra Brown. She lived with an abusive and violent Coleman and violence became a part of their relationship. The propensity for violence became an integral part of their killing. On at least one occasion, she followed Coleman's lead when she killed an elderly couple in Cincinnati beating them to death using a four-foot wood candle stick, a crow bar, vise grip pliers and a knife. She is thought to have been killed as many as eight persons in the company of Coleman. Even after the trial and the incarceration on death row, Brown remained loyal to her lover and signed legal documents to become common law partners.

Conclusion

There are indications of an increasing number of women involved in serial murder. Priscilla Ford, Charlene Gallego, Thelma Barfield and others are all examples of an emerging number of women serialists who pose a disturbing danger to our society. Though women represent a small percentage of offender cases in serial murder, changing characteristics of the female offender may be impacting their representation. For example, Hickey offers only two such changes:

Over the past few years, females offenders killed fewer family member (Comfort) while increasingly targeting strangers . . . (and) Those who had male partners were much more likely to use violence in killing their victims . . . (1991, 127).

Although some research suggests many women kill for financial (material) gain, other more intrinsic and complex explanations need to be explored which address sociopathy and psychopathology. These differences, combined with public perception, have resulted in most of the research and literature being devoted to the male serialist.

Bibliography

Bernick, B. and Spangler, J. 1985. Rovers kill up to 5,000 each year, experts say. *Deseret News.* September, Las Vegas.

Blackburn, D. 1990. *Human harvest: The Sacramento murder story.* New York: Knightsbridge Publishing Co.

Eckert, A. 1985. *The scarlet mansion.* New York: Bantam Books.

Elkin, P. 1989. *The death shift.* News York: Onyx Books.

Hickey, E. 1991. *Serial killers and their victims.* Pacific Groves, CA: Brooks/Cole Publishing Co.

Holmes, R. and DeBurger, J. 1985. Profiles in terror: The serial murderer. *Federal Probation.* September. 29-34.

Holmes, R. and DeBurger, J. 1988. *Serial murder.* Newbury Park, CA: Sage Publications.

Holmes, R., DeBurger, J. and Holmes, S. 1990. Inside the mind of the serial murderer. *American Journal of Criminal Justice.* Vol. 13. No. 1. Fall. 1-9.

Levin, J. and Fox, J. 1985. *Mass murder: America's Growing Menace.* New York: Plenum Press.

———— Report to the nation on crime and justice. 2nd Ed., Washington, DC: Bureau of Justice Statistics

Ressler, R., Burgess, A. and Douglas, J. 1988. *Sexual Homicides: Patterns and Motives.* Lexington, MA: Lexington Books.

Reynolds, B. This is the beginning of the end for murderer. *USA Today.* August 30.

Schreiber, F. 1984. *The shoemaker: The anatomy of a psychotic.* New York: Signet Books.

van Hoffman, E. 1990. *A venom in the blood.* New York: Donald I. Fine, Inc.

PART II

——————————

THE MIND OF
THE SERIAL KILLER

No one truly understands the mind of the serial killer. There have been valiant, impertinent, academic, yellow-page journalism, and mass media approaches to do so, but all have fallen short of gaining access to the mind of this most dangerous predator. In studying serial murder for the past 15 years, Ronald Holmes has looked for the basic compelling motivations inside the mind of the serial murderer but has also fallen short. The pop culture books have made simplistic attempts to explain this most unanswerable query and have placed the answer at the doorstep of the domineering and abusive parent, usually the mother. Others have stated that the answer really rests within the triangle of youthful behaviors: cruelty to animals, bedwetting, and firesetting. Certainly, there are very disturbed people who commit these acts, but these commissions do not necessarily *cause* one to be a serial murderer. The true answer is not simple, and we probably will spend the next 100 years looking for the answer(s). However, there are some who seriously doubt that we will ever find the part of the brain or the niche in society that accounts for fatal sequential predation.

Perhaps the one serial killer whom most Americans know is Hannibal Lecter, the main character of Thomas Harris's two books *The Red Dragon* and *The Silence of the Lambs*. His insights into the minds of Francis Dolarhyde and Hannibal Lecter are interesting, insightful, and accurate.

But unfortunately, in real life, this rarely occurs. Academics and researchers have carefully examined senseless acts of violence committed on hundreds of people per year. These effects provide us with more than a glimpse into the mind of the serial killer. This is the focus of the first three chapters in this section.

Dr. Robert Hale is an emerging figure in the academic study of serial murder. A sociologist by education, he is currently an assistant professor at Southeastern Louisiana University. Combining his interest in serial murder with his educational exposure to various criminological theories, Hale offers the reader a view into the mind of the serial killer and the influence of the total environment as a causative factor. Can it be that the mind of the serial murderer can be molded by the unique combination of biology and the environment? This is the thrust of Hale's "The Application of Learning Theory to Serial Murder." Can "frustration" as a child be the prime cause of one becoming a serial killer? Using a learning theory developed more than 40 years ago by two psychologists, Hale offers one possible explanation for the etiology of the serial killer.

Dr. Al C. Carlisle was a prison psychologist at the Utah State Prison. Recently retired, Dr. Carlisle spent his professional career in psychological sessions with killers such as Gary Gilmore, Ted Bundy, and many others. From more than 25 years of almost daily contact with violent personal offenders, he has developed a theory of causation of at least the sexually motivated and power-motivated serialists. Carlisle has found dissociation to be an important factor in the personality and mindset of the serial killer. Using his years of experience as a prison psychologist and his exposure to many serial killers, Carlisle discovers a small part inside each killer that compels him to kill. Different killers call it by different names: "the shadow," "the beast," "the entity." Is it this 1% of a killer's mind that takes over the other 99%? Using his notes from his interviews, Dr. Carlisle treats the subject matter with academic rigor and scientific objectivism.

Just as Bundy eluded to the "entity" as one small part of his personality that overcame and ruled his entire personality, Carlisle learned that many other serialists also have the "one percent" that takes over the "ninety-nine percent" and compels the murderous acts.

Ronald Holmes includes a chapter in this section titled, "Sequential Predation: Elements of Sequential Fatal Victimization." In this chapter, he lists and explains various elements that he has learned from interviews with serial killers. These elements are fantasy, symbolism, ritual-ism, and compulsion. By blending these elements, the deviant sexual predator launches into the fatal acts of predation. It is the unique com-bination of these elements that accounts for the manner in which serial killers murder their victims. The information from this chapter was gath-ered from interviews with the "real experts," the serial killers them-selves. It was from the interviews that the final chapter became a reality.

Holmes, DeBurger, and Holmes explore further the mind of the serial killer by examining the behavioral sources of the serial killer, looking at the types of expected gains by serial killers, the methods and patterns of the murderous events, the role of the victim, victim selectivity, and victim relationships. Valuable insight, from a much different perspective from Hale or Carlisle, adds to the arguably meager amount of knowledge about the mind of the serial killer.

The final chapter is penned by a man imprisoned for murder. A "true expert" on personal violence, this offender practiced on his victims hei-nous acts of violence that placed their lives in jeopardy. In his own words, he speaks from a perspective of a serial killer. He is intelligent, educated, verbal, and charming, and it is not surprising that he was able to secure victims. He does not appear to be a violent personality. He is charming, witty, and wishes to place the unwitting victim into his comfort zone to commit acts of personal violence. There are many law enforcement pro-fessionals who believe he is responsible for more than a score of other unresolved murders. He is in prison, not on death row but in the general population. There is a remote chance that he will be free someday, and this is a truly frightening prospect.

5

The Application of Learning Theory to Serial Murder, or "You Too Can Learn to Be a Serial Killer"

ROBERT HALE

Serial murder is often viewed as the most senseless and violent form of criminal behavior. Many researchers in criminology have attempted to uncover the factors that would lead an individual to commit such an act. In 1988, Holmes and DeBurger published what is considered the first systematic and most comprehensive examination of serial murder. Focusing on serial murder as a particular form of homicide, they outline the social characteristics of serial murder and provide a typology of the murderer. In their efforts, however, the authors make a mistake common among those who research this behavior by disregarding the internal motives of these crimes.

Operating from this orientation, Holmes and DeBurger give little attention to the psychological motives of the serial killer, focusing instead on the external drives and motives that lead to serial murder. To ignore these internal drives is to overlook an important source of motivation for the serial killer. This source is rooted in Sigmund Freud's notion of the basic drives of Eros and Thanatos (1961); it is furthered in Dollard and Miller's theory popularly known as the "frustration-aggression"

Author's Note: This chapter first appeared in 1993 in the *American Journal of Criminal Justice*,17(2), 37-45. Reprinted with permission.

hypothesis (1950). This report provides a synthesis of the notion of internalized humiliation as a motive and discusses how this behavior could be explained from a learning perspective.

Serial Murder Reviewed

Serial murder is a specific form of violence in the category of multicide. Multicide differentiates between the crimes of serial murder, spree murder, and mass murder. Holmes and DeBurger list five primary elements in serial murder, focusing largely on the traits of the perpetrator. First, serial murders are usually one-on-one relationships. There are rare exceptions, but the pattern typically involves only two people, the assailant and the victim. Second, the relationship between the victim and the assailant is usually that of stranger. Although the individuals might be slight acquaintances, serial murder seldom occurs between intimates. Holmes and DeBurger call this a "non-Affiliative" relationship. Third, the serial killer's motives are not immediately obvious. Clear-cut and obvious motives are lacking, due to the "stranger-perpetration" of the crime, therefore the killer's motives appear to be non-rational. Fourth, the serial murderer is motivated to kill. Whatever other brutality is visited upon the victim, the final insult will be death. Holmes and DeBurger do not see these deaths as a crime of passion in the conventional sense (1988: 19), nor do the deaths arise from victim precipitation. Finally, the central element is repetitive homicide. The serial killer kills, and will continue to kill if not stopped (Holmes and DeBurger, 1988: pp. 18-19).

Characteristics uncovered by Holmes and DeBurger are important for providing a foundation for looking at the specifics of serial murder. Most serial killers do not become as sensationalized or proficient as a Ted Bundy or a Jeffrey Dahmer. Unlike these killers, most serial murderers kill only 10 or 12 times, and these are usually spread out over a period of several years. Most maintain a low profile, living a private existence. They give the appearance of being socially responsible, often holding a job. They do not give the impression of being "crazy," to draw attention to themselves could mean detection and arrest. Because of their cunning and the "non-Affiliative nature" of the relationship to their victim serial killers may lead "normal," undetected lives for years. Often their identification and apprehension occur quite by accident, as in the case of Dahmer. For these reasons, it is difficult to arrive at an accurate measure of the number of serial killers.

Holmes and DeBurger also examine the relationship between the victim and offender. It has been stated previously that the perpetrator and victim typically do not have an intimate relationship, if in fact there is any relationship at all between the two. Holmes and DeBurger write that "the victim need not have taunted, threatened, or abused the killer." They further claim that there are not any motives of "hatred, rage, fear, jealousy, or greed at work" (1988: p. 24). The serial killer is thought to kill for motives other than internal emotion.

This report diverges from the views of Holmes and DeBurger on this point of the relationship; between the victim and the perpetrator concerning motive. The roots of intrinsic motive toward killing are passed over and handled as inconsequential by Holmes and DeBurger. As a result, intrinsic emotions are not explored or examined at any length in their writings. The primary concern of *Serial Murder* is to provide a formulation of typologies of serial killers and killings. However, without a deeper and more complete understanding of the internal motives and drives of the serial killer the knowledge provided in *Serial Murder* is blunted. This understanding is provided through a look at internal motive. What will be shown is that the serial murderer is releasing a humiliation in an attempt to regain lost power.

Learning Serial Murder

Katz (1988) details the steps involved in killing as a means to overcome humiliation and lost power. The killer has previously experienced some type of interaction that has left the killer humiliated. The act of murder, in Katz's view, becomes a passionate attempt to perform a sacrifice to restore what is "Good" or "Right." Despite the irrational or chaotic surroundings of the murder, the killer has justified the act as necessary to restore a previous wrong.

A situation involving humiliation involves an attack on a personal claim of moral worth. The killer feels compelled to answer a challenge to his (or her) self-worth. Ted Bundy, for example, is reported to have chosen his victims based on their resemblance to a former girl friend who

had broken a marriage engagement she had with him. Bundy purport-
edly selected his victims based on their having brunette hair, parted
down the middle of the head, looking much like his former fiancée (Rule,
1980) Jerome Henry Brudos felt he was never accepted by his mother
Brudos transferred his hatred for his mother to other women through his
mutilation of their bodies. For Brudos, the murder of strange women
served as a catharsis for the humiliation he endured through his
mother's rejection. During a confession, Brudos admitted killing one
victim only because he had "absolute control" over her life; he continued
by stating he had never felt control over any other woman before this
time (Rule, 1988: p. 145). Ed Gein is another serial killer who transferred
an early humiliation into a later quest for power. Gein is described as
"the little recluse who had hated his mother so much that he had killed
her and other older women and made vests of their dried flesh. . . . Ed
Gein had been a life-long bachelor, absolutely ruled by his hated mother"
(Rule, 1988: p. 137). Gein's maternal rejection would have been amplified
since Gein's father was a heavy drinker who often abused both Gein and
his mother (Gollmar, 1982: pp. 66, 70). A similar example of humiliation
emerges in the case of the Hillside Stranglers, Kenneth Bianchi and Angelo
Buono. Bianchi "created" an alternate personality as a "repository for all
his hateful feelings toward his mother" (Levin and Fox, 1985: p. 150).
These three examples represent an early humiliation that can trigger a
serial murder rampage. Other examples provide further support.

Richard Biegenwald lives in the Trenton (New Jersey) State Prison
convicted of multiple murders of both males and females. His humiliation was rooted in his father, "an alcoholic who had no interest in his
wife and child, (and) often beat his young son" (Linedecker, 1988: p. 125).
Also, during the period of a decade, Robert Hansen murdered at least 17
women in Anchorage, Alaska. Hansen was described as "the skinny
stutterer with the pimply face (who) was virtually shut out of the dating
game during his teenage years." His humiliation over being rejected
socially led to a "deep-seated hatred" for young, beautiful women.
Hansen justified his murders through a rationalization that he was killing women; most of his victims were prostitutes or barroom dancers
(Linedecker, 1988: p. 137). In this manner Hansen was internally justified
in releasing his naked prey into the Alaska wilderness before hunting
them down with a rifle.

The proposed hypothesis that an early humiliation can translate into
the most vicious of criminal acts applies only if the killer recognizes and

internalizes humiliation as a motive. All people experience some form of humiliation in their lives but do not turn to murder as a recourse. However, for some psychological reason the serial killer has internalized the wrong and uses it as a rationale for murder. An explanation is found in Abraham Amsel's frustration theory (1958).

The killer associates certain cues from the situation in which the humiliation occurred with the humiliation. The humiliation is referred to as a "nonreward" situation, which means that a reward did not occur in a situation in which a reward previously occurred. Nonreward presented in a situation in which reward previously occurred produces an unconditional frustration response (RF). The cues which were present during the humiliation (RF) become conditioned to produce an anticipatory frustration response. The anticipatory frustration response also produces a distinctive internal stimuli (SF) which motivates the individual to avoid potentially humiliating situations (as indicated by similar cues) in the future.

For Bundy and Hansen it was a frustration rooted in a humiliation that occurred out of a social and dating scheme; others were able to obtain dates, fall in love, and be married. Out of frustration they had to ask why they were being denied. Maternal deprivation was the basis for the behavior of Brudos, Gein, Bianchi, and Buono. And for Biegenwald it was the denial of both maternal and paternal bonding that caused frustration. They could see others receiving this type of love, but they were denied. These killers internalized cues from their environment which in turn directed their behaviors. It is this internalization that differentiates the serial killer from other functioning members of society.

The killer has internalized the cues that predict (in the killer's perception) a frustration. This occurs, and can be explained, through Hull-Spence theory of discrimination learning (1943; 1946). According to this theory, exposure to SD indicates that reinforcement is available; SBlock indicates that reinforcement is not available. The serial killer has encountered SBlock in various situations described previously, but has not experienced any, or else very few, SD through which discrimination might occur. Thus, in all situations in which the cues that indicate a potential humiliation to the killer are present, the killer associates the nonreinforcement of a SBlock situation. A dearth of SD situations does not allow the killer to discriminate. The further role of discrimination will soon be discussed.

The question that needs to be answered with regard to serial murder remains: Why does the serial murderer not go back to the originator of the humiliation and kill this person to set right the humiliation? Why did Bundy choose not to kill his ex-fiancee, nor Brudos kill his mother, nor Biegenwald kill his father, all of whom are said to be the causes of humiliation in these killers' lives?

The answer lies in Dollard and Miller's (1939, 1950) theory of learning. According to the Dollard and Miller theory, the individual is "instigated" toward a behavior. An instigator is "some antecedent condition of which the predicted response is the consequences" (1939: p. 3). The instigated behavior serves as the origin for all related subsequent actions. The concept of an instigator is broader than that of stimulus which refers only to the energy exerted on a sense organ; according to Dollard and Miller, an instigator can be any antecedent condition, either observed or inferred, from which a response can be predicted, and this condition can either be a stimulus, a verbally reported idea, image, or motive, or some state of deprivation (1939: p. 4).

The serial killer is no different than any other individual who is instigated to seek approval from parents, sexual partners, or others. In other words, all individuals learned to seek approval (Dollard and Miller, 1950: p. 92). Upon the successful completion of the instigation, it is said that "goal response" has occurred. When an instigated goal response occurs at its proper time then all parties involved are satisfied with the resolution. However, in the example of the serial killer this successful resolution does not occur. The interference that occurs, as mentioned previously, is called "frustration."

Frustration occurs when a motivated individual encounters some barrier that prevents the person from reaching a desired goal. Social frustrations that were perceived by the serial killers have never been previously introduced. For Ted Bundy, frustration was rooted in his broken engagement, and for Robert Hansen it was a rejection that occurred as he tried to enter the social scene through dating; for Jerry Brudos, Ed Gein, Kenneth Bianchi and Angelo Buono, it was rejection by their mothers that inhibited the goal response of maternal acceptance. In each of these instances (and other examples exist for other serial killers), a frustration is experienced and internalized involving some critical period of social development which causes these individuals not to experience the social successes of other persons.

In each of these cases an aggressive drive has been blocked. According to this theory, the aggressive drive is seen as a basic impulse or drive.

However, this drive may be blocked by objective danger (such as a realistic fear of retribution) or by anxiety about the expression of aggression (due to prior punishment for aggressiveness) (Dollard and Miller, 1950: p. 211). Gein and Bianchi experienced the former type while Bundy and Hansen experienced the latter. In all cases, the emotion of aggressiveness is suppressed by the individual, but eventually must be released. This leads to feelings of either frustration or anxiety by the individual. When direct discharge is blocked or not possible, aggressive impulses must be released indirectly through displacement to less threatening objects, a concept that Dollard and Miller borrowed from Freud (1939: p. 22). The suppressed aggression is rechanneled and is displaced onto a less threatening object, a concept that Miller and Dollard borrowed from Freud (1939: p. 22). The suppressed aggression is rechanneled and is displaced onto a less threatening object that cannot retaliate. This is accomplished through the concept of "transference," in which a "learned equivalence" increases the extent to which responses can be transferred from one object to another through "generalization" (Dollard and Miller, 1950: p. 101).

Applying this to serial murder, the killer remains under the control of the person who originally forwarded the humiliation. If it were possible the serial killer might release his (or her) aggression on the individual who originally frustrated the killer. However, this person holds control over the individual by the humiliation they have visited upon the killer. This control, and the degree of accompanying humiliation, prohibits the killer from approaching this person.

By creating the humiliation, this person has blocked a basic drive within the killer, that being the free expression of a particular behavior. This behavior could involve any action aggressively pursued by the killer. The killer cannot confront the real cause of the humiliation; if this were possible the humiliation would have been challenged earlier and would not have become suppressed and internalized. The feelings and problems experienced during a particularly formative period in the killer's life are transferred to stimuli that appear similar to the killer through the process of generalization. For example, Bundy and Hansen had been rebuked in sexual relations while Brudos, Bianchi, and Gein had experienced humiliation through familial relations. Of course, these rebuffs occur for many people over the course of time; the key here is that the insult was internalized and not corrected, allowing an internal humiliation to set in that the killer is trying to rectify. As a result, the actual murder victims are serving as scapegoats for the intended victim. During a police interrogation, Gein provided an insight into the notion of generalization, describing how a victim reminded him of his mother:

> Q. What do you think about Mrs. Worden?
>
> *Gein.* I did take her for the resemblance of my mother; her height and every-thing was the same and she had resemblance in the cheekbones (Gollmar, 1982: p. 72)

Unlearning Serial Murder

Most persons would judge the serial killer as being beyond rehabilitation. However, Dollard and Miller include a discussion of a treatment process that might be extended in application to the treatment of the serial killer, acting on the assumption that serial murder is the result of a learned behavior. Dollard and Miller (1950: p. 311) quote Alexander and French (1942: p. 21) who claim "(B)y reviving the past emotional actions . . . we enable the patient to develop the power to differentiate between the original childhood situation and his present status." A major problem within the serial killer is the lack of ability to discriminate (Dollard and Miller, 1950: p. 50). Discrimination involves the ability to specify the differences and similarities between comparable stimuli. The similarity or difference between stimuli are specified by a "gradient of generalization." The example given by Dollard and Miller (1950: p. 52) discusses how a child bitten by a dog will be afraid of other animals and more afraid of dogs than of cats and horses. The serial killer is confusing cues in the present with cues from the past: Ted Bundy generalized that all women with a body shape, hair color, or hair style similar to that of his ex-fiancée represented a threat. Based on faulty discrimination, Bundy transferred his humiliation onto innocent victims.

According to the Alexander and French hypothesis, the therapist could concentrate the serial killer's attention on the past to uncover the basis for these faulty generalizations in an attempt to expand the learning processes of the killer. The killer may then retrieve past descriptions about incidents that have been repressed into the unconsciousness and the conditions (the killer's perceptions) that caused these descriptions to be repressed. The therapist could then expose to the killer that these situations need not be taken so seriously by the killer, that the perceived humiliation is not as serious as originally inferred. As faulty associations are pointed out, extinction of behaviors and generalizations can begin to occur. Through this process of extinction the killer can begin to overcome the unconscious humiliation that has resulted in the expression of these aggressive behaviors.

Of course, the public concern to this approach would be the fear that "spontaneous recovery" might occur. This phenomenon was discovered by Pavlov (1927). According to Pavlov, the initial inhibition of the conditioned response which occurs as a result of extinction is only temporary. The arousal of the inhibitory state which is blocking the behavior declines following the initial extinction. As the strength of the inhibitory state diminishes, the ability of the conditioned stimulus to elicit the conditioned response returns. Thus, the monster within the serial killer would re-emerge.

A peculiar situation is at work which compels the serial killer to kill over time when other types of killers seem to overcome their humiliation in a single act. The theories of Luckenbill are used toward presenting an explanation. Luckenbill (1977) noted the effect that having an audience has on a killer's satisfaction with the act. When a potential humiliation occurs in public, the aggrieved party cannot simply walk away from the challenge. This would merely serve to reinforce the humiliation and the acceptance of the situation by the victim. Consequently, the response must occur in public, and preferably in front of the same audience that witnessed the insult. Only in this way can the humiliation be rectified and what is right be restored. Through the previous challenge to his self-worth, the killer feels justified in answering the challenge in an equally forceful fashion.

However, the serial murderer does not perform in front of an audience, or at least in front of an audience that survives to bear witness. The serial murderer experiences a certain humiliation during some stage in his life. Until the serial killer can correct this humiliation, the killer must continue in his quest to set matters right. Unfortunately, an ambivalent situation confounds the circumstances. The serial killer must kill to overcome humiliation, while, on the other hand, no audience survives to verify that right has been restored. Consequently, serial killers are destined to kill for dual reasons: no audience is present to bear witness to the fact that the killer has restored "right," and perhaps more importantly, the killer is failing to remove the actual target of his humiliation. As a result, the killings must continue.

References

Alexander, F. and French, T. (1946). Psychoanalytic theory. New York: Ronald Publishing.

Amsel, A. (1958). "The road of frustrative nonreward in noncontinuous reward situation." Psychological Bulletin, 55: pp. 102-119.

Dollard, J., Miller, N., Doob, L., Mowrer, O., and Sears, R. (1939). Frustration and aggression. New Haven CT: Yale University Press.

Dollard, J. and Miller, N. (1950). Personality and psychotherapy. New York: McGraw Hill Book Co.

Freud, S. 1961. (1931). Civilization and its discontents. New York: W.W. Norton and Co.

Gollmar, R. (1982). Edward Gein: America's Most Bizarre Murderer. Delavan, WI: Charles Halberg and Co.

Holmes, R. and DeBurger, J. (1988). Serial murder. Beverly Hills, CA: Sage Publications.

Hull, C. (1943). Principles of behavior. New York: Appleton.

Katz, J. (1988). Seductions of crime. New York: Basic Books.

Levin, J. and Fox, J. (1985). Mass murder: America's growing menace. New York: Plenum Press.

Linedecker, C. (1988). Thrill seekers. New York: Paper Back Book Co.

Luckenbill, D. (1977). "Criminal homicide as a situated transaction," Social Problems, 25:176-187.

Mills, C. (1940). "Situated actions and vocabularies of motive," American Sociological Review, 5: 905-913.

Pavlov, L. (1927). Conditioned reflex. Oxford: Oxford University Press,

Rule, A. (1980). The stranger beside me. New York: W.W. Norton and Co.

——— (1988). The Lust Killer. New York: W.W. Norton and Co.

Scott, M. and Layman, S. (1968). "Accounts," American Sociological Review, 33: 46-62.

Spence, K. (1936). "The nature of discrimination learning in animals," Psychological Review, 44: 430-444.

Wolfgang, M. and Ferracuti, F. (1967). The subculture of violence. London: Social Science Paperbacks.

6

The Divided Self

*Toward an Understanding of
the Dark Side of the Serial Killer*

―――――――――

AL C. CARLISLE

"I knew myself, at the first breath of this new life, to be more
wicked, sold a slave to my original evil; and the thought, in that
moment, braced and delighted me like wine."

—Robert Lewis Stevenson,
The Strange Case of Dr. Jekyll and Mr. Hyde

The Jekyll and Hyde story is a fictional account of a person who, through
chemical experiment, becomes transformed into two separate entities,
each with his own set of realities, and each having diametrically opposite
intentions. Even though it is fiction, this story is often used as a simile
to describe opposing personality states of offenders whose violent
acts appear incongruent with the image others have of them. Ted Bundy,
Christopher Wilder, and John Wayne Gacy, for example, were each perceived as upstanding citizens, yet each was a vicious killer. Each was
intelligent, energetic, and actively involved in the community. Bundy
graduated from college and later went to law school. He worked on a
crisis line in an attempt to help others, and was a field worker in political
campaigns. He obtained adequate grades in his law classes even though

Author's Note: This chapter was first printed in 1993 in the *American Journal of Criminal Justice,* 17(2), 23-36. Reprinted with permission.

he was simultaneously killing victims. He is believed to have killed over 30 victims.

Wilder was a wealthy co-owner of a construction business, owned Florida real estate worth about a half million dollars, always had plenty of girlfriends and was liked by those who lived around him. He killed eight victims, torturing many of them. Gacy had a successful business, would dress up like a clown to cheer up sick kids in hospitals, and was Jaycee "Man of the Year." When the snow became deep he would hook up a snowplow and clean out the driveways of the homes on his block. Each year he sponsored a celebration for about 400 people in Chicago at his own expense. He killed more than 30 victims. Each of these was admired by many, yet each was a serial killer whose dark side was demonstrated by the vicious manner in which a victim's life was taken.

Were they originally good people who went astray or were they born evil and had the ability to hide their sadistic homicidal tendencies from those around them? The evidence accumulated on each would suggest the first postulation to be the accurate one. The pathological process that leads to the development of an obsessive appetite (and possibly an addiction) to kill is still one of the most perplexing psychological mysteries yet to be solved.

Is the Serial Killer Mentally Ill?

While it is tempting to explain the behavior of these killers by labeling them psychotic, or insane, psychiatric data usually contradict such a conclusion. Each of these three, for example, was able to carry out a fairly high level of daily functioning while committing crime. Each made logical, and often creative, decisions in his work. Those closest to each of them generally did not see indications of mental illness, nor of violent tendencies, and were surprised when the person was arrested for murder. While most serial killers are not insane in the legal sense (that is, they knew the difference between right and wrong at the time of the crime), it is commonly accepted that there is some deviant or pathological process occurring within them which is directly related to the commission of multiple homicides.

A second frequently used explanation in the attempt to understand the serial killer is to label him a psychopath, a term which refers to a person who has a clear perception of reality, but one who seems to lack feelings of guilt, and commits criminal acts for his own immediate gratification, having little regard for the pain and suffering caused by his acts. In other words, a person who has no conscience. While this term may describe the killer's behavior, it still doesn't explain the psychological processes that go on within the person that cause him to "kill for pleasure." No more does it answer the question of whether this lack of conscience resulted in the killing, or if psychological pain caused violent tendencies which in turn resulted in suppressing moral prompting. There are many indications that some serial killers experience strong remorse when they kill, at least in the beginning, which shows some capacity to experience guilt. Yet, in spite of the regret for their act, they go on to kill again. Clearly, there have to be some ingredients in the process of the development of the serial killer which have excepted our focus. It is not acceptable any longer to use the terms "monster" or "psychopathic killer" as explanatory mechanisms. An increased understanding of the psychological processes that take place within the offender prior to, during, and following the criminal act may help in recognizing and alleviating the problem earlier in the person's life.

While there are many explanatory possibilities, one area which has been minimally explored utilizes the concepts of fantasy, dissociation and compartmentalization which result in what many offenders refer to as a dark, sinister, twisted self that hungers for sordid and depraved experiences which would have created deep feelings of revulsion earlier in the killer's life. The purpose of this article is to suggest how this sinister dark side of the person is sparked into existence and develops through common psychological processes. The utility of understanding the process for the mental health profession is in recognizing and redirecting this process in youth. For law enforcement, the utility is towards the development of investigation and interviewing techniques which can enhance the detection and conviction process.

Dissociation and the Separate Self

The concept of an altered self, or altered identity, has its scientific roots in the findings of such persons as Sigmund Freud, Carl Jung, Pierre Janet and Josep Breuer (see Ellenberger, 1970). Freud postulated the subconscious mind, a "hidden" level of consciousness generally not accessible to the conscious processes. He demonstrated fairly conclusively that traumatic memories and emotions from a person's past could be housed in the subconscious which could later have a strong effect on the emotional life and behaviors of that person. Breuer and Freud (1957) found a connection between behavioral symptoms and subconscious memories which they referred to as a "splitting of consciousness" or dual consciousness processes (p. 12).

The concept of separate parts or personality types are the basis for Eric Berne's *Games People Play* and the field of Transactional Analysis which hypothesizes the interplay of personality structures within each of us called the "child," "adult," and "parent" states. Ernest Hilgard (1977) comments regarding simultaneous, dual levels of thinking:

> Even more intriguing and puzzling is the possibility that in some instances part of the attentive effort and planning (which a person may engage in) may continue without any awareness of it at all. When that appears to be the case, the concealed part of the total ongoing thought and action may be described as dissociated from the conscious experience of the person (p. 2).

John and Helen Watkins (1978) have found the presence of "ego states" within many people which are more than simply attitudes or moods, and which are parallel to Hilgard's finding of a Hidden Observer (see Hilgard, 1977). Following up on the findings of Paul Federn, they postulated that these ego states are personality systems which have split off from the main personality. They found these fractioned personality states to be fairly common in many people, to be somewhat independent from each other and to have a strong controlling effect on the person.

The process of dissociation is a normal psychological process which provides the opportunity for a person to avoid, to one degree or another, the presence of memories and feelings which are too painful to tolerate. Dissociation is a continuum of experiences ranging from the process of blocking out events going on around us (such as when watching a movie) to Multiple Personality Disorder (MPD) where personalities are separate compartmentalized entities. The ego states referred to by Watkins and Watkins, the Hidden Observer referred to by Hilgard, and the concepts of the entity, dark side and shadow referred to by various homicide offenders are somewhere between the two extremes. These are sub-MPD level states of consciousness which have been created by the person in an attempt to better adapt to his world.

The Role of Fantasy

While in the usual case of dissociation traumatic memories are buried, allowing the person to avoid experiencing the pain, on the opposite side of the coin is the process of creating fantasy imagery, or illusions, for the purpose of avoiding pain and generating excitement. Walter Young (1988) found that a traumatized child who became MPD would incorporate fantasy imagery into a personality identity. In the same manner, a child who experiences excessive emptiness and engages in extensive daydreaming may reach the point where the identity or entity generated through the fantasy becomes a compartmentalized and controlling factor in the person's life.

A fantasy is an imagery process in which a person attempts to obtain vicarious gratification by engaging in acts in his mind which he currently isn't able to do (or doesn't dare to do) in reality. Fantasy is a mechanism by which a temperament, such as anger, begins to take a form with a specified purpose and direction. Ongoing and intense fantasy is also a mechanism by which hate and bitterness can begin to become dissociated and compartmentalized from the more ethically focused aspects of the mind. Intensely painful memories and deep emptiness can lead to intensely experienced fantasies, which over time take on a greater and greater degree of reality. When a person is totally absorbed in a fantasy, he dissociates everything around him. Anger and emptiness become the energy and motivating forces behind the fantasy. While in the fantasy the person experiences a sense of excitement and relief. However, when it is over there is still a feeling of emptiness because the fantasy has whetted an appetite for the real thing, which he anticipates will be even more enjoyable than the fantasy. Thus, through fantasy, the person creates a make-believe world wherein he can accomplish what he can't do in reality. Over time, the person may turn to this pseudo-existence with increasing rapidity when he feels stress, depression or emptiness. This leads to a dual identity, one being that associated with reality and the people he associates with every day (Carl Jung's Persona) and the other the secret identity which is able to manifest the power and control he would like over others (Carl Jung's Shadow concept). If the person is angry and bitter, this alter identity is usually an animal of destruction. The major problem is that heavy fantasy is inexorably linked to the process of dissociation and compartmentalized. As the person shifts back and forth between the two identities in his attempt to meet his various needs, they both become an equal part of him, the opposing force being suppressed when he is attempting to have his needs met through the one. Over time, the dark side (representing the identity or entity the person has created to satisfy his deepest hunger) becomes stronger than the "good" side, and the person begins to experience being possessed, or controlled by this dark side of him. This is partly because the dark side is the part anticipated to meet the person's strongest needs, and partly because the good side is the part which experiences the guilt over the "evil" thoughts, and therefore out of necessity is routinely suppressed. Thus, the monster is created. Bill (a pseudonym), a person who became a multiple homicide offender, describes the need he had for fantasy as a child:

> Without that (hero fantasies) I would have had to live with myself. What would have been the alternative? I go out into the garage and I'm in there reading a book or reading one *Reader's Digest* article after another. If I'm not doing that I'm back inside the house where I'm a nobody. If I'm not doing that, I'm out there on the school yard playing ball, maybe, but still a nobody (personal correspondence).

Bill would become absorbed in the fantasies to the point that he had a difficult time living his day-to-day life with them:

> "I think that anybody who would look upon me, at least for the first hour after reading the book would think I was preoccupied. . . . With most people when they put the book down they are back to the real world . . . whereas in my case, these would provide scenarios that I would yearn for, and wish could happen. I was in there (the story). I could almost smell the smells, see the sights. I was gone. I was in another world." (Ibid)

Over the years, Bill relied on his fantasy life for his major satisfaction, always still yearning for the fulfilling social life which would replace the fantasies. However, when it didn't come bitterness and revenge fantasies replaced the hero fantasies. Still wanting to be a socially respected person, he attempted to suppress his violent urges while concomitantly relying on his increasingly more violent fantasies to gratify his urges for retribution. This created a serious motivational imbalance in his mental system which resulted in a compartmentalization of the opposing motivational forces (the desire to be a respectable citizen and the opposing desire to get revenge) so that he could have some sense of balance in his life. Ted Bundy described an attempt to keep the two opposing forces separate:

> . . . as we've witnessed the development of this darker side of this person's life, we'd expect to see how very closely controlled and separated this part of him became, and how he was able to keep it, ah, more or less, from those around him who thought he was normal. And because this separation was so distinct and well maintained, we would find it unlikely [that] the roles could get confused (Michaud and Aynesworth, 1989, p. 195).

However, the roles do begin to get confused which results in an even greater attempt to keep these identities or forces separate in order to maintain the appearance of normalcy. The process of suppression results in the development of the sinister or dark side of the personality.

The Creation of the Shadow

The vicarious enjoyment of fantasy is enhanced through a self-sustained hypnotic trance, and it creates an appetite which gets out of control. Ted Bundy, in telling Michaud and Aynesworth (1989) how a psychopath killer is created, stated:

> there is some kind of weakness that gives rise to this individual's interest in the kind of sexual activity involving violence that would gradually begin to absorb some of his fantasy . . . eventually the interest would become so demanding toward new material that it would only be catered to by what he could find in the dirty book stores . . . (p. 68).

As this process continues, it begins to dominate his life. Bundy continues:

> By peeping in windows as it were, and watching a woman undress, or watching whatever could be seen, you know, during the evening, and approaching it almost like a project, throwing himself into it, uh, literally for years. . . . He gained, you'd say, a terrific amount of . . . at times . . . a great amount of gratification from it and he became increasingly adept at it as anyone becomes adept at anything they do over and over again . . . and as the condition develops and its purposes or characteristics become more well defined, it begins to demand more of the attention and time of the individual . . . there is a certain amount of tension, uh, struggle between the normal personality and this, this, uh, psychopathological, uh, entity (Ibid, p. 70).

Bob (pseudonym), a homicide offender, described his experience of the development of this entity, dark side, or shadow within him prior to his homicide:

> The beast can take over to complete an identity if you leave a hole in yourself. In other words, it seeks a vacuum. In a healthy person the vacuum doesn't exist. There's a sense of identity that prevents a need for the dark awareness.
> It was very much like a battlefield in my head, wrestling with what I as a human being felt to be reasonable alternatives. It was a battle between two very different parts of myself—goodness and evil. When you feel evil, there is a sense of power. It can consume you. There is not much intellect involved with making an evil decision. It is a more gripping thing, more animalistic. It's so much simpler and so much easier to give into it than to hang on to a moral structure that you don't understand, or an ethic or value or commitment, all the things that make us human beings (personal correspondence).

The offender may attempt to curtail the problem which is developing:

> I just kept trying to shake it off and physically I would shake my head to rid myself of the thoughts. I wondered where it could come from, or without my pulse going, how I could consider such an ugly sequence of events (Ibid).

When this doesn't work, he attempts to indulge in the fantasy rather than fight it to see if that would work. He continued:

> Let's give in to the thoughts. Let's not try to resist it. Let's grovel in it for maybe 20 minutes. Maybe that will dissipate it. Maybe it will blow off some steam. Let's have a fantasy, OK? What happened was, I became preoccupied with the fantasy. It did not resolve itself (Ibid).

This process begins to get more and more out of the person's control, as evidenced by the Boston Strangler:

> I could not stop what I was doing. This thing building up in me—all the time—I knew I was getting out of control (Frank, 1966, p. 326).

Ultimately, when a person has visualized killing over and over again, a time may come when an actual event, similar to what he has been fantasizing about, presents itself. At such time, under the right circumstances, the offender finds himself automatically carrying out an act he has practiced so many, many times in his mind. Finally, inevitably, this force, this entity, makes a breakthrough. Bundy commented:

> The urge to do something to that person (a woman he saw) seized him— in a way he'd never been affected before. And it seized him strongly. And to the point where, uh, without giving a great deal of thought, he searched for some instrumentality to, uh, uh, attack this woman . . . there was really no control at this point . . . (Ibid, pp. 72-73).

The offender may partially, or completely, dissociate the crime (see Carlisle, 1991). Following the event, the offender's mind returns to the realm of the real world and he often experiences surprise, guilt, and dismay that such an act could have happened. Bundy adds:

> What he had done terrified him. Purely terrified him. And he was full of remorse . . . and, you know, he quickly sobered up, as it were. . . . The sobering effect of that was to . . . for some time, close up the cracks again. And not do anything. For the first time, he sat back and swore to himself that he wouldn't do something like that again . . . or even, anything that would lead to it . . . within a matter of months, slowly but surely, the impact of this event lost its, uh, deterrent value. And within months he

was back, uh, uh, peeping in windows again, and slipping back into that
old routine (Ibid, pp. 74-75).

By acting out the fantasy, the dark side or shadow, now becomes a
more permanent part of the person's personality structure. Bundy adds:

> Well, we, we . . . ah, described this individual and found that his behavior,
> which was becoming more and more frequent, was also concomitantly
> . . . occupying more and more of his mental and intellectual energies. So
> he's facing a greater, ah, more frequent challenge of this darker side of
> himself to his normal life (Ibid, p. 171).

Within the offender there is a revulsion of the act, but there is also a
sense of excitement, satisfaction, and peace. If the feeling of peace is
profound, as if a great load has been taken off the person's shoulders, he
is especially likely to become a serial killer. The Shadow becomes
stronger because the person has now transcended that final boundary
and most inhibitions against killing are gone and overwhelmingly painful guilt is suppressed. Still, there are some feelings and beliefs against
killing. The good side isn't dead. Just pushed away. Thus, there is generally a period of time before another homicide occurs.

The offender may begin tempting the fates a little by allowing himself
to engage in some of his earlier pre-homicide activities, thinking this will
help satisfy the need that is still growing within him, yet promising to
himself he will never go as far as he did the last time. However, a time
comes when the urge to again feel that power and control becomes so
strong the offender gives into it. Bob describes his experience of the
fantasy about the plan to commit homicide.

> My mouth would dry up, my peripheral vision would narrow, and I
> would be at peace. This was a plan that whatever cost would accomplish
> what I wanted and would create balance in my life. There is a sweetness
> in surrendering to any plan. To allow yourself to commit provides a
> platform in your life where you're not at drift . . . Here there is power.
> Here there is meaning, logic and order and stability. If I have to give in
> to an evil thing to do it, it is worth it (personal correspondence).

Another homicide is committed. He may again experience guilt and
may again promise to himself that it will never happen further. However,
his identity has now drastically changed.

The Obsession

He has become the very being he had so often visualized in his fantasies, even though the possibility of becoming such was so abhorrent to him. He has stepped over the line and cannot step back. The only way he can handle the guilt is to compartmentalize it and thus not consciously experience it. But the guilt doesn't go away. It remains hidden beneath the surface grinding on the offender, which often produces an eventual deterioration in the killer's personality.

The homicides are often not as satisfying as the first one was, and do not reach the level of satisfaction of his fantasies. The killer's search for the ultimate high becomes an obsession. Usually by this time the offender senses the entity within as being a dark side that is very evil and is controlling him, and it terrifies him. He detests it, is fearful of it, yet he basks in its power. He may continue his attempt to fight against its controlling influence, but soon he gives up his struggle against it and allows it to dominate him. His new life becomes a secret existence, often known only to him.

A drastic identity change has occurred, with the opposing identities being farther apart than ever before. Strong self-hate is engendered and in order to avoid it, the offender has to idealize the pathology. The Shadow has advanced to the level of having become the Controller and is now the dominant force in the offender's life. He can't undo what he has done nor can he face the guilt or accept the responsibility for his behavior. By doing so he would have to face what he has become.

Thus, his sickness becomes his idol and he places himself on a pedestal and worships his own image. For Bill, the two most common traits he experienced at the time of the killings were, "my 'SENSE OF BEING PERFECT' and my sense of feeling that I was 'ALMOST LIKE A GOD'" (personal correspondence). To be divine is to be sinless. To be sinless abnegates blame, and the "evil" act becomes mentally transformed into a divine judgement. The ego dystonic becomes ego syntonic. The offender is hooked. An addiction begins to build, due partly to the attempt to chase the high, and partly in an attempt to find the gratification in reality which the person has found through fantasy.

The offender may begin to flaunt his prowess and feelings of superiority, such as did the Son of Sam (Life-Time Books). He may toy with the police. He savors the knowledge that he is skillful, he can kill people and no one can catch him. He plans, stalks, observes and executes his crimes with great skill, at times taking great chances because he feels invulnerable. Edmund Kemper, who killed his grandparents, six college-age girls, his mother, and finally his mother's friend, stated:

> It was getting easier to do. I was getting better at it. . . . I started flaunting that invisibility, severing a human head, two of them, at night, in front of my mother's residence, with her at home, my neighbors at home upstairs, their picture window open, the curtain open, eleven o'clock at night, the lights are on. All they had to do was walk by, look out, and I've had it. Some people go crazy at that point. I felt it. It was one helluva tweek (Home Box Office, 1984).

The uncontrollable nature of the urge is expressed by Charles Hatcher, a serial murderer who began his killing spree in the early 1960s, murdering 13 adults and three children. His spree finally ended when he committed himself to a mental hospital the day after he abducted and murdered an 11-year-old girl in St. Joseph, Missouri. He admitted to FBI agent Joe Holtslag:

> I kill on impulse. It's an uncontrollable urge that builds and builds over a period of weeks until I have to kill. It doesn't matter if the victims are men, women, or children. Whoever is around is in trouble. (Ganey, 1989, pp. 216-217).

Bob described it this way:

> It was like obeying somebody else. I felt as though I was taking orders and the Shadow was about to say, "No longer will you think of other alternatives" (personal correspondence).

Regarding the compulsion, Bill stated:

> once the compulsion is there, it is not a matter of should I or shouldn't I. At this point it's too late. It's a psychological impossibility to stop that activity (personal correspondence).

The compulsion is a combination of the planning, the hunt, the capture, the power and control over the victim, the terror she shows and the possession of the person, often both before and after death.

The excitement combined with the need for companionship and possession is demonstrated in the Dennis Andrew Nilsen and Jeffrey Dahmer cases. Nilsen, a 37-year-old executive officer at the Jobcentre in Kentish Town, London, killed 16 young men at Cranley Gardens and 13 at his residence on Melrose Avenue. He would invite the victim to his apartment for an evening of companionship and then would kill him. He stated:

> It was intense and all consuming . . . I needed to do what I did at the time. I had no control over it then. It was a powder keg waiting for a match. I was the match. . . . The kill was only part of the whole. The whole experience which thrilled me intensely was the drink, the chase, the social seduction, the getting the "friend" back (meaning the essence of the 'friend' would still be there), the decision to kill, the body and its disposal.
>
> The pressure needed release. I took release through spirits and music. On that high, I had a loss of morality and danger feeling. . . . I wished I could stop but I could not. I had no other thrill or happiness (Masters, 1985, p. 241-243).

There may be dissociation during the act as indicated by Albert De-Salvo regarding looking in a mirror and seeing himself strangling a Scandinavian woman a week before he killed Anna Slesers:

> I looked in a mirror in the bedroom and there was me strangling somebody! I fell on my knees and I crossed myself and I prayed, 'Oh, God, what am I doing? I'm a married man. I'm the father of two children. Go, God, help me! . . . Oh, I got out there fast. It wasn't like it was me, Mr. Bottomly—it was like it was someone else I was watching (Frank, 1966, p. 313).

Or, dissociation of the event may occur following the crime, as indicated in another of the Boston Strangler's crimes:

> You (meaning himself) was there, these things were going on and the feeling after I got out of that apartment was as if it never happened. I got out and downstairs, and you could of said you saw me upstairs and as far as I was concerned, it wasn't me. I can't explain it to you any other way. It's just so unreal. . . . I was there, it was done, and yet if you talked to me an hour later, or half hour later, it didn't mean nothing, it just didn't mean nothing (Ibid, pp. 320-321.).

Habituation, Decline, and Fall

Habituation occurs and the act does not produce the anticipated satisfaction. In an attempt to obtain the level of excitement and fulfill ment so desperately sought for, the killer escalates his activities in the form of increased frequency of the crimes and/or increased sadistic acts. Parallel to this there is often a deterioration in the self-image of the offender. He becomes very repulsed by his acts and he begins to hate himself. He feels out of control and helpless in the presence of the Shadow he has created. He feels mastered by his Dark Side. The moralistic side of himself fights against the killer within which thirsts for blood. The killer may then reach out for help in some manner. After his eighth victim, the Zodiac Killer of the 1960s wrote a letter to attorney Melvin Belli:

> Dear Melvin, This is the Zodiak speaking.
>   I wish you a happy Christmas. The one thing I ask of you is this, please help me. I cannot reach out for help because of the thing in me won't let me. I am finding it extremely difficult to hold it in check. I am afraid I will loose control again and take my ninth and possibly tenth victim. Please help me. I am drowning . . . (Graysmith, 1976, p. 207).

The Zodiac Killer went on to take at least 49 lives. In another case, Bill Heinrens wrote a plea for help in red lipstick on a wall of the apartment of his victim just before he killed her:

> For heavens
> Sake catch me
> Before I kill more
> I cannot control myself" (Freeman, 1956, p. 15).

The overpowering urges to kill pitted against the hate he has developed for himself, results in a deterioration in the consistency of his emotions and behavior and it is more difficult for him to continue to kill as singularly in intent as he had done so in the past. He becomes more sloppy in his criminal activities, almost as though he were trying to get caught. The Chi Omega killings, for example, were very different from the approach Bundy had used in the past. Arthur Bishop, an offender who sexually molested and killed five boys, began to engage in criminal activities in an attempt to get caught by the police following the fourth homicide. When he got caught following the fifth victim he fully confessed all of the details of each crime to the police and later said that was a tremendous relief to get rid of the load he was carrying. Charles Hatcher voluntarily committed himself to a mental hospital the day following his final homicide and confessed to the other killings, partly because another person had been found guilty of his first three victims. Westley Dodd attempted to abduct another victim from a movie theater. The boy fought him and Dodd was able to narrowly escape. However, the following week he attempted the same thing in another theater and got caught. Two contract killers I have worked with each reached the point where they had so much self-hate because of their crimes that they ceased to care whether they got caught or not, and thus they were apprehended easily while committing an amateurish crime. Once the offender has been caught and placed in prison, he often seeks psychological counseling out of a need to understand how he developed into the person he became.

While every serial killer does not fit the model suggested here, many do. Finding that a killer has an inner part, or some internal entity that becomes an overwhelming force in his life and compels him to kill again and again doesn't excuse or justify the person's actions. There is no way to rationalize away a killer's responsibility for his crimes. There may have been some event or events which started the process, but the person himself fed it and allowed it to build and to get out of control. Thus, the person created his own monster which then controlled him, causing him to do the things he actually wanted to do in the first place. An understanding of the psychological processes regarding splitting and compartmentalization will aid in the detection process. If this process is not recognized and corrected, it continues unabated. The final product is best summarized by a statement Bundy made to the Florida police when they were interrogating him:

> "I'm the most cold blooded son of a bitch that you will ever meet" (Michaud and Aynesworth, 1983: p. 113).

References

Breuer, J. and S. Freud (1957). Studies on hysteria. New York: Basic Books.
Carlisle, A. (1991). Dissociation and violent criminal behavior. *Journal of Contemporary Criminal Justice*, 7, 273-285.

Damore, L. (1981). In his garden: The anatomy of a murder. New York: Dell Books.

Ellenberger, H. (1970). The discovery of the unconscious. New York: Basic Books.

Frank, G. (1966). The Boston strangler. New York: Signet.

Freeman, L. (1956). Before I kill more. New York: Kangaroo Books.

Ganey, T. (1989). Innocent blood. New York. St. Martins Press.

Graysmith, R. (1987). Zodiak. New York: Berkeley.

Hilgard, E. (1977). Divided consciousness: Multiple controls in human thought and action. New York: John Wiley and Sons.

Home Box Office. (1984). Murder: No apparent motive. American Undercover Series.

Jacobi, J. (1973). The psychology of C. G. Jung. New Haven: Yale Press.

Jung, C. (1983). Psychiatric studies: The collected works of C.G. Jung (Vol 1). New York: Bollingen Series XX/Princeton University Press.

Masters, B. (1985). Killing for company: The case of Dennis Nilsen. New York: Stein and Day.

Michaud, S. and Aynesworth, H. (1983). The only living witness. Linden Press/Simon and Schuster.

Michaud, S. and Aynesworth, H. (1989). Ted Bundy: Conversations with a killer. New York: Signet Books.

Serial Killers. (1992). New York: Time-Life Books.

Stevenson, R. (1963). Dr. Jekyll and Mr. Hyde. New York: Scholastic Book Service.

Watkins, J. (1978). The therapeutic self. New York: Human Sciences.

Young, W. (1988). Observations of fantasy in the formation of multiple personality disorder. Dissociation, I. P. 13-20.

7

Sequential Predation
Elements of Serial Fatal Victimization

———————

RONALD M. HOLMES

Introduction

Perhaps nothing galvanizes the public's attention as fatal serial or sequential predation. The names of serial offenders, killers and rapists alike, capture the media and become perverse societal icons. Ted Bundy, Gerard Schaefer, Henry Lucas, John Wayne Gacy, and others demanded and received immense attention to such a degree that the names of such sequential predators became household names.

Books, movies, TV shows and documentaries have become a part of the pop and serious culture of our times. Thomas Harris' books, *The Red Dragon* and *The Silence of the Lambs,* are literary icons. Everyone wants to be a profiler like Clarice Starling! But the real star of the books and movies was the serial predator himself, Hannibal Lecter. So it is not only the real predators who capture our imagination; the fictional ones also are as equally famous or infamous.

It is a sad commentary when we can recite the names and life histories of serial predators but few know or can recall those names of the victims. This is indeed an area of study that demands some attention. But what this article is concerned with is the manner in which the victims are selected as part of the fantasy requirement, as well as how the role of the elements of predation are intertwined and become a script for action.

Author's Note: This chapter was first published in 1997 in the *Journal of Sexual Compulsivity,* 4(1). Reprinted with permission.

Literature Examination

In addition to a plausible explanation for the etiology of the serial offender (Nagayama, Hirschman, and Beutler, 1991; Newton, 1992), the selection process of victimization has received meager academic attention. Norris (1998), for example, briefly examines victimization but neglects any in-depth analysis. Ressler (1992), Douglas and Olshaker (1995), Hickey (1997), and others have examined the serial predator and also crime scene assessment. Recently the role of geography is also examined by Holmes and Holmes (1996), Gresswell and Hollin (1994), Rossmo (1994), and Brantingham and Brantingham (1981).

Jenkins (1990) remarked that there appears to be a subculture of recreational serial killers who prey upon victims who are selected if only by a circumstance of location. This is especially true in the manner in which women select their victims (Segrave, 1992), who select their victims usually from family members or other intimates.

Race is a factor in the selection of a victim because typically serialists will victimize those who are in their own race cohort (Holmes and Holmes, 1992, 1994, 1996; Meyers et al., 1993). Serial homicide perpetrators usually select strangers; this has been reported by many researchers including Williamson, Hare, and Wong (1987).

The role of the victim in the serial murderer's cycle of personal and fatal violence is lacking. The focus of the literature thus far has centered around a wide variety of variables which have hope for the eradication of this very serious social problem.

The purpose of this paper, however, is different. It is to examine the various components of the victimization process; this process of victimization rests within the mindset of the predator. The predatory process, then, becomes a vehicle for examination. To understand the mindset is to gain insight into the predatory process.

The Sexual Components
of Sequential Victimization

In interviewing serial predators in correctional institutions throughout the United States, certain behavioral scripts were common. This community of thought concerning serial predation became apparent during the interviews of twenty-one serial murderers and rapists. The commonality of thought, especially in sexual victimization, often enveloped attitudes and values of sexual themes. These themes were typically centered around a thought process of control, brutalization (often fatal) and an increasingly shorter period of regret, remorse, and fear of apprehension.

The victimization process is composed of four elements: fantasy, symbolism, ritualism, and compulsion. It is the interaction of these elements that provide a scenario for predation. These identified elements and the related contents were discussed by the serialists with remarkable consistency. They uniformly spoke of the necessary elements of gratifying violence and the sequence of actions that are necessary for such gratification. The first is fantasy.

A. FANTASY

Fantasy as an element of deviant sex is integral to the understanding of the mindset of the serial predator. It is through this mindset that the crime indeed makes some sense to those who are seriously interested in gaining knowledge into the mind of the serial predator.

The fantasy of most, if not all, sexually active people is never truly realized to its ultimate goal. Recognizing that crimes of violence are often accompanied by a sexual element that is ritualistic and sexually compulsive, there are behavioral urges to perpetrate in congruence with the behavioral script which lies within the fantasy of the offender.

One serialist said his fantasies typically centered around an ideal victim type (young Chippendale model types), and the desire to make them into his personal "love slaves." To accomplish this task, to realize his fantasy, he drilled holes into their skulls and filled them with acid. He also ate body parts. But despite these attempts he was never able to realize the total fulfillment of his fantasy. His name was Jeffrey Dahmer (Bauman, 1991).

The fantasy for the serial predator is sexual. This may appear strange because of the manner in which most people view "normal" sex. Certainly, fulfilling sex varies from one person to another and from one time to another. The developing violence that occurs in many acts of sequential predation demands an escalation of violence to achieve personal satisfaction for the psychological addiction. The predators themselves stated that they believed that it was truly an addiction that they developed since they started their career of serial predation. If this is true, this addiction, as with many addictions, demands an increasing amount of personal violence to accomplish gratification.

It is, perhaps, this unrequited fantasy that keeps some violent serialists always in search for the perfect act of victimization. It may also be why some victimizations perpetrated by one serialist do not match the serialist's unique M.O.; that particular victim or that particular victimization scenario did not "fit." Something, or somebody, was wrong. This "wrongness" did not fit and marred the fantasy resulting in a damaged act of victimization. The murder or rape was completed but it fell short of desired gratification because the act did not parallel the fantasy.

B. SYMBOLISM

Sex is very symbolic. The symbols in sex are one of two types: fetishes and partialisms. Since men appear to be more visibly oriented to sex, it would be logical to assume that men who are sexual possess both. Women, conversely, are not as visually oriented and are less influenced by fetishes and perhaps more by partialisms.

A fetish is an object that has been viewed in a sexual manner and erotically endowed. Jerry Brudos, an incarcerated serial killer from Oregon, allegedly had a shoe fetish. He wore high heel shoes, forced his wife to wear those same shoes, and at least one of his victims was photographed before he killed her wearing those same shoes (Hickey; Holmes, 1991). One serial killer said in an interview that he loved stockings and found them to be erotically arousing. He forces, through intimidation, his visiting girlfriend to sit with him with her shoes removed so he can touch her silk stockings with his shoeless foot.

Of course, a possession of a fetish does not make one a predator. But like the partialism (body parts) that both men and women possess (e.g., breasts, buttocks, legs, etc.), for the serial offender they become a part of the predator's fantasy, and need to be a part of the victimization process as part of the ritual, if the act is to be fully realized and personal gratification achieved.

C. RITUALISM

The compelling, singular manner in which criminal acts are perpetrated gives viability to the profiling process. The ritualistic behavior certainly becomes a part of everyday life apart from actors of serial predation. The sequence of preparing oneself for the day, the shower, shave, making of the bed (or not), the way one eats breakfast (or any meal), plus the routine of multiple other daily tasks that become a natural and mundane part of everyday life becomes part of one's everyday ritual. This becomes vital not only in the study of the crime scene in the search for the predator but also for the careful analysis of the perpetrator and the victim. True, the ritualistic behavior of the victim will sometimes contribute to the person's victimization. If there is a stalking process, for example, the offender may study the habits of the selected victims so successful intervention of these ritualistic behaviors can result in the abduction and later victimization. For example, if an unaware selected victim travels the same way and at the same time to a college class or a health club workout session, the predator can use the victim's unaware dedication to ritualism to interdict and abduct.

The sequential predators are also ritualistic in criminal behaviors. The behavior may center around the stalking process, the acts of predation, the manner in which the brutalization occurs, or even body-victim posturing and disposal. One case of a sequential homicidal offender illustrates this point quite well. This killer murdered elderly white females, following them from a night of drinking from a neighborhood bar. After murdering them, he stripped their clothing from the waist down, lifted their blouses, and left the victims' car keys and drivers' licenses on their chests. The ritualism of victimization was constant.

D. COMPULSION

Certain behavioral acts are very compulsive and this is probably most true when sex is involved. If one is sexual, and the elements of fantasy, symbolism, and ritualism are all interacting and striving for fruition, and if this contentedness is thwarted for some reason, the striving for satisfaction may become stronger. Not only may it become stronger, it may change, at least temporarily, the manner in which the crime is committed. Ted Bundy and others have reported a part of the personality, Bundy called it the Entity (Michaud and Aynesworth, 1983), another serialist calls it the Beast, and yet another has a different name, the Shadow. It becomes so strong that the one percent (the Entity) overcomes the ninety-nine percent. It indeed becomes a compulsive factor as far as the personality is concerned, not in a physical sense, but in a psychological sense.

This is no better illustrated than in the case of Ted Bundy. The known or highly suspected killings of Bundy before he went to Florida were remarkably alike. There was a fantasy, stalk, an abduction, the murder, and finally the disposal of the body. After being incarcerated for more than two years on the kidnapping of one victim and extradited to Colorado to stand trial for murder in another case, Bundy escaped, traveled to Florida, and attacked four women, killing two. The crime scene at the Chi-Omega Sorority and the soon-after assault upon another Florida State University coed did not reflect any of his previous acts (other than the selection of his ideal victim type). However, three weeks later he abducted a twelve-year-old female and murdered her in a very similar way he had done previously to coming to Florida. His senses and feeling of compulsion had been raised dramatically during his incarceration. His victimizations in Tallahassee satisfied his craving (compulsion) that resulted in a return to psychological peace. In other words, the compulsivity factor, because of the two year period of incarceration, demanded a frenzy of violence. The last murder by Bundy of Kimberly Leach was more controlled and more akin to the murders in the western states since he was victimizing on a "regular basis."

Serial Victimization

In the analysis of sequential victimization, there appears to be in many cases a tenuous relationship between the offender and the victim. In other words, victims may act, behave, or live in such a fashion as to contribute to their own victimization. Witness the example of one who falls victim to a predator who has stalked her and learned her daily routine, routes of travel, work schedule, etc. Had the victim altered her routine, perhaps she would not have been victimized. This not to say that the victim is responsible, only that by certain behaviors, one may have contributed to one's own victimization. Let us here examine the victim as it becomes an integral part of the victimization process.

Too much has been made of Ted Bundy's ideal victim type: white female with long dark hair parted in the middle. In an interview with

Bundy he said he preferred college-aged women because the college campus was an ideal "hunting ground." The partialism of hair color and type of hairstyle had nothing to do with his selection of a victim. Actually, several of Bundy's victims had short hair, at least one had red hair (Laura Aime), and another had blond hair (Susan Rancourt). Several were not college students including his first victim, 8 year old Ann Marie Burr and his last known victim, Kimberly Leach, age 12.

How does a sequential predator select his victim? Recall the symbolic elements of sex (fetishes and partialisms) and how those elements interact with the other three elements. If possible, the offender will select a victim which fits the "profile" of an ideal victim type. But this total profile is not composed entirely of sole physical attributes. There may be other items present. Bobby Joe Long did not kill one victim who later aided in the identification of Long because as he said, "something just wasn't right." She did not fit because of how she looked after she was abducted or it could have been because of the manner in which she behaved.

One serialist said his ideal victim type is "blond haired, blue-eyed, unmistakably young, very definitely female, cheerleader type." But if she was not available, another type would do, especially if the predator had not been active in a period of time (which would influence the feeling of compulsivity). This feeling of compulsion not only will change the crime scene, depending on the time since the last predation, but it will additionally alter the victim type from the ideal to what is available and vulnerable.

In the initial stage of victim selectivity, the visibility factor looms foremost in the mind of the serialist. It may also be based upon hair color, body build, clothing, etc. It may also be predicated upon certain behavioral traits. Bundy said he could evaluate the victim's vulnerability by the manner in which the person walked, the tilt of the head, or the manner in which the individual was aware of the surroundings. This truly is a chilling thought, but these types of human hunters are in the business of evaluating their intended victims.

Some offenders base their selection upon the real or suspected occupation of a victim. One offender said he selected prostitutes because they were responsible for venereal disease. Another stated that his victims were all drug abusers and pushers, and responsible for the dispensing of illicit drugs to young children in his community. So, it does not appear to be any one solitary factor involved in the selection of a suitable victim for a sequential victimizer but a subjective Gestalt predicated upon the fantasy and other interlocking elements.

The selection of a victim for a serial offender may depend more upon the type of serialist seeking a victim. The selection of victims is different from one major type of serial murderer to the other. Holmes and DeBurger (1985, 1988) offered four different types of serial killers. The Visionary type, for example, is involved very little in the selection of a suitable victim for his/her purpose. The Mission, Hedonistic (with subtypes of Lust, Thrill, and Comfort), and Power/Control male serial killers as well as some female serial killers, are more involved in the selection of an "Ideal Victim Type" (IVT). For a more detailed examination of the various types of serial killers, please refer to Holmes and DeBurger (1985, 1988), Holmes and Holmes (1994), and Holmes and Holmes (1996).

The following table illustrates the traits of victims of the various types of serial killers.

TABLE 7.1. Types of Serial Killers and Victim Selectivity Criteria

	Type of Serial Killer				
				Hedonistic	
	Visionary	Mission	Lust	Thrill	Comfort
Victims					
Specific	x	x			x
Nonspecific	x		x	x	
Random x		x	x		x
Nonrandom		x			x
Affiliative				x	
Strangers	x	x	x	x	

What is involved in the selection of a victim? As already said, Bundy could tell a victim by the way she walked down the street, the tilt of her head, the manner in which she carried herself, etc. This thought by Bundy was reinforced by the statement that the "look" of a victim may contribute to the victimization process (McCarthy, 1984:10). This is truly disconcerting to believe that a serialist can become so proficient in his "trade" that he can select a victim out at a glance. One killer stated that his victims "must be" blonde-haired, blue-eyed, unmistakably female, cheerleader type. Once he was blocked from victimizing this type, he selected what was available. On the other hand, as Egger (1984) suggested, being a victim of a serial killer may only be a factor of being in a space where the victim can be victimized. This is an uneasy perspective since there appears to be little that can be done concerning protecting oneself from becoming a victim of a serialist. This point is also shared by Levin and Fox (1985) who stated that serial killers often select their victims "who may (be) just accessible" (1985: 231). Or said another way, victims may be selected only by being at a certain place at a certain time (Egger, 1990).

Egger (1985) and Levin and Fox (1985) also agree that victims of serial killers are often members of the underclass. By being members of this social cohort, the victims are powerless, and also are members of groups whose members are vulnerable and "easy to dominate" (p. 75). Who are these "easy to dominate"? Egger lists them: "vagrants, prostitutes, migrant workers, homosexuals, missing children, and single and often elderly women" (1985: 9).

There are indeed four "hunting grounds" for serial killers: strolls for prostitutes, gay bars and gay areas, skid row areas, and women on college campuses. One "hunting ground" not mentioned, among several others perhaps, are the bars and similar sites where single women frequent and become easy prey. Bundy, for example, picked up at least one woman from a bar, Brenda Ball, and there is some thought that he was at the bar next to the Chi-Omega House in Tallahassee and saw several of the Chi-O sisters at the bar before he went into the sorority house on Super Bowl Sunday, 1978.

The victim must fulfill the fantasy. There is a need to be satisfied, and since most of the male serialists kill for sexual purposes, it is evident that the victim be female and possess attractive traits for the predation process. In other cases, such as Donald Harvey, the patients were all male and were all helpless. He had his fantasy of power and held the life of others in his hands.

The fantasy and the ritual interact with each other. The selection of the victim and the ritual that follows after the abduction in a five window killing fulfills a deep and ever unfulfilling need for the serialist. The selection of the ideal victim is desired; the fantasy can only be fully satisfied with the suitable victim. So, the fantasy and the ideal victim play important and vital roles in the serial predation activities of the serial killer. Combined with the fantasy and the victim emerges the ritual that is also part of the fantasy. So what you have is a three part act: the fantasy, the victim, and the ritual. To fulfill the psychological anticipated gain, all the components must be present and be fulfilled to a degree which is appreciated by the serial killer.

The victim plays a vital role in the selection process. Only when a suitable victim is obtained can the murder be "rewarding." This is true for all serialists. The reward may be short-lived and may initially be accompanied by guilt or a self-consuming shame. But there arises again a need to kill. This is true for those serial killers who are sexually motivated to those who kill because of voices or visions, and even for the serial murderer who kills for "creature comfort reasons."

Despite the process of selecting a victim based on a variety of criteria, it appears to be to some degree determined by the inner and consuming feeling of psychological compulsivity. Edmund Kemper, a serial killer in California, stated it the most clearly when he said the compulsive factor was "an awful, raging, eating feeling that was threatening to consume me from within" (HBO Special, *Murder: No Apparent Motive*).

Conclusion

The fatal dispatchment of innocent victims by sequential predators is a grave social problem and societal concern. The first step toward a successful reduction to this form of victimization lies not only in the apprehension of the victimizer but also in gaining some basic information about the elements of serial predation. The identification of elements in the victimization process is such a step.

The gathering of the information for this article is twofold: first, the academic research from various sources and disciplines; and second, from the incarcerated offenders who participated in this study: those in prison in the general population, on death row, and already executed. Certainly there will be some "pure" researchers who will view this article with some skepticism. This is expected. However, what is offered here is information gathered and analyzed from the real experts in the field of serial predation, the offenders themselves, as well as the academic community. It is also expected that it will serve as a springboard for other research and serious discussion.

Bibliography

Bauman, E. (1991). Step into my parlor. Chicago: Bonus Books, Inc.

Brantingham, P. and P. Brantingham (Eds.). (1981). Environmental criminology. Beverly Hills, CA: Sage Publications.

Douglas, J., and Olshaker, M. (1995). Whoever fights monsters. New York: St. Martins Press.

Douglas, J., Burgess, A.W., Burgess, A.G., Ressler, R. (1992). Crime classification manual. Lexington, MA: Lexington Books.

Eckert, A. (1985). The scarlet mansion. Boston: Little Brown.

Egger, S. (1984). A working definition of serial murder and the reduction of linkage blindness. *Journal of Police Science and Administration,* 12, 348-357.

Egger, S. (1990). Serial murder: An elusive phenomenon. New York: Praeger.

Gresswell, D. and Hollin, C. (1994). Multiple murder: A review. *British Journal of Criminology Delinquency and Deviant Social Behaviour,* 34:1, (Winter): 1-14.

HBO Special, *Murder: No Apparent Motive.*

Hickey, E. (1997). Serial killers and their victims. 2nd Ed. Belmont, CA: Wadsworth Publishing Co.

Holmes, R. (1991). Sex crimes. Newbury Park, CA: Sage Publications.

Holmes, R. and DeBurger, J. (1985). Profiles in terror: The serial murderer. Thousand Oaks, CA: Sage Publications.

Holmes, R. and DeBurger, J. (1988). Serial murder. Newbury Park, CA: Sage Publications.

Holmes, R. and Holmes, S. (1992). Understanding mass murder: A starting point. Federal Probation, 56:1, (March), 53-61.

Holmes, R. and Holmes, S. (1994). Murder in America. Thousand Oaks, CA: Sage Publications.

Holmes, R. and S. Holmes. (1996). Profiling violent crimes: An investigative tool. 2nd Ed. Thousand Oaks, CA: Sage Publications.

Jenkins, P. (1990). Sharing murder: Understanding group serial homicide. *Journal of Crime and Justice,* V 13 (2): 125-147.

Levin, J. and Fox, J. (1985). Mass murder: America's growing menace. New York: Plenum.

Myers, W., Reccoppa, L., and McElroy, R. (1993). Malignant sex and aggression: An overview of serial sexual homicide. *Bulletin of the American Academy of Psychiatry and the Law,* 21:4, 435-451.

Michaud, S. and Aynesworth, H. (1983). The only living witness. New York: Signet.

Nagayama Hall, G., Hirschman, R. and Beutler, L. (1991). Theories of sexual aggression. *Journal of Consulting and Clinical Psychology,* 59:5, (October), 619-681.

Newton, M. (1992). Serial slaughter: What's behind America's murder epidemic? Townsend, WA: Loompanics Unlimited.

Norris, J. and Birnes, W. (1988). Serial killers: The growing menace. New York: Dolphin.

Ressler, R., Burgess, A. and Douglas, J. (1988). Sexual Homicide: Patterns and motives. Lexington, MA: Lexington Books.

Rossmo, D. (1994). Place, space, and police investigations: Hunting serial violent criminals. In J.E. Eck & D.A. Weisburd (Eds.), Crime Prevention Studies Vol. 4. Monsey, NY: Criminal Justice Press.

Segrave, K. (1992). Women serial and mass murderers: A worldwide reference, 1850 through 1990. Jefferson, NC: McFarland Company, Inc.

Williamson, S., Hare, R., and Wong, S. (1987). Violence: Criminal psychopaths and their victims. *Canadian Journal of Behavioral Science*, 9:4, 455-462.

8

Inside the Mind
of the Serial Murderer

RONALD M. HOLMES
JAMES DeBURGER
STEPHEN T. HOLMES

Introduction

When one thinks of homicide in America, "smoking gun" or "dripping knife" murder immediately comes to mind. However, a new form of homicide, impersonal and stranger-perpetrated, is growing in frequency and notoriety (Holmes and DeBurger, 1985; Rule, 1986). This new form of multicide is "serial murder."

Multicide comes in at least three forms: mass murder, spree murder and serial murder. Mass murder is the killing of a number of people at one time in one place. The McDonald's massacre in San Diego by James Huberty is an apt example of such an occurrence. Spree murder is the killing of a number of people in a very short period. The number is more than two usually within a month or so. Charles Starkweather is an example of a spree murderer when he killed nine people within four weeks.

The serial murderer kills a number of people over a period of time, many times months and years. The large number who fall prey to the serial murderer has been estimated to be 5,000 a year, and the number of serial killers now at large is at least 35 (Bernick and Spangler, 1985; Rule,

Authors' Note: This chapter was first published in 1988 in the *American Journal of Criminal Justice*, 13(1), 1-9. Reprinted with permission.

1986). There is a long list of contemporary serial murderers: Ted Bundy, Gerald Stano, John Gacy, Wayne Williams, and many more. These killers are well-known. In addition, there are examples of serial killers who appeared in the literature as long as 50 years ago. Albert Fish and H.H. Mudgett were serial murderers whose cases received such publicity. Fish, a grandfatherly type, murdered as many as 400 children in New York (Holmes and DeBurger, 1985). Mudgett, circa 1900, killed as many as 200 men, women and children (Eckert, 1985).

Types of Serial Killers

The motives, methods, gains, and behavioral patterns vary from one serial killer to another and from one type to another. One interesting typology has been developed which offers four kinds of serial killers. This typology was developed by Holmes and DeBurger (1985) after interviewing serial killers in prisons throughout the United States and examining hundreds of homicide cases. These researchers stress ideal types, and there is obviously some blending of perpetrators in the world of this serial violent personal offender.

The first is the Visionary Type. This person kills because voices or visions demand lethal action against a defined and identified cohort of people. Almost certainly, a case for psychoticism could be made for this serial murderer.

However, most serial killers are neither psychotic nor insane. As an example, the Mission Type serial killer may attempt to rid the community of prostitutes because they pose a moral problem as well as a health hazard. This killer does not hear voices, and there is no vision demanding such an action. The murderer may legally be insane but not mentally ill.

The third variety of serial killer in this typology is the Hedonistic Type. This person will kill because it is pleasurable or because it enhances the murderer's social or personal status. It is within this type that the comfort-oriented subtype appears. Women sometimes are serial killers. Nannie Doss and Belle Gunness both were serial murderesses who killed family members and suitors for money and material gain (Holmes and DeBurger, 1985).

The fourth type of serial killer is the Power/Control serial murderer. The killing of this victim supports the perception of being in complete control, and as Bandy stated, " . . . what greater power can one have than over life or death" (Bundy, 1985)? This serial killer receives personal gratification from the total subjugation of the victim. The motive may not be sexual in the normal sense of the word; sex does come in different packages with different ribbons and bows. The murder occurs, but first comes the instilling of total and disabling fear. Total domination becomes erotic. This is the motive and the gratification of the murder. This has been a dominate theme by the serialists during the personal interviews by Holmes and DeBurger.

Behavioral Background

Sources. In an attempt to explain the phenomenon of serial murder, usual explanations emanate from one or a combination of three possible areas: psychogenic, sociogenic and biogenic.

In the psychogenic explanation for impersonal violence, one would look for psychological causes which contain viable reasons for the perpetration of homicide. A seductive mother, an abusive father, sibling rivalry, a rejecting parent, a poorly developed superego, the lack of psychological defenses, poor impulse control, and a variety of other psychological reasons may all play an important role in the making of a serial killer.

The sociogenic explanation would identify and examine social causes for serial murder: poverty, unemployment, societally blocked means to legitimate ends, etc. A combination of these "causes" would blend and produce a serial killer. For example, one expert of serial murder lists the following as characteristics of a serial killer: intelligent, white, charismatic, illegitimate, police groupie, jobhopper, focuses on one victim type, liar, and several other items (Rule, 1986).

The third possible explanation for the etiology of the serial murderer lies in biology and heredity: underdeveloped ears, harelips, elongated second toes, bedwetting as a child, psychomotor epilepsy, and abnormal readings on the electroencephalograms. Other studies, although not necessarily making a case for serial murder, have argued for a relationship between crime and hypoglycemia, brain wave abnormalities, nutrition, or other physical conditions. These constitutional factors play an integral role in the etiology of the violent (Dorfman, 1984).

Do these three areas of examination offer one reason for this ultimate form of impersonal violence? One practitioner disagreed and simply stated, "The harsher reality of what makes a serial killer is parental attachment or the lack of it" (Rule, 1985). This "explanation" rests within the psychological realm. It may not only be nonsensical but utterly ridiculous to think of a single cause for this ultimate form of personal violence. In reality, the "true" reason for the making of a serial murderer may lie in the combination of the psychogenic, the sociogenic and the biogenic. In other words, the basis for this illness is still unknown.

Locus of Motives. An important aspect concerning the understanding of the serial murderer must lie in motive orientation and direction. In other words, what are these motives and where do they originate? Motives of the serial killer may originate in one of two ways: intrinsically or extrinsically. In considering the types of serial murderers—visionary, mission, hedonistic, and power/control—it is important to consider this issue.

Examine, for example, the case of the visionary serial killer. He may kill because he experienced an apparition; the Lord instructed him to kill all prostitutes in town. He would feel "outer-directed" to carry out his personal commandment from God. The locus of motive is extrinsic to himself; the motive for murder was "outer-motivated." The reason for action as well as the rationalization for the killing comes from outside of his own being.

There is another type of serial murderer who kills because he has deliberately and consciously taken it upon himself to fulfill a mission. The locus of this motive lies within himself. There are no outside voices commanding him to kill or apparitions instructing him to murder. Regardless of the "merit" of his action, he will make a decision to eradicate a cohort of people because of the victim's occupation, sex, race or personal lifestyle.

Some others kill because they enjoy killing. So it is with the hedonistic serial murderer. Richard Ramirez, the Night Stalker, vividly illustrated this point. He was quoted as saying that he liked to watch his victims squirm after he shot them; he liked to see blood run from their wounds. He would kill his victims and then eat the victims' leftovers from their kitchens. The motives for Nannie Doss and Belle Gunness, both female serial killers, rested outside their psyche. They killed to improve their status in life. H.H. Mudgett was another comfort-oriented hedonistic killer. He murdered scores of hapless victims to collect insurance monies or personal properties (Eckert, 1985).

Of course, the serial killer may murder for other reasons than voices commanding him to do so, because of a perceived "wronged" to be "righted," or because it is fun. The power/control serial killer seeks control and domination over his victim. This is his motivation and his pleasure. The motive may not clearly be understood, but it rests within the psyche of the murderer. Ted Bundy, for example, stated to his interrogators, " . . . there is something deep inside of me, something I can't control" (Bundy, 1978).

To come to some understanding of the serial offender, it is important to determine the locus of the motive. With some, the motive is visible and recognized; with others, the motive may be not only unknown to the observer or investigator but to the serial murderer himself. It may be something deep down within his psyche, something he cannot control.

Explanation of Gain. Within each type of serial perpetrator there emerges an expectation of gain. There is something obtained by the killing of a series of human beings which accompanies the murder itself. Sometimes the gain is fairly obvious; other times the gain may be unknown even to the murderer.

Gain, then, may be either expressive or instrumental. It does appear that for the most part the motive behind serial killing lies within the realm of an expressive motive. It may certainly be that some serial killers dispatch their victims for some monetary or material gain. Mudgett, as stated earlier, killed for insurance money and the goods and property of his many, but illegal, wives. The "hit man" for organized crime, although not usually placed in the category of a serial killer, kills because of the material gain. In this instance, the motivation for killing is not only fundamentally extrinsic but the killer is functioning as an instrument for achieving goals sought by exterior forces.

The expressive gain motivates many other serial killers. It is a hypothesis that this serial killer's homicidal behavior is expressive of the interlocking motives and propensities which predominate in his mind and personality. His behavior is oriented toward expressive (psychological) gain. This is unlike the entrepreneurial killer for whom behavior is instrumental with material gain as the primary orientation of the comfort-oriented serial murderer such as Mudgett, Doss, or Gunness. Furthermore, some hedonistic serial killers' orientations appear on the surface to be instrumental in the sense of seeking some form of material gain. But even for these, the central motivation is toward not only creature comforts but personal pleasure.

Victims

Some killers often discriminate in their selection of their victims. The traits, selection process and relationships with their victims will certainly vary from one serial killer to the next (Holmes, 1983; Holmes and DeBurger, 1985; Hazelwood and Douglas, 1980; Rule, 1985).

Victim Traits. The selection process of the serial killer will be either a specific or nonspecific instance, for example, there may be one physical trait which will attract the murderer to a particular person as a potential victim. Chris Wilder stalked "beautiful women." Douglas Clark, along with Carol Bundy, killed prostitutes along Hollywood and Vine. Ted Bundy killed young women, many with long hair parted in the middle.

In examining other cases of serial offenders, the traits of the victims may not be as apparent. Gerald Stano confessed to the murder of forty-one young women in three states. His victims, however, did not have a specific physical or social trait other than all were females. The same was true of Ken Bianchi. His victims in California were all females. Some were white, black, or Mexican-American from fourteen to the late twenties.

Some serial killers undoubtedly are relatively nonspecific in their targeting of victims. Despite this, most stay within a sex category and their own race.

Murder Selection Event. The serial murderer's selection of his victims may either be random or nonrandom. Some killers may randomly rape and kill any female hitchhiker who may unfortunately get into their cars or greets them in a certain fashion.

In essence, some serial murderers are often described as random in their selection of their victims. In fact, however, many serial killers will carefully stalk, wait, and kill a particular type of victim. Posteal Laskey, the Cincinnati Strangler, illustrates the nonrandom pattern of victim se-

selection. He killed elderly women after carefully appraising their vulnerability. It appears, therefore, serial killing may not be as random as once thought (Wilson and Seaman, 1985).

Relationship Pattern. It is commonly thought that most victims of serial killers are strangers. This is indeed the modal situation, and this has very important implications for law enforcement. With cases such as these, luck plays an important role in the apprehension of the serial killer. Detection and apprehension become compounded not only by the spatial mobility of some serial murderers but also by the lack of information sharing by many police departments.

Affiliative serial murder cases are infrequent but not missing from police files. Affiliative serial murders are within the context of an established pattern of social relations. Nannie Doss fatally poisoned her four husbands and several other family members. Martha Beck and her lover, Ray Fernandez, killed at least twelve lovelorned women who had become romantically involved with Fernandez (Holmes and DeBurger, 1988).

Methods and Patterns

The particular pattern of methods connected with serial murder homicide cluster around the event, the planning and the organization of the murder.

Murder Event. From the analysis of the scenes of serial murder cases as well as the interviews with the serial murderers, the murdering act occurs in one of two ways: act-focused or process-focused. In the former instance, the commission of the murder is swift, incisive, and directed toward accomplishing the goal—the killing of the victim. The focus of the act is simply the murdering of the individual. This would be particularly the focus of the mission or visionary type of serial killer.

A "visionary" homicide recently occurred when an elderly female was repeatedly stabbed, sexually assaulted, and decapitated. There was no evidence of planning, and the Assaultist related that it was indeed a blitz attack motivated by the perpetrator being chased by a demon. The victim, while living in the same housing project as the alleged offender, was murdered with her own butcher knife. The gratification of the act-focused murder lies within the murder act itself.

The processed focused killing is fundamentally different. This killing is characterized by sadistic methods of torture, sodomy, rape, and murder. Moreover, the scene itself will reflect great planning and detail to minute considerations so the pre-murder fantasies will be fulfilled. In addition, mutilation and dismemberment reflect a process-focused murder. Such killings are typified in the hedonistic and power/control serial killings. The expressive gain from these murders is realized more from the brutality of the process than from the simple act of ending the victim's life. One serial murderer related in an interview that, " . . . when I pulled her head back by the hair and cut her throat, this was the best orgasm I ever had" (Author's files). The utter domination, instilling of fear and finally the murder all become a part of the process.

Planning of the Event. Another basic behavioral factor in the serial murder case is the degree of planning connected with the murder event. Some serial killers go through very long and elaborate plans which are interwoven with their fantasies. Jerry Brudos thought for years how he would capture young women and keep them underground in a cavern (Stack, 1983). Even though his killings did not follow the exact scenario of his fantasies, there was a great deal of intricate maneuvering in his stalking, waiting, and killing.

For other serial murderers, the killing event is more an outcome of some spontaneous impulse. In these cases any planning is virtually non-existent. Such was the case mentioned above with the offender finally decapitating his victim.

Organization of the Event. Planning of the murder event necessarily precedes the killing itself. The organization of the kill centers around the act of the process of the murder. Psychological profiling, for example, attempts to offer some indications of the type of person who would commit such a crime by the "presence" of nonphysical evidence of love, rage, hate, or fear. The FBI's Behavioral Sciences Unit examines the organization of the crime scenes and offers such profiles. The scenes of some kills are very difficult if not impossible to classify, but the usual classification of the organized nonsocial and disorganized asocial is offered. This judgement is predicated upon several factors, e.g., weapon used (if any), weapon is left at the scene, etc.

The crime scene itself theoretically reflects the personality of the serial killer. If the killer is organized about himself, he will be organized in his kill. This same would be true if the person was a very disorganized person. His crime scene would reflect his disorganization. Most serial killers who would kill for sex or power purposes would fall into one of these two categories.

Conclusion

The professional literature on multicide developed over the last several years has been devoted to "traditional" homicide. This paper attempts to focus upon one form of multicide, serial murder. Two methods to gain information on this paper were utilized: personal interviews with serial murderers and the examination of serial murder cases. Through these sources, motives, gains, victim selection, and other information were obtained. This knowledge base has provided the cornerstone concerning a new theoretical posture of serial murder.

Indeed, the mind of the serial killer is most intricate. And perhaps the exact motivation toward this ultimate form of personal violence may never be understood. Even if apprehended early in his killing career, there may be no possibility of rehabilitation. But if we can come to some understanding of the dynamics of their behavior, at least an early identification could become a possibility.

Bibliography

Bernick, B. and Spangler, J. (1983, September 16). Rovers kill up to 5,000 each year, experts say. Deseret News. p. 1.

Bundy, T. (1978). Taped interview. (Author's files).

Bundy, T. (1985). Personal interview.

Dorfman, A. (1984, October). The criminal mind. Science Digest, p. 44.

Eckert, A. (1985). The scarlet mansion. Boston: Little Brown & Co.

Hazelwood, R. and Douglas, J. (1980). The lust murder. FBI Law Enforcement Journal. Vol 49 (4): pp. 1-8.

Holmes, R. and DeBurger, J. (1985). Profiles in terror: The serial murderer. Federal Probation. Vol. 39: 29-34.

Holmes, R. and DeBurger, J. (1988). Serial Murder. Newbury Park, CA: Sage Publications.

Rule, A. (1986). Personal interview.

———. (1985, August). Symptoms of mass murder. Science Digest, p. 49.

Stack, A. (1983). The lust killer. New York: Signet Press.

Wilson, C. and Seaman, D. (1985). The encyclopedia of mass murder. New York: Putnam Press.

9

A Serial Killer's Perspective

ANONYMOUS

My comments pertain to various inner workings of serial murderers, offered from the perspective of someone who has been just such a killer: myself. There are various types of serial killers, so it is obvious that my input here will not be directly applicable to each and every murderer who nears that appellation. But there are many of this fold who, while appearing intelligent and rational and essentially normal to the unsuspecting eye, are nonetheless driven by a secret, inner compulsion to seize upon other human beings, usually complete strangers, for the purpose of subjecting them to deliberate terror, systematic brutalization, and then death. This is the type of killer I was. This is the type of killer I've endeavored to understand through many years of introspection. And it is upon the inner workings of this form of murderer—the sadistic serial killer—that I hope to present some insights for those who might benefit from my own unique, albeit unenviable, perspective.

Victim Selection

Among the issues I have heard discussed regarding serial killers is that of their victim selection process. The traditional school of thought has it that serial murderers, on the whole, select their victims on the basis of certain physical and/or personal characteristics which they, the

---

Note: This letter first appeared in Holmes and Holmes, *Profiling Violent Crimes: An Investigative Tool* (2nd ed., Thousand Oaks, CA: Sage, 1996), pp. 68-76.

victims, possess. This assertion presupposes that, within the mind of each individual serial killer, there evolves a synthesis of preferred characteristics and, ultimately, a clear, specific picture of his ideal victim—male or female, black or white, young or old, short or tall, large-busted or small, shy or forward, and so on. Then, as the reasoning goes, when a typical serial killer begins an active search for human prey, he will go to great lengths to capture and victimize only those individuals who closely fit the mold of his preferred "ideal."

I am personally convinced that every serial killer does indeed nurture a rather clear mental picture of his own ideal victim. However restrained the outer demeanor of many a serial murderer may appear, each is without question a hyperactive and exacting thinker, his thought-life obsessively preoccupied with the smallest details of how and what he will do to his future victims. For throughout each one, he pays particular attention to the varied modes of restraint, abuse, and destruction that will later be his options when a victim is on hand, his mind all the while deciding which of these options provide him the most in the way of self-gratification. And, just as he focuses so attentively upon the methods of violence which gratify the most, so does he pay close attention to those physical details and personal characteristics which he has determined, through his imagination, to be the ones most gratifying to find and abuse as the objects of his later violence. The ideal methods and the ideal victim, then, are fairly well established in the mind of the serial killer long before he actually seeks out his prey.

Notwithstanding this point, however, I strongly believe that in the case of most serial killers, the physical and personal characteristics of those on their respective list of victims only infrequently coincide with the desired traits of their imagined "ideal." In my own case a host of assorted factors contributed to what I finally deemed to be my ideal victim, this mental vision consisting of such specific traits: gender, sex, race, size, shape, age, length and color of hair, dress and certain characteristics concerning my ideal victim's bearing. Yet, despite this collection of "preferred" traits, none of my actual victims ever completely fit the mold of my "ideal," and only a very tiny fraction possessed slightly more than half of the desired characteristics. The remainder of my victims fit no discernible mold or pattern whatever, beyond their common trait of gender. And such is the case, I believe, with most serial killers—their ideal victim, and those whom they actually victimize, seldom are one and the same.

There are two basic, interrelated reasons for this disparity. The first centers on the extreme caution exercised by a serial killer in his predatory search for a victim; the second, upon the nature of the compulsion that drives him to violence.

Addressing the first reason, it can be said that a serial killer is among the most alert and cautious of all human beings, this arising from his foremost concern to carry out his activities at the very lowest minimum of risk to himself. However, as much as he has inwardly justified his intentions, he nevertheless does have an unacknowledged sense of awareness of the heinous nature of the acts he will commit. He is aware of the stakes involved—that there is absolutely no room for error—and therefore will mark out no one for capture unless he perceives the odds to be overwhelming in his favor. His motto might well be, "Whom I cannot seize safely and with ease, I will not seize at all."

This unremitting sense of caution has direct ramifications on victim selection in that, during the course of his search for human prey, a serial killer is seldom apt to find his preferred ideal victim in a position of safe and easy capture. However obsessed he may be with capturing his "ideal," he is frequently thwarted by the simple fact that, in actual practice, the opportunity for this hardly ever presents itself under the requisite circumstances demanded by his extreme caution. In truth, it is a difficult and time-consuming task to locate any potential victim who can be readily seized without risk to detection. And it is a task made all the more difficult and time-consuming when the parameters of selectivity are narrowed by any focus upon the "ideal." A serial killer could, of course, bide his time. He could reject all other easy prey until, at last, his ideal victim appeared in circumstances perfectly suited to his caution. In actual practice, however, he rarely will choose to wait very long.

Why is this so? Because, as the second reason given earlier, the nature of a serial murderer's compulsion for violence is such that it precludes any prolonged or self-imposed delay in acting out his brutal urges. Initially, he may set out fully determined to succeed at capturing his ideal victim regardless of how long he might have to remain on the prowl. But as time passes without his promptly accomplishing this specific end—a common occurrence within his many hunts—his ballooning compulsion for violence itself will swiftly overtake any initially held obsession for a particular mold of victim.

This speedy shift of a serial killer's priorities might be likened to the conduct of a lion who finds himself hungry for a meal. Stirred to the hunt by his initial pangs of hunger, the lion set out in search of a gazelle—that is, a gazelle in particular—because he happens to favor the taste of the gazelle meat over all other savannah fare. Early in his hunt, a hyena and then a zebra cross well within his killing range, but the lion lets them both pass unmolested and continues on with his search for the preferred gazelle. As time passes, however, he finds that the gazelles just won't cooperate; they smartly keep their distance each time the lion nears, remaining safely outside his killing range. His hunger and frustration mounting with every passing moment, the lion quickly decides that any meal will do, be it a skimpy long-eared hare or a sickly emaciated monkey. In the end, it's the meal, not the type of meal that really counts.

So it is with a serial murderer. A serial killer just will not defer acting out his violent urges simply because his ideal victim adamantly refuses to materialize at his beck and call. Instead, his intense and mounting hunger for real-life violence against a real-life captive inevitably compels him to settle for any soonest-available victim of opportunity. And it is this, the increasing mounting stresses of a serial killer's compulsivity, and not such concerns as preferred physical or personal characteristics, which ultimately determines the matter of victim selectivity.

Perception of Potential Victims

As a serial killer steps away from his home to begin a hunt for human prey, it is almost always true that he knows absolutely nothing about the person who is fated to become his next victim. And, in truth, he really doesn't care. He doesn't care whether the stranger he'll soon encounter is a person of hopes and fears, likes and dislikes, past disappointments and goals for the future. He doesn't care whether the person loves or is loved. Indeed, he doesn't even care whether the person has a name. All such personal characteristics fall with the sphere of real-life human beings. And, as far as he is concerned, his next victim is not a human being in the accepted sense of the term. So, well before he even crosses paths with his next victim, he has already stripped that person of all human meanings and worth; he has unilaterally decreed, in absentia, that the person is deserving of no human consideration whatsoever.

This, then, is a serial killer's personal perception of all his future victims; each one is nothing more than a mere object, depersonalized in advance, with each existing only for himself and only to be seized and used as he sees fit. Moreover, he perceives his unseen prey not just as objects to be used, but as objects worthy of extreme contempt, vicious abuse, and certain destruction. In the mind of a serial killer, nothing is more worthless, and no one is more contemptuous, than the nameless, faceless stranger for whom he sets out to hunt.

Why does a serial killer hold such an extreme and irrational disregard for others? How can he so utterly despise and count worthless another human being whom he has even yet to meet? The answer to these questions is that, after years of nurturing and reinforcing his compulsion for violence within his imagination, each serial killer comes to a place where he finds it absolutely necessary to act out his brutal mind-images. And this, in turn, thrusts him into the position of needing to perceive living human beings—the only pool that he can obtain real-life victims—as worthless objects deserving the violence he desires to mete out. So, he mentally transforms them into hateful creatures, because, in the twisted morality of his own making, it is only against such that he can justify and joyfully inflict his manifestly hateful deeds of violence.

Naturally this outlook does not arise spontaneously or overnight. A serial murderer does not just wake up one fine morning with the desire to hate and kill other human beings. Instead, the entire sum of his initial violent activity takes place only in his imagination, and usually minus the presence of any outwardly directed feelings of hatred. At first, he is perhaps only intrigued by the mind-pictures he allows into his imagination. Then, gradually these begin to provide him with a sense of pleasure and self-gratification, this arising from the heady sense of control and power and accomplishments he feels as he places himself in the role of the aggressor within his make-believe arena of violence. He perhaps cannot identify or articulate these sensations for what they are, but to him, all that matters is that they feel good, and so he continues mentally playing out the violence that causes them to surface. For the moment, however, his "victims" remain wholly imaginary, and he is content enough with his arrangement. At this early stage, he almost certainly gives no serious thought to the possibility of carrying out violence over to actual, living victims.

As he continues dwelling on such images, however, he becomes like the budding heroin addict who finds he requires a more powerful jolt, a more powerful means of self-gratification. And it is at some point during this stage that a future serial murderer begins taking the steps that will help transform his undeveloped appetite for mental violence into a full-bloom compulsion for the same. Gradually, he grows more and more dissatisfied with the limited collection of mind-pictures that his imagination has worn out to excess, so he begins to search out his newer and more sophisticated imagery to play out in his mind. This imagery—which he obtains from books, magazines, movies, or any other sources depicting new examples and new methods of violence—is introduced and tried out upon his still-imaginary victims, this further reinforcing mental violence as his primary means of self-fulfillment.

The next step in the progression is that violence upon imaginary victims, however refined this violence may be, begins to lose its gratifying effects upon the future serial killer. Thus he switches gears anew and starts practicing his mental violence on real, living people—people he sees or knows from his school, his neighborhood, or his workplace—these taking the place of what previously had always been fictional, imaginary victims. At the start of this new trend, he is probably convinced that, despite the fact that he might actually enjoy inflicting real violence upon, say, the librarian from his school or the girl who lives next door, he still would never consider doing such a thing to them, or to any other living human being, outside the space of his own imagination. As much as he might believe this lie, however, this imaginary brutalization of actual human beings has fateful ramifications on the course of future events. For in order to inflict injury upon the librarian or the girl next door, even if this is meant to be done strictly within his mind, he first and necessarily learns techniques that will later be used to sanction actual and willful victimization. This is exactly what he does, and he continues reinforcing the development of these techniques as he plays out, in his mind-pictures, his new game of replacing imaginary victims with real people. But even this new practice soon loses its novelty and gratifying effects. And, in part because he is now equipped with some experience at depersonalizing others, his deterring inhibitions gradually begin to dissolve in the face of his need for a more effective stimulus. For the first time, he begins seriously considering the thought of real violence against live human beings.

Finally, then, the decisive moment of choice arrives, and the inevitable occurs. He has practiced in his mind for so long and has derived such intense feelings of personal fulfillment from this imagery that his appetite for this, when it arises, is virtually insatiable. Imagery, however, no longer cuts the mustard. The future serial killer knows now that his brutal fantasies must be acted out, that only his real violence will give him the measure of relief that his compulsion craves. And, just as he never denied himself relief in the past, so will he not deny himself relief in the present. Indeed, by this time, he finds it psychologically impossible to deny himself the relief which now can come only through literal violence.

And so he crosses over the line and begins to look upon other human beings as potential victims, and as the mere props they must later become on the stage of his acted out violence. And as he continues thinking about them, he grows to despise them, even if for no other reason than they are walking free somewhere, as yet uncaptured, thereby denying him the relief he craves and is convinced he deserves. They are "denying" him and he "deserves" them. By these and other such twisted rationalizations, he provides for himself all the reasons he needs to justify hunting down people as if they were vermin.

All such self-serving justifications, of course, are nothing but willful self-delusion and deliberate lies. To a serial killer, however, such lies are entirely necessary. For deep inside of himself, each serial murderer does have an unacknowledged awareness of the fact that his future victims are innocent beings deserving nothing of his wrath. Yet to admit to this fact directly, he would also have to openly admit that he—and the violence he intends to inflict—is altogether unjust and wrong. And, for a man grown accustomed to the goodness and the pleasure it provides, any such admission of actual wrong is intolerable. Not only intolerable, but impossible.

Perceptions During Violence

Once a serial killer is in possession of a live victim, the acts he carries out on this person are very often done as if on autopilot, these almost always being a close reenactment of what he previously did only in his imagination. The reason for this is that he already knows from the countless mental scenarios of his past the degree of self-gratification he can obtain throughout certain specific methods of violence. So, from among all these violent fantasies, he picks and chooses the individual cruelties which he feels will assure the most in the way of self-fulfillment. These selections, then, comprise the process from start to finish that he carries out upon the victim he has on hand.

Yet if the serial killer has this kind of special emphasis on the careful and systematic acting out of his favorite mind-pictures, it is only because of the tremendous meaning and pleasure he derives from watching the degrading, dehumanizing effects they have on his victims as he methodically carries them out. To him, nothing is more important than to see his victim reduced to the very lowest depths of misery and despair. For if there is any single reason for why a serial killer does what he does, it is so he may seem enlarged and magnified in his own eyes through the willful and violent degradation of another human being.

This need for self-magnification is always, I believe, a mandatory prerequisite to any episode of violence. Just prior to his every decision to victimize, a serial killer always first experiences a sudden and precipitous psychological fall, an extreme low, which he can neither tolerate nor deal with in any rational fashion. Throughout his day-to-day existence, all of his meaning is derived from the fact that he thinks himself profoundly special, unique, and perfect over all other human beings on the face of the earth. So, within the sudden onset of this mental low, he finds it virtually impossible to respond to it, especially to the crushing sense of anomie it gives rise to with anything else but unbridled inner rage. And it is this very same boiling rage that, in turn, fires up and triggers his preestablished compulsion for violence. The acting out of his cherished fantasies, he knows, will elevate him from his intolerable and infuriating psychological low; they will make things "all right" and cause him to feel good about himself; they will "prove," without any shadow of doubt, that he is really somebody.

This, then, aids in understanding the motivations and perceptions of a serial killer as he performs his actual deeds of violence. For when he finally has a live and helpless victim in hand, the violence he inflicts is not carried out just for the sake of violence alone, but, more so, for the purpose of reestablishing and reaffirming his own great worth via the brutal degradation of his victim. The long experience of his imaginary violence has already reinforced and "proved" the notion that, to become a real somebody, he needs only to display his power to debase, his power to break, and his power to destroy whomever he succeeds at capturing. So, in the twisted logic of a serial killer, he "proves" his own personal power and superiority by "proving" his victim's "worthlessness" through the demeaning violence he metes out.

The specific methods of violence he chooses to act out then are perceived as "good" and "righteous," perfectly appropriate for the present, as they have already been tried and tested in the imagination for their ability to restore his feelings of supremacy. And, once he actually begins, he is so intensely focused upon the careful performance of this script-like process, and upon the restoration sensations they give rise to, that he leaves virtually no room whatsoever for perceiving his victim as anything other than a mere object, a lowly stage prop, a piece of meat necessary only for the literal acting out of his own self-serving drama.

The consequences of this outlook are that the struggles, the pain, and the outcries of a serial killer's victim inspire nothing in the way of pity; his victim is a worthless object, wholly depersonalized, and is therefore ineligible for such a human expression as pity. Rather than empathy, a serial killer feels a tremendous surge of excitement and euphoria at the sight of his victim's anguish, for this, to him, is what the whole violent episode is all about. His victim's misery is the elixir that thrills him beyond all measure, for it is his tangible assurance that all is proceeding according to his well-ordered plan; it is his visible "evidence" that he is the magnificent, all-powerful creature he always knew himself to be.

His real gratification comes from the subjugation, terrorization, and brutalization of his victim, and almost not at all from the actual murder of the victim. Thus, from a serial killer's viewpoint, his victim might be likened to a disposable paper cup, from which he takes a long and satisfying drink of water. Once the water is gone, his thirst quenched, the cup has served its purpose; it is useless and therefore can be crushed without thought and thrown away, as if it never existed. Similarly, once a serial killer's violence has run its course, providing the desired self-fulfillment, his battered victim is of no more use to him than a soggy, used-up paper cup. Since he no longer needs to terrorize or abuse, his victim is perceived as an object of inconvenience, a worn-out piece of luggage he no longer needs.

PART III

INVESTIGATING
SERIAL MURDER CASES

Possibly the most important, and also the most difficult, task in the investigation of a serial murder case is to determine if it is indeed a case of serial murder. At first blush, this would appear to be a statement that is not needed, but there are problems in the investigation of a high-profile serial murder case that are not present in a typical "smoking gun" or "dripping knife" homicide. Police departments across the United States, and in foreign countries as well, are concerned with murder rates and the number of unresolved murder cases they have on hand. These murder cases occupy a great deal of manpower and financial resources that apparently lead to no quick resolution of a case. Some departments, especially those with financial resources, have devoted some of those resources to using outside experts in the field of criminal justice. For example, Dr. Ron Holmes has consulted with many police departments across the United States as an expert in criminal investigation assessment. This same statement could be made for Dr. Joseph Davis. Davis is becoming a well-known expert in psychological profiling, and his portfolio is expanding at a dramatic rate. In this section, some of Davis's work on the investigation of stalker cases has been included. Davis is also cited in this section in his profiling of an actual murder case in California.

Other police departments are instituting cold case squads. This movement is recent and led by the influence in no small part of Sergeant

David Rivers in Florida. This section contains a chapter by Sgt. Rivers about his Cold Case Squad with the Metro-Dade (Miami, Florida) Sheriff's Office.

As said above, the determination of a case currently under investigation as the work of a serial killer requires a much different mode of law enforcement operation from other homicide case investigation. How is this so?

Various types of serial violent personal offenders use different forms of stalking behaviors. Dr. Ronald Holmes examines motivations as well as the anticipated gains of stalkers in his chapter, "Stalking in America: Types and Methods of Criminal Stalkers." Again in the examination of various types of stalkers, e.g., the political stalker, the celebrity stalker, the professional hit stalker, the lust stalker, and the domestic stalker, his research found that different stalkers use different methods in their criminal behavior. Also, there are different perceived gains they hope to realize. It is true that not all stalkers become serial killers (e.g., John Hinckley II); some may stop if for no other reason than the stalker is apprehended by the criminal justice enterprise (e.g., Sirhan Sirhan). Others may become mass murderers, such as Julio Gonzales. This chapter aids in the understanding of the mindset of the stalker, which is especially helpful when stalking is involved in the commission of serial murder.

Dr. Joseph Davis, from the University of California system, is internationally known as a criminalist, criminologist, and psychological profiler. Chair of the department in forensics at his university, Davis has the academic experience as well as the practical experience in the criminal justice system. He is the founder of the Center for Applied Forensic-Behavioral Sciences, and he has also been declared an expert witness in sex crimes and fatal violence. In addition, he has profiled numerous cases for police departments in the United States. In his chapter, "Profiling the Clairemont Serial Murder Case," Davis goes through the steps in this murder case and the manner in which an academic can lend a unique expertise to the practitioners in a case. This killer was later apprehended in no small part because of the accuracy of Davis's assessment of the homicide case.

The third chapter in this section, by Ron Holmes, discusses the use of psychological profiling in serial murder cases. Offering a short history of the criminal investigation process, profiling in fantasy and fact (including a profile completed by Holmes in a lust murder and suspected serial murder case), Holmes discusses the basic goals and assumptions of the profiling enterprise. The method of operation, the signature, and other important components of the profiling process are discussed.

The final chapter in this section was written by Sgt. David Rivers, commander of the Cold Case Squad of the Metro-Dade (Miami, Florida) Sheriff's Office. Sgt. Rivers gives the reader a practical guide to the investigation of cold cases, many of which are suspected serial murder cases. The 10 steps in the reopening of an old case has proved valuable to many departments in the resolution of "cold cases." These steps are being followed by police departments across the nation. Sgt. Rivers is the president of the National Center for the Study of Unresolved Homicides, Inc.

10

Stalking in America

Types and Methods of Criminal Stalkers

———————————————

RONALD M. HOLMES

Introduction

When Robert Bardo went to the door of Rebecca Schaeffer, of the TV series *My Sister Sam,* and fatally shot her, the level of consciousness was raised concerning the dangers of stalkers. Several years earlier, Arthur Jackson stalked and stabbed actress Theresa Saldana. Recently, John Hinckley, Jr., shot at Ronald Reagan in an attempt to impress actress Jodie Foster. A farmer in Canada has written scores of letters to singer Anne Murray.

Not only those in the entertainment field or politics are stalked. Husbands and wives seek out their former mates to terrorize. Unbalanced persons send letters and make phone calls to athletes and targeted strangers for purposes of terrorizing and even sexually assaulting and murder. There may be no one truly safe from a predatory stalker.

Little is known about the mind and mentality of one who stalks. Meager research has been done to empirically study this phenomenon. What has been done is often lacking in research rigor and theory testing. Therefore, we are truly only in a beginning stage in our analysis and scientific study of this most serious personal concern.

———————————

Author's Note: This chapter was first published in 1993 in the *Journal of Contemporary Criminal Justice, 9,* 317-327. Reprinted with permission.

Also lacking is an analysis of different types of stalkers, differences influenced by behavioral patterns and expected rewards, material or psychological. This is the purpose of this endeavor.

What Is Stalking?

More than two dozen states have initiated laws to combat this social problem of stalking. Kentucky, for example, has passed House Bill 445 which defined stalking as " . . . an intentional course of conduct which is 1. Directed at a specific person or persons; 2. Which seriously alarms, annoys, intimidates or harasses the person or persons; and 3. Which serves no legitimate purpose."

Of course there are other definitions of stalking. Other states too have passed laws with similar language. But as varied as the laws or definitions, just as divergent are the persons and the behaviors involved in these predatory acts.

Stalking takes many forms: phone calls, letters, personal confrontations, etc. For example, in Oregon, a 24 year old man sent letters and presents to a 11 year old girl. Professing his lasting love for the child, the man wrote letters to her which said, "When I seen (sic) her, when I look into her eyes, my mind goes black. . . . I will wait for ten years. I will, and about sex I don't want none until our honeymoon." The man is now serving a sentence at the Oregon State Correctional Institute (Hallman, 1992).

Methods within the stalking process become an important and integral part of the act. Norris (1988) discusses the process of the stalk as it concerns the sex offender. It appears as a starting point in the selection process of the serial predator. Holmes (1989, 1990) has also examined the stalking of the sexual predator. He lists "the stalk" as one of the five steps in the selection and the execution of serial murder. Hazelwood (1991) extends a similar discussion with the serial rapist.

Literature Review

Criminal stalking has only recently been an area of examination by those interested in the criminal mind. Dietz et al. (1991) analyzed threatening letters sent to members of the U.S. Congress. This study attempted to gauge the seriousness of the threats. Realizing the numbers of such letters range in the hundreds each year, and rising, a need was realized to develop an index of personal safety to these public servants.

Other people are targets of a different type of stalker, the Erotomaniac. This person suffers a delusional belief that one is passionately loved by another. In The New Statesman and Society (1990: 32), five basic characteristics of this form of stalker were listed:

1. The person comes from a difficult and psychologically troubled domestic environment.
2. A domineering parent.
3. A transference of love and devotional interest to a person who is unobtainable.
4. A history of dramatic demonstrations of love including threats of suicide, dangerous and very public acts and sometimes physical attacks.
5. Irrational and inappropriate attempts to dissuade the love object and turn the rejections into a gesture of love.

Historically diagnosed as paranoids, Arieti (1959) suggests that erotomaniacs suffer from a "monodelusional disorder" with "good prognosis" for successful rehabilitation. This is hardly encouraging remarks for those who suffer at the hands of these stalkers.

The academic literature has centered its discussion of stalkers in terms of a medical model. Only recently have other articles appeared which examine this behavioral phenomenon from a different perspective. Vernon Geberth (1992), a retired New York homicide detective, for example, lists two types of stalkers. One is the Psychopathic Personality Stalker. Invariably a male, and representing the largest population of stalkers, he comes from a dysfunctional family; violence is the norm. He stalks because he has lost control over a subject, e.g., a former girl or a wife, and exercises too frequently fatal violence.

The Psychotic Personality Stalker is the second type. This stalker, either male or female, becomes obsessed with an unobtainable love object. Geberth places erotomania in this category.

Geberth lists three types of stalking: Erotomania, almost 10% of all stalkers, Love Obsession, which includes 43% of all stalkers where the victim is a stranger to the stalker who is obsessed and mounts a campaign

Selected Stalkers and Their Victims

Stalkers	Victims
Joni Penn	Sharon Gless, actress
Mark David Chapman	John Lennon, musician
Arthur Jackson	Theresa Saldana, actress
	John F. Kennedy, president
	Teresa Berganza, singer
John Hinckley, II	Jodie Foster, actress
Tina Ledbetter	Michael J. Fox, actor
Stephen Stillabower	Madonna, musician
	Sean Penn, actor
Ken Gause	Johnny Carson, TV host
Nathan Trupp	Michael Landon, actor
	Sandra Day O'Connor, Supreme Court Justice
Ralph Nau	Olivia Newton-John, singer
	Marie Osmond, singer
	Cher, singer
	Farrah Fawcett, actress
John Smetek	Justine Bateman, actress
Robert Bardo	Rebecca Schaeffer, actress
Billie Jackson	Michael Jackson, singer
Margaret Ray	David Letterman, TV host
Roger Davis	Vanna White, TV star
Brook Hull	Teri Garr, actress
Ruth Steinhagen	Eddie Waitkus, baseball player
Daniel Vega	Donna Mills, actress
Robert Keiling	Anne Murray, singer

NOTE: Information for the stalkers and the victims in this table was obtained from sources including Geberth (1992); U.S. News and World Report, 1992. In the mind of a stalker, Vol 1112. February 17. 28-30; People Weekly, 1990. When fans turn into fanatics, nervous celebs call for help from security expert Gavin DeBecker. Vol. 33. February 12. 103-106. People Weekly, 1989. Vicious crime, double jeopardy, Vol. 31. June 5. 44-49; People Weekly. 1990. Vanna White and Terri Garr ask the courts to protect them from fans who have gone too far. Vol. 34. July 16. 41. People Weekly. 1989. Justine Bateman becomes the latest celebrity to be menaced by an obsessive fan. Vol. 32. September 25. 112-113; People Weekly. 1989. An innocent life, a heartbreaking death. Vol. 32. July 31. 60-66. Lurie, R., 1990. Guns and roses. Los Angeles Magazine. Vol. 35. February. 88-94. Time. 1989. A fatal obsession with the stars. Vol. 134. July 31. 43-44. New Statesman and Society. 1990. Erotomania. Vol. 3 July 27. 31-32.

of harassment to make the victim aware of the stalker's existence, and finally the Simple Obsession Stalker who accounts for 47% of the stalkers who knows the victim, perhaps a neighbor or a former boss, and begins then a campaign of harassment. Geberth remarks that this typology was gathered from research done in Los Angeles.

Regardless of the number of articles which appear in both the professional literature as well as trade magazines, e.g., *Time*, the *Los Angeles Magazine*, and *U.S. News and World Report*, stalking is a formidable problem. Moreover, stalking had been viewed from little more than a cursory position. It is only now that serious efforts are made to examine stalking as a major social enigma.

Typologies of Stalkers

As evident in any specific type of human behavior, people behave differently from disparate motivational factors and anticipated gains. These variations in behavior stem from many constitutional and/or physical factors. It may indeed be biology, environment, or personal chemistry or more likely a unique combination of these factors which we do not at this time understand. Social and behavioral scientists, neurologists and physicians, psychologists and psychics all have their theories which explain human behavior. What is only true is that we do not understand the human condition, criminal or not.

One initial endeavor is to develop a typology of stalkers. This has been done in the case of serial murder (Holmes and DeBurger, 1985, 1988). Developing such a typology based on motivation and gain, four types of serial killers were developed. From this exercise, a better understanding was gained to investigate crimes of sequential killers.

Below a typology of stalkers will be described. Within each type of stalker the motives and anticipated gains will be examined. Within each type these two elements function for the predator as a personal justification. In addition to the motivational and gain factors, we have offered other discriminating elements which are unique to each type of stalker: Celebrity, Lust, Hit, Love-Scorned, Domestic, and Political.

By analyzing more than six score of stalking cases, trained raters were given the task of placing each individual case into one of six types. The raters were trained using test cases, and the variables (Victims, Methods of Selection, Motivation, Anticipated Gain, Fatal Violence, Personal Affinity, and Sexual Motivation) were coded by a university professor, a

Typology of Stalkers

	Celebrity	Lust	Hit	Scorned	Domestic	Political
Victims						
Nonstranger				x	x	
Stranger	x	x	x			x
Selection						
Random		x				
Planned	x		x	x	x	x
Motivation						
Intrinsic	x	x		x	x	x
Extrinsic			x			
Anticipated gain						
Psychological	x	x		x	x	x
Material			x			
Intended fatal violence						
Yes	x	x	x		x	x
No				x		
Sexually motivated						
Yes		x				
No	x		x	x	x	x

doctoral student in criminal justice and a masters-level student in the administration of justice.

CELEBRITY STALKER

The Celebrity Stalker is one who stalks someone famous. Typically, the victim is in the entertainment profession: recording artist, actor or actress, or athlete (football, baseball, etc.).

This type of stalker will pursue a personal stranger. Although this victim is well-known on an impersonal level, a famous TV star for example, the target is personally unknown. Robert Bardo sent Rebecca Schaeffer love letters two years before he killed her. At one time he traveled by bus from Arizona to Hollywood to personally deliver flowers and a giant Teddy bear. Refused admittance, he later obtained her address from a private detective. He rang the bell at her front door and when she opened it, he fatally wounded her. Bardo had written to his sister months before and confessed an imaginary love affair with Schaeffer but wanted to eliminate something he could not obtain.

The victim is carefully selected by the Celebrity Stalker. The motivation is inward and the anticipated gain is psychological. As with the case of Bardo-Schaeffer, violence is often fatal. Sometimes when it is not, it is only because the stalker was unsuccessful. This is illustrated by the case of Arthur Jackson's knife-wielding assault on Theresa Saldana. A delivery man just happened to come upon the attack and wrested the knife away from Jackson only after he had stabbed her eleven times. His intent was to kill.

With the Celebrity Stalker, there is no personal affinity, no lines of bloodship by family or marriage. And, of course, the act itself is not sexually motivated.

THE LUST STALKER

The Lust Stalker is motivated by a perverse sense of sexual predation. This type of sexual offender is typically a serialist and if a serial murderer is of the Hedonistic or Power/Control type (Holmes and DeBurger, 1985, 1988). Despite many claims that this type of stalker will select ideal victim types, e.g., those with specific physical, personal, or occupational traits, the victims themselves are typically strangers. The hunt itself may be quite involved or a spur of the moment occasion. What is the anticipated gain is a sexual experience, a psychological gain. Too often the Lust Stalker will undergo an escalation into violence which includes the murder of the victim. Again, there is no personal relationship, through blood or marriage, with the selected victim.

Jerry Brudos, a serialist from Oregon, would be an excellent example of the Lust Stalker. Using a ruse to "arrest" his victim, taking them to his home, he killed at least four women. To one woman, he cut off an ankle; another he cut off a left breast; to a third, both breasts; and finally with his fourth victim, he sent electrical shocks through her body while she hung from a rafter in his garage. Brudos was arrested while stalking his fifth victim, a young college woman (Stack, 1983).

THE HIT STALKER

The example of this stalker is the professional killer. Such a stalker would be the murderer. The victims are strangers. They have been carefully selected by the employer of the professional murderer. The anticipated gain is material, the money or other monetary goods which will be realized from successful predation. Fatal violence is the norm; no sexual acts are demanded. Again, there is no personal relationship.

An example of the Hit Stalker is Richard Kuklinski. An admitted professional killer (*The Ice Man*, HBO Special, 1991), Kuklinski coldly and dispassionately described his selection of victims and the manner in which he disposed of his victims. He even relates leaving his home on Christmas Eve while assembling toys for his children to go into town to kill a man.

THE LOVE-SCORNED STALKER

Unlike most stalkers, the Love-Scorned Stalker intends violence, usually not fatal violence, against someone known. The victim, then, is known to the stalker. There is psychological gain. The predator believes the victim, once realizing how much the stalker really cares, will return that affection. A personal relationship exists between the stalker and the victim, though not by blood or marriage. There has been at one time or another a personal relationship in which too many times the stalker has misunderstood the depth of that relationship. There is no sexual component to the stalking although the act may take on a sexual element.

A young 18 year old college coed, Melissa (not her correct name), went to the police for protection. She said that a young man, also a freshman at the same university which she attended, had been writing her letters and following her to her part-time job as well as walking behind her darting behind bushes and buildings on the campus. She had known the stalker since their freshman year in high school. Upon further investigation, it was found that the young man had broken into her house, went through her bedroom, and stolen panties and bras. Upon developing an analysis of the situation, the man was encouraged to seek hospitalization for his mistaken belief that the Melissa was in love with him and wanted to have his babies.

THE DOMESTIC STALKER

The Domestic Stalker at one time shared an intimate part of the victim's everyday life. This is a factor which differentiates the Domestic Stalker from the Love-Scorned Stalker. The former at one time shared an equally shared relationship and life experience. This relationship was inclusive of, but not limited to, love.

All too frequently a case is reported when an estranged husband hunts his former wife. Often the stalking is a long-term affair, and the confrontation between the two results in tragic consequences. His motivation is psychological, "to get even" with that individual who once shared an important part of the stalker's life.

Recently an estranged husband was stalking his wife for days. He finally approached her outside a daycare center where she had left their only child. Getting into her car to travel to work, he ran up to her car, shot her in the face and then shot himself. He died at the scene. The anticipated gain is perversely psychological, fatal violence is too often the goal. The target was one whom he shared an intimate connection. Again, there is no sexual motivating factor involved in the selection of the victim or the perpetration of violence in the finalization of the stalking episode.

THE POLITICAL STALKER

The intended victim of the Political Stalker is a personal stranger. It may be the President of the United States, the mayor of a large city, a minor city leader, or someone else in the citizen's eyes. The history of this country has more than its share of those who have stalked public officials including our presidents. In many cases, the public officials have been only wounded. Unfortunately, in too many other cases, the victims have been murdered.

The victims of the Political Stalker are carefully selected and the process of stalking is planned. There is usually a political ideology which precipitates the stalking and the intended fatal violence which ensues. As noted, sexual motivations are missing in this form of predation. When Lee Harvey Oswald shot President Kennedy, the President was not personally known to the assassin. They were strangers. There was no money exchanged, as far as we know, from a terrorist organization to Oswald

Presidential Stalkers

Year	President	Stalker	Age	Location	Weapon	Injury
1835	Andrew Jackson	Richard Law	35	U.S. Capitol	Handgun	None
1865	Abraham Lincoln	John Wilkes Booth	26	Ford Theater	Handgun	Death
1881	John Garfield	Charles Guiteau	38	Train Station	Handgun	Death
1901	William McKinley	Leon Czolgosz	28	U.S. Exposition	Handgun	Death
1912	Teddy Roosevelt	John Shrank	36	Hotel	Handgun	Injury
1933	Franklin Roosevelt	Guiseppe Zangara	32	Public Park	Handgun	None
1950	Harry S Truman	Griselio Torresola / Oscar Collazo	25	Blair House	Handgun	None
1960	John Kennedy	Richard R. Pavlick	69	Motorcade	Explosives	None
1963	John Kennedy	Lee Harvey Oswald	24	Motorcade	Rifle	Death
1974	Richard Nixon	Samuel Byck	44	Airport	Handgun	None
1975	Gerald Ford	Lynette Fromme	26	Public Park	Handgun	None
1975	Gerald Ford	Sarah Moore	45	Hotel	Handgun	None
1981	Ronald Reagan	John Hinckley, Jr.	25	Hotel Sidewalk	Handgun	Wound to body

NOTE: Adapted from Sifakis, C. (1991). *Encyclopedia of assassinations.* New York: Facts on File.

146

for killing the President. Apparently it was a political ideology which accounted for the motivation to murder. John Wilkes Booth killed Lincoln because of political ideologies which were different from those espoused by the President. Lynette Fromme shot President Ford, almost certainly motivated by the influence of the relationship with Charlie Manson and the Family's political leanings.

The Political Stalker is fundamentally different from the other stalkers we have mentioned. The Lust Stalker is motivated by a predatory sense of sex as conquest. The Hit Stalker anticipates a material gain. The Celebrity Stalker hopes to bask in the reflected glory of the celebrity or believes the target shares the affectionate relation which is in his mind only.

So it is that within each type we have discussed a type of stalker and the behavioral and psychological dynamics involved with each. This is the first step in the understanding of the stalker and perhaps, then, a step toward prevention.

Conclusion

Stalking is a social condition which is attracting more attention not only from those in the criminal justice system but also those in the social and behavioral sciences. As criminal justice practitioners we are concerned with the early identification of those who stalk their victims. By gaining some insight into the mentality and the mind-set of the stalker this may be the first step in the detection of those who will start this form of violence.

There must be an effort at early identification of the stalkers. One initial step is to make differential judgments concerning various types of stalkers. This has been the focus of this article. By the development of such a typology, this is the first step into an analysis of stalking as well as the personal risk of the potential victim.

References

————. 1989. A fatal obsession with the stars. Time. Vol. 134. July 31. 43-44.

————. 1989. An innocent life, a heartbreaking death. People Weekly. Vol. 32, July 31. 60-66.

Arieti, S. American Handbook of Psychiatry. 1st Ed. Vol. 1, New York: Basic
    Books. 525, 551.
Dietz, P., Matthews, D., Martell, D., Stewart, T., Hrouda, D., and Warren, J. 1991.
    Erotomania. New Statesman and Society Vol. 3, July 27. 31 32.
Geberth, V. 1992. Stalkers. Law and Order. Vol. 40. No. 10. October, 138-143.
Hallman, T. 1992. Stalker robs girl of innocence. The Oregonian. Monday. March
    9. A1-A8.
Hazelwood, R., and J. Warren. 1989. The serial rapist: His characteristics and
    victims. FBI Law Enforcement Bulletin. 58(2), 18-25.
Holmes, R. and DeBurger, J. 1985. Profiles in terror: the serial murderer. Federal
    probation. 39. (September): 29-34.
Holmes, R. and DeBurger, J. 1988. Serial murder. Newbury Park, CA: Sage Pub-
    lications.
———. 1989. Justine Bateman becomes the latest celebrity to be menaced by an
    obsessive fan. People Weekly. Vol. 32. September 25. 112-113.
Lurie, R. 1990. Guns n' roses. Los Angeles Magazine. Vol. 35. February. 88-94.
Norris, J. 1988. Serial killers: The growing menace. New York: Dolphin Books.
Rudeen, M., J. Sweeney, and A. Frances. 1990. Diagnosis and clinical course of
    erotomania and other delusional patients. American Journal of Psychiatry.
    Vol. 147. No. 5. May. 625-628.
Sifakis, C. 1991. Encyclopedia of assassinations. New York: Facts on File.
Stack, A. 1983. The lust killer. New York: Signet Books.
———. 1989. Vanna White and Terri Garr ask the courts to protect them from
    fans who have gone too far. People Weekly. Vol. 34. July 16. 41.
———. 1989. Vicious crime, double jeopardy. People Weekly. Vol. 31. June 5.
    44-49.
———. 1990. When fans turn into fanatics, nervous celebs call for help from
    security expert Gavin DeBecker. People Weekly. Vol. 33. February 12.

11

Profiling the Clairemont
Serial Murder Case

A Collaborative Investigative Effort

―――――――▬―――――――

JOSEPH A. DAVIS

Although homicide cases quite often bring denial, shock, disbelief, horror, and fear to many communities, no other type of offense strikes terror in the public like that of the sexual predator, or in this case, the serial killer. Furthermore, the aftermath following a high-profile serial murder case investigation frequently leaves a community psychologically traumatized and often devastated, and extensive critical incident stress debriefings (CISD) are required for law enforcement, the community-at-large, and the families of the victims (Davis, 1995a, 1995b, 1996a, in press).

This forensic-behavioral analysis and case study focuses on a series of homicides and one such sexual serial offender who became known as the Clairemont Serial Killer. The Clairemont killer stalked, predated, terrorized, and traumatized San Diego residents over a period of 9 months, from January 1990 to September 1990. According to Achenbach (1991), "The typical serial killer wants sexual gratification. Killing is a characteristic of the way he rapes. Torture and murder arouse him" (p. A9). Furthermore, according to Davis (Miller, 1990), "Serial killers typically kill without remorse and have no compassion for human suffering" (p. 5). When investigating any murder case where the suspicion of a series is theorized, human motive, drive, purpose, criminal intent, and ultimately, the specific "signature" aspect of the unknown predator's violent behavior must be analyzed and examined closely. In time, once this process is carefully done, the results will give local law enforcement feedback so that they can further focus, direct, and plan their criminal investigation (Miller, 1990, p. 5).

Homicide in America

A homicide is the willful, nonnegligent killing of one human by another (Harries, 1990). According to the Federal Bureau of Investigation (FBI), one violent index offense occurs every 19 seconds. Furthermore, one homicide occurs approximately every 25 minutes in the United States (FBI, 1994). Many different types of homicides exist. A single homicide has one victim in one homicidal event, a double homicide has two victims in one event, and a triple homicide involves three victims in one location during one event. A mass homicide involves the killing of four or more victims in one location within one event without a cooling-off period. A spree murder is a multiple homicide occurring in *more than one location* with no emotional or psychological cooling-off period (Douglas & Burgess, 1986; Holmes & DeBurger, 1988). A serial murder is a series of connected or linked killings involving at least three victims, at different times, but there is a cooling-off period between the homicides that can last for days, weeks, months, and even years (Davis, 1996a; Egger, 1984; Hickey, 1991; Holmes & DeBurger, 1988; Ressler, Burgess, & Douglas, 1988).

Profiling the Clairemont Series From Victimology

VICTIM #1

On January 12, 1990, Tiffany Paige Schultz was found murdered in the Canyon Ridge Condominium complex on Cowley Way. Ms. Schultz, age 20, was a part-time dancer and undergraduate college student at San Diego State University. Her partially nude body, found in a supine position in her roommate's bedroom, had been traumatized with approximately 57 stab wounds, primarily to the upper left quadrant of her chest. Approximately 30 or more deep, penetrating stab wounds, suggesting overkill (piquerism), were noted in a grouped pattern in that quadrant.

The assailant did not leave many clues except for trace evidence. The murder weapon was not found but was later determined forensically to be a type of carving knife or butcher knife.

Evidence of sexual activity at antemortem was present at the scene. Investigators did not disclose whether this was due to the suspected killer or to Ms. Schultz's boyfriend (the boyfriend was initially a suspect in the investigation, but he was cleared 5 days later). Neighbors residing in Clairemont, a suburb of San Diego, reported that they heard scuffling from Ms. Schultz's second-floor Canyon Ridge residence (Platte & Granberry, 1990, p. D2).

VICTIM #2

On February 16, 1990, Janene Marie Weinhold, age 21, was found stabbed to death in her Buena Vista Gardens apartment on Cowley Way, also located in Clairemont. Located only 2 blocks away from the previous murder scene on January 12, police began to wonder if there was a connection to the Tiffany Schultz case. Ms. Weinhold, an undergraduate college student attending the University of California at San Diego, was found also in a supine position in her roommate's bedroom. She had been stabbed multiple times, also in the upper left chest region. Her apartment appeared ransacked, and some clothes were taken from the premises. Several other clues were left for investigators. The murder weapon, a bloody knife from Ms. Weinhold's kitchen, was found in the sink at her apartment. House keys were found by the front door under a basket of wet laundry, suggesting that the victim was surprised, ambushed, or "blitzed" by the assailant. Forensic evidence confirmed that she had been sexually assaulted (Okerblom & Fried, 1991, p. B2).

VICTIM #3

On April 3, 1990, Holly Suzanne Tarr, age 18, was stabbed to death in her brother's Clairemont apartment. She also died as a result of sharp force trauma from a knife to the chest region. The death scene was the same as the crime scene. As in the Schultz and Weinhold murders, her brother's apartment was also an upstairs unit, and it was located at the Buena Vista Gardens apartment complex on Cowley Way. Ms. Tarr was

TABLE 11.1. Author's Comparison Victimology Profiles

Name of Victim and Age	Date of Death and Location
Tiffany Paige Schultz, age 20	January 12, 1990. Cowley Way in Clairemont
Janene Marie Weinhold, age 21	February 16, 1990. Cowley Way in Clairemont
Holly Suzanne Tarr, age 18	April 3, 1990. Cowley Way in Clairemont
Elissa Naomi Keller, age 38	May 21, 1990. 52nd Street and Trojan Avenue
Amber Clark, age 18	September 13, 1990. Honors Drive in Univ. City
Pamela Gail Clark, age 42	September 13, 1990. Honors Drive in Univ. City

Additional Victimology	Victim to Offender Profile
All victims lived within minutes of Prince	Prince lived in the same complex as three victims
Of the six victims, five were also students	Offender had a possible acquaintanceship with victims who lived at Buena Vista Gardens
All the victims were athletic, outgoing, well-liked, and charismatic	Offender killed all six victims in their residences or apartments during the daylight hours
Many victims had visited the Family Fitness Center on the day of their deaths	Offender killed in the late AM or early PM hours; he would walk or drive his car to each scene

a high school student from Michigan and an aspiring actress who was visiting her brother during spring break. Before her death, Ms. Tarr was seen playing tennis and lounging by the pool in the Buena Vista Gardens complex. She then went to her brother's apartment to shower. At 12:30 p.m., Clairemont neighbors heard screams from Richard Tarr's apartment, and a friend went to check on Ms. Tarr. When she did not answer the door, an apartment maintenance worker was called to gain access to the premises. Upon entrance to the apartment, the maintenance worker saw a knife-wielding man with a white T-shirt pulled over his face. Ms. Tarr was lying on the ground, face up, wearing only panties, a bra, and a bloody towel over her chest partly covering her face. The attacker rushed through the now-open door and ran west on Dakota Street, dropping the knife and shedding the T-shirt. A bloodstained butcher knife was found on the grass behind the apartment complex by a young boy walking home from a local school. The knife was later

TABLE 11.2. Profile, Signature, and Modus Operandi

Offender Modus Operandi	Victim to Offender Profile
Selects young and attractive white females	Background: All victims are Caucasian
Shoulder-length light brown or blonde hair	Employment: All victims were employed
Strikes in the early morning/early afternoon	Residence: Crime scene same as death scene
Weapon of choice: Carving/butcher knife	Majority of victims are members of the Family Fitness Health Club and Gym in Miramar
Location of multiple stab wounds in upper left chest over the heart (overkill noted and determined to be the criminal signature)	Prince was a member of the same fitness center
Cooling-off period over a period of weeks or months between each death	Prince worked only minutes away at the local Miramar Naval Base and Naval Air Station
Prince took personal items (trophies)	Prince lived in the same complex as three of the victims and within minutes of three others
Prince was noted to be at work on the days the murders had been committed	Shultz, Weinhold, and Tarr lived in Clairemont
Prince had a possible passive acquaintanceship with the victims at the gym	Keller and Pam and Amber Clark lived minutes away
Victim surveillance or preplanned attack	Many victims were determined to be killed after returning home from the gym
	All victims suffered multiple stabbings in the chest

identified as the murder weapon, taken from Richard Tarr's apartment (Okerblom & Fried, 1991, p. B2).

VICTIM #4

On May 21, 1990, Elissa Naomi Keller was found murdered in her east San Diego apartment on 52nd Street and Trojan Avenue. The death scene was determined to be the same as the crime scene. Ms. Keller's nude body was found propped up against her bed by her 18-year-old daughter. The 38-year-old woman had been stabbed multiple times. Consistent with the previous serial crimes and death scenes, the victim received multiple sharp force trauma in the form of stab wounds (over-kill) to the upper left chest region.

VICTIMS #5 AND #6

The next victims were involved in a double homicide. Pamela Gail Clark, age 42, and her daughter, Amber Clark, age 18, were killed in their four-bedroom home in University City on Honors Drive. Their home was located only 3½ miles from the other killings. As before, the death scene was the same as the crime scene. Each victim had been stabbed approximately 11 times in the upper left chest quadrant. The elder Clark was found laying supine and completely nude near the hallway entrance to her daughter's bedroom. Amber, partially nude, was found between her bedroom door entrance and the hallway. Police arrived on the scene at 12:41 p.m. after a neighbor found the body of Pam Clark.

Neighbors who lived next door and across the street in University City had their windows open but heard no unusual noises until the police helicopter hovered over the house at about 1:00 p.m. (Sullivan, 1990, p. B1)

Community Response and Police Reaction

When the public became aware of a serial killer was on the loose in the Clairemont and University City area, the entire city was very concerned. The once peaceful neighborhood on Honors Drive quickly was in a near state of panic. According to Gary Learn, the neighborhood is made up of primarily retired people and they are home most of the day. Because their community appeared to be immune to crime, many of the residents were in the habit of leaving their doors unlocked and their windows open. That all changed after the murders of Pamela and Amber Clark. Almost overnight, doors and windows were locked tight. San Diego Police assigned extra officers to patrol the University City area. Even Guardian Angels expanded their nightly patrols to cover Honors Drive (Krueger, 1990, p.B1).

Profiles of an Organized Versus
a Disorganized Killer

After the death of the third victim, Holly Tarr, the San Diego Police Department contacted several forensic experts as consultants to the Clairemont serial investigation. They were brought in to study the victimology and analyze the crime scene data. The evidence provided in the Clairemont series did not fit the "classic" textbook serial murder pattern (Miller, 1990, p. 5). According to Alan Davidson, a San Diego psychologist, "If it's one person as the police say, he doesn't fit either of the templates [patterns]" (Sullivan, 1990, p. B1).

The FBI's Behavioral Science Unit (BSU) has researched and categorized serial killers as being organized, disorganized, or mixed-type offenders (Douglas & Burgess, 1986; Ressler et al., 1988). An analysis of the crime scene and victimology shows that the criminal and psychological personality makeup of the killer is a mixture of both types (Sullivan, 1990), which is not unusual. According to Vernon J. Geberth, a retired New York homicide commander, "Many serial killers can provide a mixture of both organized and disorganized characteristics" (Sullivan, 1990, pp. B1, B2).

The classic organized killer is a sadistic, psychopathic predator who ruthlessly plans his murders so that he will not get caught. An individual who is sadistic has a sexual perversion in which gratification is obtained by inflicting physical or emotional pain on others. A psychopathic person behaves in an antisocial way and has no guilt or remorse for any antisocial acts. In his criminal behavior, as well as in other areas, he may show a lack of judgment and foresight that is almost beyond belief, yet he may score well on intelligence tests (Miller, 1990, p. 5; Holmes & DeBurger, 1988; MacDonald, 1961).

The classic disorganized killer is typically psychotic. An individual who is diagnostically labeled as a psychotic is suffering from a severe mental disorder and is generally out of contact with reality. He suffers from a deterioration of normal intellectual, cognitive, psychological, and social functioning that leads to partial or complete withdrawal from reality (Davis, 1996b; Douglas & Burgess, 1986; Feldman, 1977; Hickey, 1991; Holmes & DeBurger, 1988). See Table 11.3 for crime scene differences between organized and disorganized killers (mixed offenders will provide

TABLE 11.3 Crime Scene Differences of Organized and Disorganized Killers

Organized Offender	Disorganized Offender
Offense planned	Spontaneous offense
Victim is targeted stranger	Victim of location known
Personalizes victim	Depersonalizes victim
Controlled conversation	Minimal conversation
Crime scene reflects overall control	Crime scene random and sloppy
Demands submissive victim	Sudden violence to victim
Restraints used	Minimal use of restraints
Aggressive acts prior to death	Sexual acts after death
Body hidden	Body left in view
Weapon or evidence absent	Weapon or evidence often present
Transports victim or body	Body left at death scene

SOURCE: Reproduced from Ressler et al. (1988), p. 123.

a complicated "blend or balance" of both categories without the greater weight of either category being present in the profile construction).

The Clairemont Killer as a Possible Organized Offender

The Clairemont assailant displayed traits that are associated with an organized killer. First, he preyed almost exclusively upon attractive and physically active white females with shoulder-length brown hair who were between the ages of 18 and 21 (except for Elissa Keller, age 38, and Pamela Clark, age 42, who were both physically fit and appeared to be younger than their reported age). Ms. Clark, who did not fit this description because of her blonde hair, appeared to have been murdered because the Clairemont killer did not anticipate her being home. Organized killers target particular victims to fulfill their fantasies.

Common characteristics of victims selected by an individual murderer may include age, appearance, occupation, and hairstyle. In one particular sample, targeted victims included adolescent male youths, hitchhiking female college students, nurses, women frequenting bars, women sitting in automobiles with a male companion, and solitary women driving two-door cars (Ressler et al., 1988, pp. 122-123).

An organized offender fantasizes about the murder, going over the details repeatedly. Mental notes are made to correct previous mistakes and to create the ultimate fantasy (Achenbach, 1991, p. D8). To heighten the fantasy and to help relive it, they often take souvenirs or artifacts from the victim or the crime scene (Miller, 1990, p. 5; Ressler et al., 1988).

As an organized offender, the Clairemont killer entered the residences without signs of forced entry, in broad daylight, and without attracting suspicion or attention. He came in through an open door or window, or else he broke in. He may have been thinking like a burglar (Sullivan, 1990, p. B1), which would indicate good or at least average intelligence and careful planning. Another possibility is that he talked his way into the residencies.

> The organized offender is socially adept and may strike up a conversation with the victim as a prelude to the attack. Offenders may impersonate someone else as a method of gaining access to the victim. The offender's demeanor is not usually suspicious. He may be average or above average in appearance, height, and weight, and he may be dressed in a business suit, a uniform, or neat, casual attire (Ressler et al., 1988, p. 123).

Third, there was evidence of sharp force trauma, overkill, mutilation, and sexual assault in the murders. With the exception of Holly Tarr, all of the victims were stabbed numerous times. According to Vernon J. Geberth, based on the number of stab wounds at other crime scenes, Holly Tarr most likely would have received more wounds had the killer not been interrupted.

> It is that sort of sexual aggression that points to the organized killer's primary motive, one that separates him from the "ordinary" sadist and the disorganized murderer: the need to control and dominate, to flout society's values. "It's the ultimate power of life and death over a human being that the organized killer is interested in. He's not insane. He's fully cognizant of his criminality . . . but he acts without any concern for the social welfare" (Krueger, 1993b, p. B2).

The Clairemont Killer as a
Possible Disorganized Offender

The Clairemont assailant also demonstrated traits that are associated
with a disorganized killer. First, an analysis of the crime scene showed that
he sometimes used a "blitz" or ambush attack on his victims with little
regard for the clues that were left behind (Ressler et al., 1988). This was
displayed in the assailant's second victim, Janene Marie Weinhold.

Second, the proximity of the murders suggested that the killer operated in his "comfort zone." The assailant probably knew the area well
because he lived there or had friends or family that lived in the area.
Because he was familiar with the area, he was able to blend in with the
residents and not arouse suspicion. Operating in his comfort zone also
allowed him to know the personal and occupational habits and trends
of his victims and the community patrol patterns of the police (Miller,
1990, p. 5). Obviously, this knowledge served to his advantage and might
have been used to provoke or taunt police and other authority figures.
Being able to get away with a series of violent crimes right under the
watchful eye of the police contributed to the offender's grandiose sense
of feeling in control, and to his overall accomplishment and confidence
in carrying out his premeditated acts (Miller, 1990, p. 5; Ressler et al., 1988).

Third, according to Special Agent Larry Ankrom of the FBI, the crime
scene for the Clairemont murders was the same as the death scene. In all
of the killings, the assailant did not try to hide the bodies. Although he
did position the arms and legs in a specific way, he left them basically in
the same position in which they were killed (Krueger, 1993a, p. B4).

One of the most distinguishing features of a disorganized killer is the
manner in which he obtains his murder weapon. The disorganized killer
does not bring a weapon; rather, he finds it at the scene of the crime
(Davis, 1996b; Douglas & Burgess, 1986; Hickey, 1991; Holmes & DeBurger,
1988; Ressler et al., 1988). Likewise, after the commission of a crime, the
weapon is not taken from the scene. With the exception of the Tiffany
Schultz murder, all of the weapons were obtained from, and found in,
the victim's residence.

FBI Profile of the Serial Killer

Although the Clairemont offender demonstrated character traits associated with both organized and disorganized killers, the majority of

TABLE 11.4. Author's Comparison Profile of the Clairemont Killer

Organized Offender	*Disorganized Offender*
Offense planned—Yes (minimally)	Spontaneous offense—Possibly blitz attack[a]
Victim is targeted stranger—Possibly	Victim of location known—Yes[a]
Personalizes victim—Not seen	Depersonalizes victim—Not seen
Controlled conversation—Possibly	Minimal conversation—Possibly[a]
Crime scene reflects control—No	Crime scene random and sloppy—Possibly
Demands submissive victim—Unknown	Sudden violence to victim—Yes[a]
Restraints used—No	Minimal use of restraints—Yes
Aggressive acts prior to death—Yes[a]	Sexual acts after death—Yes[a]
Body hidden—No, left in plain view	Body left in plain view—Yes
Weapon or evidence absent—Yes, minimal	Weapon or evidence often present—Yes[a]
Transports victim or body—No	Body left at death scene—Yes (crime scene)
Geographically stable—Yes (local murders)	Geographically transient—No
Transportation: Functional	

a. Mixed characteristics found between organized and disorganized categories.

characteristics fell toward the latter. I believe that the suspect provided indications of preplanning but demonstrated disorganized characteristics, which suggested a mixed approach to executing the serial crimes.

According to Gary Learn, a lieutenant with the San Diego Police Department,

> The FBI profile indicated that the Clairemont killer is a violent young male with poor interpersonal skills. He is probably a loner and an underachiever with barely a high school education. He may work at night. Immediately before or after he strikes, the killer acts in an extremely agitated or bizarre manner. (Sullivan, 1990, p. B2)

Developing and distributing a profile of the murderer provides authorities with leads about the yet-unknown suspect. The profile gives investigators a better idea of the personality of the criminal (Davis, 1995a).

My Constructed Profile of the Serial Killer

While team teaching a forensics course on death investigation with a police homicide lieutenant, I was asked to provide forensic investigative support and a criminal psychological personality profile during the Clairemont series. My profile (similar to the FBI profile) suggested that the offender also demonstrated characteristics that were associated with both organized and disorganized killers, with the majority of characteristics falling toward the latter. However, I also suggested that a blend of both categories was possible, and that a "mixed type" offender who demonstrated both characteristics was represented in the criminal investigative personality profile from both antecedent crime scene evidence and postmortem records.

My profile of the predator stated that the Clairemont killer was a young male—someone who, on the surface, projected a confident persona but had problems with structure, rules, regulations, and authority figures (e.g., supervisors, bosses, etc.) It was possible that he had a prior police record of petty theft, property crime (burglary), or assault.

I further suggested, based on feedback taken from additional criminalistic evidence (feedback filter) later gathered in the ongoing investigation (trace evidence, pubic hair, and semen found at the crime scenes), that he was a black male between 20 and 30 years old. (Most documented serial killers are white males between 25 and 35 years old; many start their predatory behavior, leading potentially to murder, in their late teens or early 20s.) I also suggested that the offender was superficially responsive and outgoing but severely psychologically and sexually immature; that he would psychologically and behaviorally present with what seems to be adequate interpersonal skills; and that he would possibly be in a relationship (not necessarily a functional one) at the time of the murders. I also believed that the offender superficially attempted to establish rapport with others but often failed and was probably an underachiever of at least average intelligence (Full Scale range score with his higher skills being in the Performance Scale Range on a standard WAIS-R; the Wechsler Adult Intelligence Scale).

I hypothesized that the offender would have at least a high school level education or GED diploma (but due to his underachievement he might not have graduated from high school). Finally, I hypothesized that the level of intelligence of the perpetrator would be determined by several factors: (1) to be due to, at least in part, the amount of time he continued to elude, evade, and escape the watchful eye of Clairemont residents and local police surveillance and investigation efforts, (2) the stalking, preplanning, and level of mental preparation with each crime, and (3) the level of sophistication and cognitive ability to premeditate, enter, and escape with confidence from each crime scene in broad daylight. Furthermore, I suggested that he may work unusual or odd hours or be employed in a job that does not require a lot of supervision or social interaction such as in a semi-skilled or skilled vocation like that of a mechanic, technician, landscaper, or service repairman who possibly has access to the common grounds near or around the Buena Vista Garden Apartments in Clairemont.

I believed that the individual was physically fit because of his job (also evident because of the physical rage and overkill found from victim to victim at each crime scene) but that he was nondescript because he could blend easily into any crowd or community. He was geographically stable (rather than transient) and lived within a 2- to 5-mile radius of the death scenes or within the suburbs of Clairemont. He was mobile and drove a nondescript, possibly late model domestic car such as a Ford, GMC, or Chevrolet. Also, I suggested that the offender was possibly right-handed (90% of Americans are right-handed) because of the angle and direction of the sharp force trauma and wounds inflicted on each victim (upper right quadrant of each torso). I believed that possible artifacts, souvenirs, or tokens (evidence linking the perpetrator to each scene and crime) were taken from the victims and would be found in his possession when apprehended, or at least within his personal property. Later in the Clairemont investigation, Prince's girlfriend at the time, Charla Lewis, whom he had also been living with, at one point had in her possession gold jewelry he had given her (a gold ring later determined to be one of the murdered victims').

Later in the investigation through the discovery and introduction of additional forensic evidence (pubic hair) and feedback, the author revised the preliminary criminal personality profile and investigative hypothesis. A suggestion was made to include placing anyone under surveillance that would be a black male (fitting the psychological profile) who lived near or in the suburb of Clairemont (his comfort zone) and belonged or regularly visited a local fitness center or workout gym where several victims had been active members (testing the hypothesis for accuracy because the victims were watched, tracked, stalked with precision the day of each murder and attacked at their residencies).

I agreed with Larry Ankrom, the FBI special agent assigned at that time to the BSU (who also constructed a profile in the case) when he stated that "immediately before or after he strikes, the killer acts in an anxious demeanor" (Krueger, 1993a, pp. B1, B4). Later in the investigation, through the discovery and introduction of additional forensic evidence and feedback, I revised my preliminary criminal personality profile and investigative hypothesis, and I suggested to police that they place under surveillance any black male fitting the profile who lived near or in Clairemont and belonged to a local fitness center or workout gym where several victims had been members.

Hundreds of membership records were meticulously examined. At a nearby fitness center, a search of records revealed several potential suspects that fit both membership and demographic characteristics from the investigative profile and hypothesis.

Identification and Apprehension of the Suspect

"There's no such thing as the perfect crime" is an old axiom sometimes used in the law enforcement realm. This axiom is based on the premise that no one is perfect. Even with the most careful and meticulous planning, criminals will inevitably make mistakes and give police a break in the case. Murphy's Law—which states that anything that can go wrong, will—applies in criminal investigation as well as elsewhere in life.

On February 3, 1991, a young woman finished her workout at the local Family Fitness Center on Miramar Road (approximately a 10- to 15-minute drive from the San Diego suburbs of Clairemont and University City). She drove her car 2 miles to her apartment on Caminito Aralia in the Scripps Ranch area of San Diego. As she was preparing to take a shower, she heard a strange noise and went to investigate. She saw a man trying to break into her apartment. She ran to a neighbor's apartment and together, they confronted the man, who quickly fled in a car. Police were called to the scene, and Officer R. P. Shields took a report on what appeared to be, by the resident's description, an attempted burglary.

Officer Shields began to suspect that the incident might be related to the Clairemont case because during her interview, the resident had just arrived home from a Miramar gym. Officer Shields intuitively believed that the man could have followed her from the gym and knew that she was inside (Fernandez, 1993).

On her own initiative, Officer Shields made up a bulletin describing the burglary suspect and the possible car he was driving. The bulletin was then shown to the employees and patrons of the local Family Fitness Center on Miramar Road where the woman worked out. The other investigators and I had a particular interest in the same fitness club located in Miramar because Pamela Clark, the sixth victim, had also been there shortly before she was murdered. Two other victims, Amber Clark, who was Pam's daughter, and Tiffany Schultz, the first victim in the series, were also members of that same fitness gym.

From the point of distribution of the burglary suspect's physical description and car, police did not have to wait long for additional results. The next day, an employee of the Family Fitness Center where Tiffany Schultz, Pam Clark, and Amber Clark were members called to report that someone matching Officer Shields's description of the burglary suspect was sitting in the Miramar Family Fitness Center parking lot in a car similar to the one described in the police media distribution bulletin.

On February 4th, the man that police found sitting in the gray, nondescript 1982 Chevy Cavalier was Cleophus Prince, Jr. Inside the car, police found a butcher knife approximately 15 inches long. Prince was arrested but released contingent upon the submission of DNA blood samples to be tested. Later, Prince was again arrested on an outstanding traffic warrant and attempted burglary. Because of the patterned similarities between the attempted burglary and the Clairemont and University City murders, Prince became the prime criminal suspect in the Clairemont murder series (Okerblom, O'Connell, Fried, Himaka, & Jahn, 1991, p. B1).

Background of the Clairemont Suspect

At the time of the attacks, Cleophus Prince, Jr. was 22 or 23 years old and listed his job on his Buena Vista Gardens Apartment application as a drywall installer. Originally from Birmingham, Alabama, Prince enlisted in the U.S. Navy in March 1987 and underwent training as a mechanic and machinist. Four months later, he was assigned to his first duty station, the Miramar Naval Air Station in San Diego, which was only a few blocks from the Miramar Family Fitness Center and a 10- to 15-minute drive from the suburbs of Clairemont and University City (Fernandez, 1993).

Prince's record in the military showed a somewhat dismal career, blotched with several nonviolent property crimes. He was convicted on one count of stealing postal money orders from a private party, sentenced to 27 days in the base's correctional brig, and fined $466. He was also disciplined for other acts of larceny and wrongful appropriation. In October 1989, Prince was discharged from the Navy (Okerblom et al., 1991, p. B1).

Evidence Against Prince as a Prime Suspect

Several pieces of physical forensic evidence linked Prince to the Clairemont and University City murders. First, in the slaying of Weinhold, a smear of fresh sperm was found on the victim's clothing. This sperm smear provided another piece of evidence linking the suspect because it provided investigators with a DNA fingerprint. According to Okerblom (1991), "The DNA from the blood sample Prince gave is an exact match to the DNA from the sperm found on Weinhold" (p. B1).

> DNA, deoxyribonucleic acid, is the basic material of heredity and is the same in all of an individual's cells. Each individual's personal traits—racial characteristics, eye and hair color—is determined by his or her unique genetic code. Except for identical twins, no two people share the same DNA sequence. Applied to forensics in 1987, DNA typing was hailed by prosecutors as a nearly infallible method for placing a suspect at the scene of the crime. (Cantlupe, Okerblom, & Fried, 1991, p. B2)

Second, Prince was seen at at least one of the murder sites. Tim Buckingham, age 18, lived in the same apartment complex as the first three victims (Schultz, Weinhold, and Tarr). Buckingham reported to police that on the day of Holly Tarr's murder, he saw Prince, whom he knew, in the Chevy wearing a red shirt and a white pillowcase on top of his head, and he was driving down an alley about a block and a half from Holly Tarr's brother's apartment. Witnesses from the Holly Tarr murder scene later reported during an interview that they saw a fleeing suspect who fit the description of a medium- to dark-complexioned male with dark, wiry hair who had an athletic build.

Furthermore, they stated that the suspect appeared to be between the ages of 18 and 25; was approximately 5 feet, 8 inches tall; and weighed about 150 pounds. According to Okerblom and Fried (1991),

> Witnesses reported seeing a young black man, wearing a red shirt with a white cloth on his head, running from Richard Tarr's apartment after the murder. Witnesses also reported that the killer drove away in an older or early model car with primer paint on it, which was described to police as possibly a Ford Pinto. (p. B2)

Third, another connection to the Tarr murder involved Prince's own handwriting. As noted above, on the day of her death, Holly Tarr played tennis and later lounged by the apartment's outdoor swimming pool. A written sign-in log of all guests using the Buena Vista Gardens' pool revealed that Prince's name was written directly beneath Holly Tarr's. Prince probably spotted Tarr at the tennis court and followed her to the swimming pool. Antecedent behavioral events suggest that Prince then quickly went to her home and waited to attack her, catching her off-guard by ambush or blitz.

Fourth, according to Gary Wiersema, a trace evidence specialist, other types of physical forensic trace evidence linked Prince to the Clairemont murder scenes. Shoe impression prints at the sites of two of the slayings were consistent with the shoes obtained from Prince's closet at the time of his arrest (Okerblom & Fried, 1991, B2). According to Okerblom and Fried (1991, p. B2), a half-inch forensic evidence specimen of pubic hair was also found on victim Janene Weinhold's body. Prince could not be eliminated as the person who left it. Prince also had in his possession some jewelry from several murder victims. It also appeared that he gave some of these token possessions to his girlfriend. This jewelry theft collaborates the earlier observation that assailants often take tokens, trophies, postmortem artifacts, or souvenirs from their victims (Davis, 1996a; Hickey, 1991; Holmes & DeBurger, 1988; Miller, 1990, p. 5; Ressler et al., 1988).

Fifth, the suspect lived very close to his victims. Between December 1989 and May 1990, Prince rented a second-floor, two-bedroom apartment in the Buena Vista Gardens apartment complex on the corner of the

3300 block of Clairemont Drive and Dakota Street. He lived in an adjacent apartment building to Tiffany Schultz, half a block from Janene Weinhold, and across the courtyard from Richard Tarr, Holly's brother. The Clarks lived only about 3½ miles from the previous murder sites—still well within the suspect's area of local spatial mobility and his comfort zone.

Police Investigative Problems

Like criminals, police are not immune to Murphy's Law, and their mistakes were clearly demonstrated in this particular serial investigation. Immediately after Holly Tarr's murder, police questioned Prince and eliminated him as a potential suspect (Fernandez, 1993). The local newspaper published the story that after an interview with Tim Buckingham, the police officer walked over to Prince's apartment across the Buena Vista Gardens common area and courtyard. While talking to the officer, Prince went inside his apartment to retrieve a red shirt on a hanger, which he thrust out the door and displayed to the officer. The investigating officer returned to Buckingham and said, "He's not a suspect." Prince did not appear nervous during questioning, and he said things to convince detectives that he was not the killer (Okerblom & Fried, 1991, p. B2).

Other factors may have played a role in eliminating Prince as a potential suspect. First, the FBI criminal psychological personality profile of the Clairemont killer suggested that the killer was a loner who had trouble holding down a job and who was in a state of high anxiety or emotionality after each slaying. In my profile, I agreed with the FBI on a few points but differed on many others. People who knew Prince stated that he had a girlfriend and was a gregarious person, and he went to work on the days the Clairemont victims had been killed (Okerblom & Dayna, 1991, p. B3). Second, Prince did not look like the composite drawing that was circulated based on witness accounts of the man fleeing the Tarr murder scene.

Third, an initial forensic examination of blood and DNA testing at first caused investigators to discount the likelihood that Prince was the killer. According to Edward Blake, a noted DNA expert, the genetic material recovered from hairs found clutched in the hand of the first victim, Tiffany Schultz, did not match Prince (Krueger, 1993b, p. B2).

After investigators determined that Prince was the prime suspect, he could have gotten away easily. After Prince was arrested for attempted burglary, he was mistakenly released from jail. According to Deputy Police Chief Cal Krosh (Okerblom, 1991), "The paperwork did not get to the jail in time and Mr. Prince was released on his own recognizance" (p. B4). Prince did appear for his arraignment on February 15 but again was released on his own recognizance on the condition that he submit a blood sample for forensic DNA testing. One month later, while visiting his family in Alabama, Prince was arrested on theft charges. Again, he was released without bail. San Diego police then notified Alabama law enforcement authorities that Prince was wanted on suspicion of murder. Prince returned to jail a few hours later on his own, but only after police convinced him that he needed to sign more paperwork (Okerblom & Dayna, 1991, p. B3).

Other Crimes Possibly Involving Prince

According to Abrahamsen (1960), sex offenders also commit other types of crimes, including robbery, burglary (often called fetish burglaries), and theft. Thus, after Prince was arrested and charged with the Clairemont murder series, detectives began to investigate all prior local burglaries, hot prowls, and armed assaults to see if Prince could possibly have been involved. Because some of the murder victims were members of a local Family Fitness Center, investigators concentrated their efforts on that site.

> Police are checking the names of 13,000 people whom records indicate were members of or had applied for membership at the Family Fitness Center on Miramar Road to determine if they were victims of a burglary. Investigators believe Prince may have committed burglaries in addition to the slayings as fitness health club members could be among the victims. (Okerblom & Dayna, 1991, p. B3)

According to Gary Learn, it is safe to assume that the assailant selected his victims from inside the fitness club or from a secluded vantage point in the attached parking lot. In fact, neighbors of Pamela and Amber Clark reported that a man fitting the suspect's physical description was seen in their neighborhood 2 or 3 days prior to the Clark killings (Krueger, 1993b, p. B2).

Police also investigated a number of other unsolved homicide cases and found a link to Prince in the Elissa Naomi Keller case. Although a number of similarities and dissimilarities were found in the Keller murder, police were quick to discard the theory that the woman died at the hands of the Clairemont serial killer. Later, police learned that on May 6, 1990, Cleophus Prince had moved to the Top of the Hill apartment complex in the 5200 block of Orange Avenue, only yards away from Keller's residence. Prince's apartment complex was located on a hill almost directly above the victim's back bedroom and bathroom windows. "A sprint from Ms. Keller's apartment, up the hillside, through the church parking lot to Prince's apartment would only take a minute or two," said Okerblom and Fried (1991, p. B2).

A thorough investigative analysis from the victim's profile in that crime also showed a significant signature similarity and quality to the previously serialized victims. Although Ms. Keller was 38, she had a youthful athletic appearance and an outgoing, charismatic personality that closely resembled that of the other victims. A woman who did not want to be identified said of Ms. Keller, "If you saw her from a distance, you'd think she was 20 years old. Plus, she lived with her 18-year-old daughter. Maybe he [Prince] thought they were roommates." Because of these and other similarities, Prince was charged with the crime. In fact, during the trial, Larry Ankrom, the FBI agent assigned to the case, testified that the way each of the six women was stabbed showed a common pattern in all of the killings (Krueger, 1993a, p. B1).

First, all of the victims were white women who were stabbed with a knife in their residences. Second, except for Holly Tarr, all of the victims were stabbed more times than was needed to kill them, with the majority of the wounds concentrated in the upper right chest quadrant. Third, all of the victims' bodies were found face up and nude or partially nude. (The fact that the bodies were in a supine position may indicate that the assailant was trying to personalize his victims—a trait associated with an organized killer.) The killer appeared to have moved the victims' arms and legs into particular positions. Fourth, all of the women were apparently killed between 10 a.m. and 2 p.m. Furthermore, Ankrom stated, "it was my opinion, after reviewing all six cases, that they were perpetrated by the same offender" (Krueger, 1993a, p. B1).

Implications of the Profile and Serial Case

The Clairemont serial killer exhibited many criminal psychological personality traits that are shared by both organized and disorganized killers. Although having mixed traits is not unusual, other characteristics of the assailant were somewhat inconsistent with the profile of the typical serial killer. Assailants are usually the first born in the family. They typically are white males between 25 and 35 years old, and they generally kill female victims of their own race (Douglas & Burgess, 1986; Ressler et al., 1988). By no means does this imply that only white males are serial killers. Prince is black (few serial killers documented through history to date are black) and one of 8 children in his immediate family.

A serial killer can be any sex, race, or age. Statistics show that before the 1970s, serial killers were a rare breed. Today, however, there are as many as 50 to 300 serial killers roaming the United States at any given time (Holmes & DeBurger, 1988). But with new forensic technology to solve murders, why are there so many still on the loose? The answer is both simple and scary—every time a killer commits a crime, he learns from his mistakes, gains confidence, and becomes more sophisticated in his predatory behaviors (Davis, 1996a; Hickey, 1991; Holmes & DeBurger, 1988). The method of operation may change, but the signature aspects of each killer will typically remain the same from crime to crime and victim to victim (Davis, 1996b; Hickey, 1991; Holmes & DeBurger, 1988; Ressler et al., 1988). Often, the key is getting law enforcement within or across geographic jurisdictions to communicate to avoid "linkage blindness" (Egger, 1984; see also Figure 11.1).

Conclusion Regarding the Prince Investigation and Series

Cleophus Prince, Jr. stood trial in 1993 for slaying six women in San Diego County. In July/August of 1993, after approximately 200 witnesses had testified in the 5-month trial, the jury deliberated for 7 hours over a 2-day period before reaching a verdict. Prince was found guilty on all six counts of first-degree criminal homicide. On October 12th, the 26-year-old Prince was formally sentenced and received the death penalty. In addition, Prince was charged and found guilty of 21 counts of burglary that occurred during the same time as the Clairemont serial killings. (The burglaries showed a geographic mapping pattern similar to that of the linked murders.)

Today, Prince currently sits on death row in a California penitentiary, denying his crimes and actions. He is awaiting his eventual execution in the gas chamber at San Quentin.

If it were assumed for a moment that Prince was not found guilty, then one must speculate that Prince must have felt like he was "getting away with murder." One only has to look at the facts to support this conclusion. Prince lived in the same area as the first three victims, Shultz, Tarr, and Weinhold. Furthermore, Prince was questioned by police after the Holly Tarr murder incident but was not considered a viable suspect. In addition, he lived almost directly behind Elissa Keller, yet investigators initially made no connection (linkage blindness) to Prince and the previous murders until later in the major case investigation. And after being arrested for relatively petty crimes, Prince was released on three different occasions on his own recognizance by police (Davis, 1996b; Fernandez, 1993).

Is it any wonder that serial killers, sexual predators, and repetitive career criminals have such a grandiose, inflated, and narcissistic sense of themselves? Fortunately, the San Diego public trust in this high-profile serial case was not a prosecutorial disappointment.

Prince, as well as many other violent offenders who currently sit in prison or on death row and who have the unfortunate, infamous, and dubious honor of being called serial killers, can probably tell you. But, like so many, Prince continues to preach his innocence and is not talking.

The Prince case, adjudicated since 1993, still affects many who worked the series, some more personally and emotionally than others. Although realizing that the six victims can never speak from the grave, the numerous law enforcement and forensic experts who worked the Prince case and brought him to justice did have the chance to speak in their place.

For myself, the investigative criminal psychological personality profile predicated from each Prince victim and crime scene revealed a different investigative and forensic message. In the end, the criminal profile did not catch Prince, but it did ultimately assist local law enforcement in focusing their investigation, which eventually led to Prince.

Overall, psychological profiles alone never catch serial killers. However, with a little luck and hard work, a collective team effort between many forensic scientists, forensic-behavioral scientists, investigators, and local law enforcement almost always does.

In this case, I had some help from at least one victim because she was, perhaps symbolically, talking to me in some unexplainable way after her death. Empirically, it cannot be explained, but somehow I knew that the final victim, Pam Clark, was doing just that. Pam was perceived by many as a warm and caring person and mother, but one thing made her different in this case—she was also one of my clinical psychology students.

In Eric Hickey's (1991, 1997) well-written and -researched book, *Serial Murderers and Their Victims,* I think he summed it up best: "To the victims, both the living and the dead. May their suffering not be ignored or forgotten."

Pam, I still remember. This chapter is dedicated to both you and Amber. Your killer has been caught. Rest in peace.

References

Abrahamsen, D. (1960). *The psychology of crime.* New York: Columbia University Press.

Achenbach, J. (1991, April 14). Serial killers: Shattering the myth. *Washington Post,* p. A9.

Cantlupe, J., Okerblom, J., & Fried, D. L. (1991, February 12). Serial task force reported using DNA testing. *San Diego Union,* p. B2.

Davis, J. A. (1995a). The behavioral-forensic scientist: The use of psychologists with forensic training as consultants to law enforcement. *Forensic Examiner,* 4(5 & 6), 16-19.

Davis, J. A. (1995b). The police psychologist: The emergence of behavioral scientists in law enforcement. *The Police Chief,* 12(11), 36-38.

Davis, J. A. (1996a). The Clairemont serial killer case: Part I and II. *Medical Scope Monthly,* 3(4 & 5), 18-23, 20-23.

Davis, J. A. (1996b). *Criminal investigative analysis: Case studies in criminal psychological personality profiling.* Unpublished manuscript.

Davis, J. A. (in press). Psychologists and behavioral scientists as human factor and performance consultants to law enforcement. *Journal of Human Performance in Extreme Environments.*

Davis, J., Douglas, J., Streed, T., Danto, B., & Rosengard, D. (1996, December). *The "mind hunter" panel: Serial murder case presentations.* Paper presented at the 4th Annual American College of Forensic Examiners Scientific Conference, San Diego, CA.

Douglas, J. E., & Burgess, A. E. (1986). Criminal profiling: A viable investigative tool against violent crime. *FBI Law Enforcement Bulletin, 55,* 9-13.

Egger, S. A. (1984). A working definition of serial murder and the reduction of linkage blindness. *Journal of Police Science and Administration, 12,* 348-357.

FBI. (1994). *Uniform crime report.* Washington, Government Printing Office.

Feldman, M. P. (1977). *Criminal behavior: A psychological analysis.* New York: John Wiley.

Fernandez, V. (1993). *The Clairemont killer.* Unpublished manuscript.

Harries, K. D. (1990). *Serious violence: Patterns of homicide and assault in America.* Springfield, IL: Charles C Thomas.

Hickey, E. W. (1991). *Serial murderers and their victims.* Belmont, CA: Wadsworth.

Hickey, E. W. (1997). *Serial murderers and their victims* (2nd ed.). Belmont, CA: Wadsworth.

Holmes, R. M., & DeBurger, J. (1988). *Serial murder.* Newbury Park, CA: Sage.

Krueger, A. (1993, June 9). Prince trial goes secret: Sheriff concerned about disclosure. *San Diego Union,* p. B3.

Krueger, A. (1993a, June 10). Prince trial expert: Same person killed 6. *San Diego Union,* pp. B1, B4.

Krueger, A. (1993b, June 10). Witness can't link DNA sample to Prince. *San Diego Union,* p. B2.

MacDonald, J. M. (1961). *The murderer and his victim.* Springfield, IL: Charles C Thomas.

Miller, C. (1990, September 26). On guard: The Clairemont serial murder case. *The Daily Aztec,* pp. 5-8.

Okerblom, J. (1991, May 12). Lone cop's instinct finally resulted in suspect's capture. *San Diego Union,* p. B1.

Okerblom, J., & Dayna, L. F. (1991, March 7). Police expand scope of Prince investigation. *San Diego Union,* p. B3.

Okerblom, J., & Fried, D. L. (1991, March 6). Sixth victim may be knife stalker's. *San Diego Union,* p. B2.

Okerblom, J., O'Connell, J., Fried, D. L., Himaka, M., & Jahn, E. (1991, March 5). Prince named as suspect last year. *San Diego Union,* p. B1.

Platte, M., & Granberry, M. (1990, September 21). Eerie killings have San Diego women on edge. *Los Angeles Times,* p. D2.

Ressler, R. K., Burgess, A. W., & Douglas, J. E. (1988). *Sexual homicide: Patterns and motives.* New York: Lexington Books.

Sullivan, M. T. (1990, September 18). Profile of a killer. *San Diego Union,* pp. B1, B2.

12

Psychological Profiling

Uses in Serial Murder Cases

RONALD M. HOLMES

With the heightened interest today in serial murder and the apprehension of the killers themselves, new techniques have emerged that have a manifest purpose in aiding law enforcement. The serial murder investigation is hindered by a variety of law enforcement activities, including turf issues, linkage blindness, the mobility of many serialists, and, of course, the identification that the case is, indeed, one of serial murder (Egger, 1990; Holmes & Holmes, 1996).

It is true that the law enforcement profession has become more proficient in its investigation of serial murder cases if for no other reason than that it is becoming more aware of the serial murder problem. It is also becoming more willing to share information than in the past (reducing linkage blindness and turf issues). Still, however, there is great concern among many that the profession needs to become more proficient.

One aid to law enforcement is psychological profiling, now termed criminal investigation assessment. The Federal Bureau of Investigation (FBI) led the way in establishing these profiles in the early 1980s. Today, the media present us with images of profilers who receive mental pictures that usually recreate the murder scene and remarkably see the face of the killer, usually a serial killer, and the commission of the crime. These TV series (e.g., *Profiler* or *Millenium*) borrow information from practitioners and academics to lend a semblance of authenticity to their programs. The "organized" or "disorganized" offender is often mentioned.

The typology of Visionary, Mission, Hedonistic, or Power/Control serial killer was mentioned in one episode of *Millenium*, giving me credit as an academic studying serial murderers. The profilers in these TV programs are either retired (*Millenium*) or an active agent (*Profiler*) of the FBI

Despite the limitation and skepticism of many, it appears that criminal investigation assessment has received adequate support to become another aid in the investigation of a range of crimes, including serial murder.

History of Psychological Profiling

Perhaps no one case announced the advent of psychological profiling more than the Mad Bomber (Brussels, 1968). A psychiatrist, Dr. James Brussels, provided his expertise to the New York Police Department in developing a psychological profile that accurately predicted many social and behavioral traits of this unknown perpetrator. Brussels predicted that when the offender was arrested, he would be wearing a three-piece suit. This proved to be accurate.

Other profiles have captured the attention of those interested in the profiling assessment process. For example, in World War II, the Allies wanted to know what the chances were of capturing Hitler, and, if this did occur, how they should handle him. Therefore, the Office of Strategic Services sought the help of Dr. Walter Langer. Langer and his associates developed a profile that was never actually needed because Hitler committed suicide (Langer, 1972). It did, however, give historians and others insight into the mind and mentality of one of the world's most evil men (Holmes & Holmes, 1996, pp. 16-17).

Psychological profiling, and the interest in its activities, have grown radically in the past two decades. Numerous fiction books have been written and published that have placated this growing interest in the criminal investigation assessment process. Many works are fiction but gleaned from true cases of serial killers. Others are works that have been blended from the murders of two or more serial killers. There are still other books, less interesting, certainly, that give the reader some insight as far as the profiling process is concerned.

Profiling In Fiction

Two fiction books by Thomas Harris (1981, 1988) have ignited and galvanized our attention not only to psychological profiling but also to serial murder. The first, *The Red Dragon*, featured the work of Will Graham, a retired agent for the FBI. He was called back into service by his section chief, Jack Crawford, at the Behavioral Science Unit at the FBI Headquarters in Quantico, Virginia. Two families had been viciously assaulted and murdered, one in Atlanta and the other in Birmingham. Graham was the best profiler the FBI could offer, and with some reluctance, he left his own family in Florida and went to the crime scenes. He tried to put himself into the mind of the serialist as he examined the rooms where the killings occurred. He knew the killer had opened the victims' eyes after he killed them; Graham wondered if the victims were "witnesses" to the acts of sex and horror that occurred after the family members had been killed. Were they an audience? He carried on a monologue with the unknown killer, saying,

> Why did you move them [the children] again? Why didn't you leave then that way? There's something you don't want me to know about you. Why, there's something you're ashamed of. Or is it something you can't afford for me to know?
>
> Did you open their eyes?
>
> Mrs. Leeds was lovely, wasn't she? You turned on the light after you cut his throat so Mrs. Leeds could watch him flop, didn't you? It was maddening to have to wear gloves when you touched her, wasn't it? (Harris, 1981, p. 19)

The Red Dragon provides a fictional introduction to the real world of profiling and to the art involved in the profiler's immersion in a case. In this novel, there is little real science; it is, indeed, an art. *The Red Dragon* is fascinating reading, and Harris told me that the agents at Quantico aided him in his research.

Harris's next book, *The Silence of the Lambs,* gives the reader a chance to examine the mind of the psychopath, Dr. Hannibal Lecter, as well as a new agent-in-training, Clarice Starling. In their developing relationship, Lecter provides Starling with vital information about the criminal mind. Under the direction of the recurring figure of Jack Crawford, who, as Harris told me, is not patterned after any one figure in the FBI, Starling hones her skills as a profiler. She receives her education from two sources: Jack Crawford and the real expert, Hannibal Lecter. Certainly, Lecter provides Starling with more information about the mind of the serial killer she is hunting than do the FBI agents at the Behavioral Science Unit. The more veteran agents had been unable to develop a relationship with Hannibal Lecter; thus, the serialist is arrested because of the profile and Starling's activities.

Profiling in Fact

There are relatively few who perform psychological profiles in the United States. Several retired FBI agents have organized such an enterprise as a business venture, and they do "profiles for profit." Others offer their services free of charge as a service to the criminal justice system.

I developed the following profile for a police department that was investigating a bizarre murder and wanted insight into the mind of the perpetrator.

Dear Detective Morgan:

Thank you for the opportunity to review the case of Ms. _____. I have reviewed the two-page fact sheet, the pathologic-diagnoses-of-the-body document, the forensic anthropologist report, the map of the county and surrounding area, the photos, and the video. I have not talked with you or anyone else about a potential suspect and am offering the following as my general impressions of the type of person you may be looking for as a viable suspect in this case.

Age   The age of this suspect would be 32 to 36. Perhaps the age could be a couple of years older. There are several reasons for this belief. First of all, I don't see this as the first time the killer has done this type of murder. What I am saying is that he has fantasized about killing a woman in this manner for several years. His fantasies have to become real, and the acts that he did to this victim take a long time to finally emerge. In addition, he has perhaps committed a murder or two before this particular murder. Other items that indicate that he would be about this age are the age of those who would "hang out" in the bars as well as those who would have the energy needed in the commission of this crime.

Sex   The sex of the offender is male.

Race   I believe that this suspect is white. There are several reasons for this. First of all, most murders are committed by people who are the same race as the victim. There was no evidence that would indicate that the race of the offender is anything other than white.

Intelligence   I think that this person is of average to less-than-average mental ability. I do not believe that this person is a "rocket scientist" but one who would blend in well with the other people with whom he associates, and he probably has the ability to work in jobs with little supervision. I also think that he is not viewed as a mental retardant but is also, on the other hand, one who is a loner and one who is viewed by others who know him as being of average ability but a little strange or weird.

Education   I believe that the suspect has a high school education or less. I also believe that while in school, he adjusted well and presented no behavioral problems of any significance. He attended a local school in your part of Ohio. I don't believe he attended college, or if he did, he stayed less than a year. His mental ability would not stop him from enrolling in college, but his mental status and disorganization would prohibit him from staying in college. In the school situation, he would have been an average student, probably not a behavioral problem.

Family   This person is either an only child or one from a small family with another sibling. His father was a passive person while the suspect was growing up and may have been deceased or absent from the family. The mother was a domineering person, aggressive, and was the center of power within the family. She was the judge, jury, and executioner. Whatever she said was the law for the family. I also believe that the mother has recently died. In the family, the child lived under her control, and the mother was constantly verbally abusing the offender.

Residence   At the time of this present murder, the suspect lived in this local area and perhaps still does. There is something of a comfort zone in the manner in which he brings the "dying" victim back to the area with which he is most familiar and most comfortable. There appear to be four dump sites here. The first one is the place in your county where the torso was found; the other three sites are less comfortable for him, and the dumping occurred at a later date. I think he lives closer to the first dump site than the others.

The place where the torso was dumped is interesting for consideration. The residence of this offender is within driving distance, and perhaps even within vision. The house itself is nondescript and blends in with the other homes in the area. This person is a long-time resident of this community. He is a person who is well-known and probably lived with his mother for a long period of time, perhaps even to the time that she died.

Vehicle   I think that this person drives a car that is in poor cosmetic condition. The car is 8 to 10 years old, a domestic car, Ford, Chevrolet, etc. It is dirty, unkempt, and also in relatively poor mechanical condition. The trunk of the car would also be littered, and there would be blood in it that would match the blood of the victim.

Employment   This person is involved in a steady job situation. I think he works in some type of construction work—something that demands physical labor. He may also be a truck driver. I don't see him as being in a white-collar position. He shows some knowledge of the various counties, and the manner in which the parts were dumped shows some knowledge that police may not always share information. He may have been at one time, or presently, an auxiliary police officer, deputy, EMT, fireman, etc.

Psychosexual Development   This killer is a seriously disturbed individual. The savagery of the dismemberment depicts someone who has anger directed toward women. The anger also appears in the manner in which he disfigured her: the permanent "smile" he has placed on her face. The way in which he cut up the body shows determination and anger, plus it makes the victim less than a human being. In other words, "Not only are you a nothing, you now become little bits of nothing."

The killer has placed the parts in a descending order of preference. First of all, the torso is found days before the other parts. But the ice particles found in the arms, legs, head, etc. show that he has a lower interest in the torso area, or perhaps he attaches less importance to the torso despite it being cut again with a "pocket" cut. The other parts are more important because they were kept longer. What is especially interesting is that the person has kept the body from the neck to the waist, or at least it has not been found. This is the most important part for him. I can see him skinning this body part and wearing it at night or around the house.

The person may be a transsexual, preoperative one, and may have tried to get counseling for sexual problems. I must stress here that I do not believe he is a homosexual. I think he has tremendous problems with his sexuality. On one hand, he admires women for whom they are, and he wants to be like them; that may be the reason he keeps the breasts and has looked inside the reproduction area of the victim. On the other hand, he hates women for the manner in which they (the mother?) have treated him. He also demonstrates this in the manner in which he selects women. The victimology shows that the victim was sexually active, frequented lower-class bars, drank, and "ran around on her family." The "victim was deserving" may have been a theme in the fantasy of the killer.

Recommendations

- Secure a task force and get the investigation under one umbrella.

- The manager or bartender of the bar must again be interviewed. The killer may have been at the bar several times before.

- You might want to check out people in the area who have meat-cutting experience, but I don't think this should occupy too much time.

- You might want to get this case on *Unsolved Mysteries*, etc.

- Check out the list of the local sporting clubs. This person is a hunter and may belong to several hunting or sporting clubs in this area.

- Check building permits for anything that could be used as a building or renovation for this type of activity, e.g., bathrooms, cutting area. You might also check for electrical upgrading permits.

- Check with people who might have permission to hunt in the areas where the body parts were found.

- Check the deaths of older women who have passed away within the past 1 to 2 years.

- Do you have ice houses locally? Check them out for customers.

Assumptions in the Profiling Process

There are four assumptions in the profiling process. These four are outlined in detail in Holmes and Holmes (1996, pp. 39-43).

THE CRIME SCENE REFLECTS THE PERSONALITY

One basic assumption of psychological profiling is that the crime scene reflects the personality of the offender. This assessment of the crime scene should aid the police by providing for their investigation of the crime, the type of personality of the offender, and narrowing of the scope of the investigation.

The manner in which a victim has been killed is very important, but other physical and nonphysical evidence also can be very valuable in the assessment of the murderer's personality. The amount of chaos at the scene, for example, might indicate that a disorganized personality was involved in the crime. If this is true, then certain assumptions can be made about the social core variables of the perpetrator. On the other hand, if a crime scene is "neat and clean," or if the murders appear to be a "five window killing" (Holmes, 1988, pp. 1-5), then other assumptions might lead to an offender with a different set of social core variables.

The focus of the attack may also indicate certain information that can aid in the apprehension of an unknown offender. An example of a case in which this was true is one in which an elderly woman was killed in her own home in a midwestern state. She was stabbed repeatedly and suffered multiple deep wounds to her upper legs and genital area. The profile offered an assessment of the crime that, in part, resulted in the arrest of the killer, a man who was not considered a suspect at the beginning stages of the law enforcement investigation.

THE METHOD OF OPERATION REMAINS SIMILAR

It is the behavior of the perpetrator, as evidenced in the crime scene, and not the offense per se that determines the degree of suitability of a case for profiling (Geberth, 1993, p. 401). The crime scene contains clues that an experienced profiler may determine to be the "signature" of a criminal. Just as no two offenders are exactly alike, it is equally true that no two crimes are exactly alike. As certainly as a psychometric test reflects psychopathology, the crime scene reflects a personality with a pathology. To understand the crime, one needs to first understand the criminal! The method of operation—how the crime was committed—will certainly tell us not only about the offender but it will also tell us about the possibility of the crimes being related and committed by the same person.

THE SIGNATURE WILL REMAIN THE SAME

The signature of a perpetrator is the unique manner in which he or she commits crimes. A signature may be the manner in which the person kills, certain words a rapists uses with victims, a particular manner in which a perpetrator leaves something at crime scenes, or some other indicator (Hazelwood, 1994).

There is some confusion concerning the difference between a signature and a method of operation. The signature is the unique manner in which the offender commits his crime. The method of operation is more akin to the way in which he kills, rapes, etc. For example, a rapist may stalk and abduct women who shop at malls. This is his method of operation. But the killer who leaves the victim's car keys and driver's license on top of her chest every time is leaving a signature.

THE OFFENDER'S PERSONALITY WILL NOT CHANGE

Many personality experts agree that the main core of an individual's personality is "set" by the time he reaches his teenage years, or even younger. It does not change fundamentally over time. A person, criminal or not, may change certain aspects of personality, but the central elements of the personality are set, and only minor alterations may be made due to time, circumstances, pressure, and other activities.

Holmes and Holmes (1996) argue that the criminal personality takes years to form, and that they (the criminals) will not change radically. Moreover, the criminal may not want to change, and even if the offender does indeed wish to change, he or she may not be able to do so. So, the criminal may not only commit the same crime over and over again, but may force his victims to perform the same ritualistic behavior.

By blending these assumptions concerning the profiling process, the profiler can be of great aid to the law enforcement community. After all, the goals of the psychological profile itself concern the benefits of the profile document in the investigation of a suitable crime. Not all crimes are suitable for profiling. For example, Holmes and Holmes (1996) list among the crimes suitable for assessment the following:

- sadistic torture in sexual assaults;
- evisceration;
- postmortem slashing and cutting;
- motiveless firesetting;
- lust and mutilation murder;
- rape;
- arson;

- bank robbery;
- sadistic and ritualistic crime; and
- pedophilia.

Once an agreement is reached concerning the type of crime and the decision to secure a psychological profile from an experienced profiler, the law enforcement agency desiring such a profile must anticipate a reward from the document itself. Thus, there are goals in the profiling effort.

GOAL 1: NARROW THE SCOPE OF THE INVESTIGATION

The first goal of a psychological profile is to narrow the range of suspects and thus narrow the scope of the investigation. At first blush, this may seem to be a simplistic statement. But let us take another look at this goal.

Say, for example, the profile suggests that the killer of a victim is a white male, single, and lives within a mile of the site where the victim's body was found. With that simple statement, there is a large number of people who can be placed aside (if only temporarily), and efforts can be directed to that group as suggested by the profiler. We have, in effect, removed from our suspects list all nonwhite males, married, divorced, widowed, and so on, and also those who did not live within a mile of the location of the victim's body. From a universe of 100% of the people who live in a community, the percentage is now down to 50% if we are not considering any females; down another 60% or so of the 50% when we are looking at only the white population, down more when we are looking only at single, white males, and so on.

We can see, then, by using the information given to us by a profiler, huge numbers of potential suspects can be radically reduced. This is not to say that others who do not fit the profile should not be ever considered. We are dealing with human beings, and nothing is ever a universal when humans are part of the population and part of the problem!

GOAL 2: SOCIAL AND PSYCHOLOGICAL ASSESSMENTS

A profile should contain basic and sound information concerning the social and psychological core variables of the offender's personality, including the offender's race, sex, social class, education, residence, marital status, type of vehicle, and other such social and behavioral items, as well as an interviewing strategy.

The social and psychological profile should hold information that can assist the law enforcement community in identifying the type of offender they are pursuing. In addition, the criminal investigation assessment may predict future crimes committed by this subject.

GOAL 3: PSYCHOLOGICAL EVALUATION OF BELONGINGS

When the law enforcement agent has a specific suspect in mind, the criminal investigation assessment should contain some information as to the materials of the crime that the suspect has in his possession. This physical and collateral evidence can help the police and others understand the subject's mentality, as well as link the suspect with the crime itself.

An example of this scenario is the case of Jerry Brudos. Jerry, a serial killer from Oregon, kept black high-heel shoes in his possession. The shoes, which he allegedly stole during the course of one of his rapes, were very important to him. He wore the shoes himself (he was a transvestite), and he also made his wife and victims wear those same shoes. In the pictures that he took of his wife and at least one victim, the shoes are visible. One victim was shown in a picture taken by Jerry with her own shoes behind her in the garage where she was a captive. She was wearing Jerry's high-heel shoes. Jerry Brudos was also involved in the sexual paraphilia of triolism. In this sexual behavior, the subject receives sexual satisfaction from seeing himself or others in sexual scenes. The police found pictures of himself, his wife, and at least two victims either nude, dressed in underclothing, or some other pose.

In examining the pictures of his wife and one victim, the heads are not part of the pictures, and the hands are down by the sides in a passive, nonaggressive, nonthreatening position. The pictures were developed at Quinseberry's Drug Store on Center Street in Salem because, as Jerry told his wife, Ralphene, "big labs process too much film to look at every picture. . . . They look at the first or last—and that's all" (Stack, 1983, p. 33).

By examining this type of evidence, an evaluation can be made of the offender and a plan of action can be developed to further pursue the suspect and make an arrest.

GOAL 4: INTERVIEWING SUGGESTIONS AND STRATEGIES

The third goal of the psychological profiling process is to offer the law enforcement agency responsible for the interviewing and interrogation process some type of interrogation and interviewing strategy. This is an obviously crucial period in the investigation of the case. The profile itself should suggest a strategy for speaking with the suspect, body language perhaps, certain words and phrases to be used or avoided, as well as a time of day or night for the interview.

Of course, not all people react in the same fashion to the interviewing process. The motivation to cooperate and what they anticipate to be the reward for them if they cooperate will shape and form the interaction they will have with the interviewing agents of the police agency. The profiler may decide to use a strategy offered by the FBI in their dealings with offenders. The organized offender, for example, may be better interviewed during a certain time of the day (e.g., daytime or nighttime). The disorganized offender, on the other hand, may be better interviewed at a different time. Regardless, the profile itself should suggest an opportune interviewing time schedule.

Profiling Serial Murder Cases

Perhaps one of the most important uses of psychological profiling occurs when analyzing serial murder cases. Profiling was used early in the cases of young black children murdered in Atlanta, and FBI agents claimed victory when questioning suspect Wayne Williams. The agents used an aggressive interrogation strategy in the courtroom, as suggested by the FBI profilers, and Williams was convicted of two murders.

Profiles are used in other cases of suspected serial murderers. When one understands the differences that exist among the different types of serial killers, their mobility, their anticipated gains, and the loci of motivations, the profiler can offer to the law enforcement enterprise a picture of the person for whom they are searching.

By being aware of the various types of serial killers and the methods and motives present in their murders, police agencies can arrange resources and personnel to the investigation of a suspected serial murder situation. This has been done in several recent serial murder cases of which I am aware. Regarding the profiles that I have done, which presently number more than 450, police have arranged their investigation in some part because of the information contained in the profile itself. Of course, there are some profiles that are completely wrong. Jenkins reports the tremendous error made by the FBI profilers in the bombing case aboard the U.S.S. Iowa; the FBI's image was tarnished because their profile in part led to the arrest of an innocent man (Jenkins, 1994).

Of course, not all profiles are going to be 100% accurate. However, I encourage departments to secure several profiles from different resources, and then use the similar information or gain useful insights from the various profiles in their investigations.

Conclusion

Psychological profiling, or criminal investigation assessment is a new aid in the investigation of crime and especially in serial murder. As it becomes more reliable, as profilers themselves become more acute in their skills, and as the knowledge base becomes more valid, more police agencies may use the skill of the profilers. There may come a time when a large department will employ a profiler on its professional staff or at least share a profiler with other departments.

There may also be a time when a "triage" team will be sent to unusual or atypical crime scenes. Each member of the triage team will have special and unique skills: a forensic entomologist, a forensic anthropologist, a forensic nurse, a medical examiner, and a psychological profiler. This team will look at the crime scene and develop an investigative document that can aid the homicide detective. The mobility of the team and the special skills held by each member could be invaluable. The other members of the team are trained in the hard sciences; only the profiler practices the "art" of criminal investigation assessment. The other members of this triage team are already accepted by those in law enforcement. Perhaps it is only a matter of time until the profiler gains equal acceptance in the investigation of atypical crimes, including serial murder.

References

Brussels, J. A. (1968). *Casebook of a criminal psychiatrist*. New York: Bernard Geis.

Egger, S. (1990). *Serial murder: An elusive phenomenon*. New York. Praeger.

Geberth, V. (1993). *Practical homicide investigation: Tactics, procedures, and forensic techniques* (2nd ed.). Boca Raton, FL: CRC.

Harris, T. (1981). *The red dragon*. New York: Putnam.

Harris, T. (1988). *The silence of the lambs*. New York: Putnam.

Hazelwood, R. (1994, March). Lecture delivered at the Southern Police Institute, Ft. Lauderdale, Fl.

Holmes, R. (1988). A model of personal violence. *Kentucky Research Bulletin, 2,* 1-5.

Holmes, R., & Holmes, S. (1996). *Profiling violent crimes: An investigative tool* (2nd ed.). Thousand Oaks, CA: Sage.

Jenkins, P. (1994). *Using murder: The social construction of serial homicide*. New York: Aldine de Gruyter.

Langer, W. (1972). *The mind of Adolf Hitler*. New York: New American Library.

Stack, A. (1983). *The lust killer*. New York: Signet.

13

Cold Case Squad

————■————

SGT. DAVID W. RIVERS

On August 3, 1960, Mr. Charles Joseph Mourey, a white male, age 56, came to Miami on vacation from his job as a butler for Ms. Hope Hampton of Park Avenue in New York. Mr. Mourey was a homosexual who had a preference for "frisky young men," according to his employer.

On August 10, 1960, a witness living at 553 North Biscayne River Drive heard six gunshots and shortly thereafter observed an old model blue vehicle, possibly a Chrysler, leave the area at a high rate of speed. Uniform officers responded to the call and discovered Mr. Mourey lying in the dirt road at that location.

The initial investigation revealed that the victim had been struck with three .22 caliber projectiles. Evidence on the scene indicated that a struggle had taken place prior to the victim being shot. The victim was fully clothed and still in possession of his jewelry and U.S. currency.

On December 8, 1986, Mr. Earl Bernath, a white male, age 40, pleaded guilty to second-degree murder and was sentenced to 10 years in the state prison. Twenty-six years had passed between the homicide and the trial.

On March 29, 1967, the body of Ms. Josephine Mildred Barnhill, a white female, age 76, was found in her trailer at 19850 West Dixie Highway, the Lone Pine Trailer Park, Lot 210.

In May 1987, Mr. Robert Ball, Jr. was placed under arrest for the first-degree murder of the victim. Within weeks, he entered a plea of guilty to a lesser charge and agreed, through his attorney, to testify against the other two subjects. More than 20 years had passed between the murder and the plea by Mr. Ball.

Cold Case Squads

BACKGROUND

In Dade County, Florida in the early 1980s, we were experiencing a rapid rise in the number of homicides. Although not unique to the Miami area, the numbers were tremendous. The command staff of the Homicide Bureau recognized that there was a void being created by open, unsolved murders.

As detectives transferred in and out of the section their cases sat open and unworked. If a lead came in, a detective, in rotation at the time and with cases of his own, had to first become completely familiar with the case; then, as time permitted, he followed up on the information. The problem with that concept is that there was never "enough" time.

The commander of the section created a small squad, headed by a sergeant, that was to be responsible for old, open cases where the original lead detective was no longer in Homicide. Originally, the sergeant was to review the open cases, make an independent determination as to which cases to work, and then work them with a team. The major evaluation factors were the apparent value of existing or new leads and the "closeability" of the case.

The squad is not responsible for investigating any cases where the originally assigned detective is still in the bureau. Neither was it asked to handle any new, incoming death cases of any kind. Originally, the squad was designed to be proactive in its choice of cases.

Soon, it became evident that the squad would be reactive to incoming leads. Very few cases were sought out by the detectives on the squad. Additionally, the Cold Case Squad tried to handle the majority of assistance calls from other homicide sections throughout the country.

CHOOSING OF DETECTIVES

When setting up a cold case squad, the detectives chosen should, whenever possible, be experienced homicide investigators, for several reasons. They need to be very familiar with the mechanics of homicide investigation. They need to be skilled interviewers and familiar with the variations in the homicide statute. Here, specifically, I am referring to the statutes of limitations and how they apply to the different degrees of murder. Why spend time and manpower on cases where the statute has expired?

Additionally, the detectives should be patient and tenacious. Cold cases are often very protracted investigations and require perseverance. Another reason the detectives need to be experienced is the courtroom and testimony. They should already be versed in courtroom procedures and the many different types of motions filed in homicide cases. All of the problems experienced in current homicide investigations are multiplied many times in a 10- to 20-year-old murder case. The detectives need experience in testifying in homicide cases so that they can anticipate the additional defense strategies available in older cases.

TIME

Cold case investigations turn the liability of time into an asset. When a case is new and fresh, most investigators agree that time is essential. The first 48 to 72 hours are generally recognized as the most critical. During this initial time period, the information is the freshest in the minds of the witnesses, and it is usually more accurate. Additionally, the witnesses are easier to locate. What usually happens when this period passes is that the probability decreases that the case will be closed quickly. However, in cold cases, time, once the enemy, eventually becomes an ally.

1. Witnesses who were friends of the subjects at the time of the homicide may not be any longer. In some cases, they may even be adversaries.
2. The witness may have been afraid of the subject at the time. Time may have made the witness stronger or the subject weaker.
3. The witness may now be in need of help with another aspect of the criminal justice system.
4. The witness may have become a better person, gotten married, found religion, and so on.
5. The witness does not mind getting involved now. People have been known to deliberately not identify people or give false information. (One witness gave a bad I.D. just so he could get on with his business.)

In virtually all of the cases closed by the Metro-Dade Cold Case Squad, the offender told at least one person about his or her involvement.

Locating these witnesses can provide the final element for an arrest and ultimate conviction.

TECHNOLOGY

Technology has advanced farther in the past 5 to 10 years than in the previous 100 years. Criminology is not a stagnant science and has made some amazing advances. Science and technology are now available that just a few years ago were considered science fiction. The advances are quickly applied to new cases, but the older cases are sometimes forgotten.

Fingerprint technology is one of the most widely used examples of this. With the advent of the cyanoacrylate latent fingerprint development system (super glue), investigators are now able to lift prints from surfaces that were previously discarded as "unprintable" (e.g., leather, cloth, etc.). The use of lasers in both "lifting" and "reading" prints has enhanced capabilities in the field greatly.

Another new and developing technology is the field of blood and semen analysis through DNA printing. This field could have an impact on the law enforcement community that is equal to, or greater than, actual fingerprints. Regarding technology, investigators must remember that as the new techniques are developed, they must be applied to the older or cold cases.

OTHER TYPES OF CLEARANCES

Sometimes, the administration of justice takes many forms. In Florida, there is no statute of limitations on first-degree murder. However, second degree, third degree, and manslaughter all have specific time limitations.

When reopening any cold case, one of the very first steps taken should be a careful review of the case. This review of the case should include, whenever possible, a state or district attorney. During this review, a determination should be made as to whether there is an applicable statute of limitations. If the statute has run and charges cannot be filed, then consideration should be given to another type of clearance.

In addition, subjects die, which makes prosecution impossible. Witnesses tend to remember more when they know they will not have to testify in court.

MEDIA

Law enforcement professionals are not in the business of intentionally making news for others to report. In the normal course of business, they tend to create news. However, good press may be beneficial. Murders make headlines in any city in the nation. Whenever arrests are made in these cases, the arrests make headlines.

When an arrest is made in a case that is 5, 10, 20 or more years old, several things happen, all of which are positive. First, any article that depicts a positive image of any police agency is always welcomed by the administrators. This alone benefits the section later. Second, it makes others in the population realize that police officers do care about the old cases. In addition, each of these types of clearances generates calls on other cold cases.

INVESTIGATIVE STEPS

When attempting to reopen old cases, whether because of a tip received or through proactive methods, the following steps should be considered.

1. Check the applicable statute of limitations for the degree of murder involved. If the case cannot be prosecuted because of the statute of limitations, then there is no need to proceed.
2. Once you have established that there is a statutory case, the next step should be to contact the property bureau and make sure that the evidence can be located.
3. At this juncture, a state attorney should become involved to ensure the proper legal approach to witnesses and subjects. For instance, if Miranda was invoked years ago, can the subject even be interviewed?
4. Try to determine who has benefited the most, financially, from the death of the victim.
5. Re-do all the background checks on the suspects/subjects, witnesses, and anyone else involved in the case. Look for criminal arrests, changes in associations and personal relationships. This should be done before any interviews are conducted.
6. Carefully review the medical examiner's file. Make sure it is complete and that the doctor who did the original autopsy is still available. Locate the person who made legal identification.

7. Contact the victim's family and see if any help can be obtained from them. Be especially careful at this point not to unjustly raise their hopes. Explain what has brought about the new, or continuing, interest and try to involve them (unless, of course, they are the suspects).

8. Begin your interviews with peripheral witnesses and associates first. Keep in mind that this may alert your suspect, so weigh this factor heavily. These types of interviews will also give you insight into changing relationships and associations.

9. Before interviewing major witnesses, see if they may be in a new situation now as opposed to when the homicide occurred. They may be in jail, on probation, or need help with some other aspect of the criminal justice system. They may have straightened up their lives, gotten married, or gotten religion.

10. If, armed with all the new information, you can obtain a warrant, do so before approaching your subject. If not, then take the best shot you have: Approach and interview the subject.

11. During this process, control and direction are essential. The use of an investigative lead sheet is just as important here as when handling a fresh case. Additionally, team conferences are important. Much of the research on an older case can be done by one detective, but conferences with the rest of the team and supervisor are also paramount. Once a definite subject is identified, then the entire team (regardless of its size) should be used.

12. Remember that the ultimate goal is the successful prosecution of the individual in court. That means that the cooperation with the prosecutor that was established when the case was opened should continue through the trial.

13. Be able to recognize cases that cannot be solved by evidence alone. If witnesses cannot be located and suspects refuse to talk, then go to the next one until something develops or someone decides to talk.

No department or individual involved in the investigation of homicides is ever going to have a 100% closure rate. And if, through some statistical maneuvering, you do, your conviction rate will suffer.

Therefore, another homicide will typically occur before the last one has been solved. How are these open cases managed, how often are they reviewed, and who is responsible once the assigned detective is either transferred or leaves the unit or the department?

If the department is small, then a review system should be established in which the case is reviewed at least once a year and someone is familiar with the facts should information come in regarding the case. This review system should include a report indicating all inquiries and information on the case.

If the department is large enough, then instituting a Cold Case Squad should be explored. The major factor in the success of this squad is that it:

1. Has the support of the administration. Without this support, success will be sporadic at best.
2. Be left entirely alone to work the old, unresolved homicides. If the members are constantly being put into rotation or having to work current cases, then their effectiveness will be greatly reduced.

Since the inception of this squad in Metro-Dade, more than 120 cases have been closed that otherwise would be sitting on a shelf, gathering dust.

PART IV

FUTURE TRENDS
IN SERIAL MURDER
INVESTIGATION
AND RESEARCH

The effective investigation of a suspected serial murder case must use the many and varied resources that are available. Although this section uses the expertise of two psychological profilers and a professional police officer, there are other disciplines that could, and should, be used. For example, forensic entomology and forensic anthropology are two such disciplines. Dr. Arpad Vass is a renowned forensic anthropologist; Dr. Neil Haskell is recognized as an expert in forensic entomology. Both instruct for the National Center for the Study of Unresolved Homicides in its Scientific Study of Death Seminars. Dr. Henry Lee, a criminalist, is involved in murder cases, including many high-profile cases such as O.J. Simpson, Jonbénet Ramsey, and the Kennedy rape case in Florida. He also contributes to the scientific study of homicide, including serial murder. To accommodate this need and interest, another book of readings is planned that will include such experts and their original writings.

In this section, we discuss a few of the future trends in the investigation of serial murder. Although there is no belief that serial murder will be a pandemic law enforcement problem in the future, there is some concern that it will need better strategies and a firmer knowledge base for the effective detection, investigation, and apprehension of serial killers. Certainly, psychological profiling has made great advances in the criminal investigation analysis process, and there is no reason to suspect that it will not continue to do so. The hard sciences of entomology, anthropology, biology, serology, and so on will also continue to advance in their work of aiding law enforcement in analyzing physical evidence left at the scene of the crime. However, there are other concerns that should be addressed because they specifically affect the serial murder investigation. Dr. Steve Egger, at Illinois State University, was one of the first academics to study serial killers and to use one—Henry Lucas—as the main subject of his doctoral dissertation at Sam Houston State University. Egger made us aware of a great issue in the investigation of serial murder: linkage blindness. In linkage blindness, a term coined by Egger, he believed, quite correctly, that agencies and departments often refuse to share information about serial murder investigations. He refers to some of the problems and issues involved in linkage blindness and the manner in which this phenomenon hinders the investigation and ultimately the apprehension of a serial killer. Linkage blindness emerges as a significant issue in the investigation of a suspected serial murder case, and readers wanting to know more about this issue should refer to Egger (1984).

In the first chapter of this section, Dr. Kim Rossmo examines the role of geography in the investigation of serial crimes, including serial murder. In his chapter titled "A Methodological Model," he examines the role of physical geography as it relates to the investigation of serial crimes. He has examined the work of others who have done similar work (e.g., Brantingham and Brantingham), but he adds special treatment to the previous work in the crimes of the serial killers. Comfort zones, modes of behavior, routes of travel, landmarks, natural and manmade barriers, and so on are all discussed. In the criminal investigation assessments done prior to Rossmo's work, many were suspicious of the worth of physical geography, but now, Rossmo has demonstrated their measurement and importance. He has emerged as one of the bright new stars in serial murder investigation.

The second chapter in this section deals with the police and the problems they may encounter with a serial murder investigation. Dr. Thomas O'Reilly-Fleming, from Windsor University, is a leading international expert on serial murder. His chapter, "Serial Murder Investigation: Prospects for Police Networking," deals with the problems in a multicide investigation, particularly with the police component of the criminal justice system. He illustrates the problems and potential solutions by citing several cases of serial killers, including Ted Bundy, John Gacy, and Clifford Olson, who was a Canadian serial killer. O'Reilly-Fleming speaks of the importance of police networking as a primary strategy in the successful resolution of a serial murder case.

The final chapter in this section, and the book itself, deals with "Problems in Serial Murder Investigations." Written by the two authors, we list several items that could hinder the serial murder case resolution: determining if the case is, indeed, a serial murder case; protection of one's turf and information sharing; deciding on the type of serial murderer under investigation; the dedication of the agency to the investigation of the case; the training and education of homicide detectives; the identification of missing persons as victims of serial murder; and the issue as raised by Egger, the existence and extent of linkage blindness. This chapter examines each issue area and offers some thoughts and strategies toward the resolution of serial murder cases.

The reader may note that there are some similarities involved in the content and direction of some of the readings in Part 3 and Part 4. However, in this final section, we wanted to alert the reader to the emerging role of geoforensic analysis (Rossmo), the problems in serial murder cases, and the ways in which future investigations can profit from the cases of the past (O'Reilly-Fleming, and Holmes and Holmes).

Reference

Egger, S. (1984). A working definition of serial murder and the reduction of linkage blindness. *Journal of Police Science Administration, 12,* 348-357.

14

A Methodological Model

D. KIM ROSSMO

Introduction

Clues derived from the locations of violent serial crimes, including serial murder, rape, and arson, can be of significant assistance to law enforcement. Such locations include encounter/apprehension sites, murder scenes, and body/property dump sites. This information allows police departments to focus their investigative activities, geographically prioritize suspects, and to concentrate saturation or directed patrolling efforts in those zones where the criminal predator is most likely to be active.

The process whereby the probable spatial behavior of the offender is derived from the information and context of the locations of the crime sites is termed geographical profiling. This form of analysis has subjective and qualitative dimensions, and is related to the broader investigative strategy of criminal or psychological profiling.

The purpose of criminal profiling is the development of a behavioral composite, a social and psychological assessment, of the perpetrator of certain types of crimes. This is based on the premise that the proper interpretation of crime scene evidence can indicate the personality type of the individual(s) who committed the offense. Certain personality types exhibit similar behavioral patterns, and knowledge of these patterns can assist in the investigation of the crime and potential suspects.

Geographical profiling is concerned with the analysis of spatial behavior. A variety of techniques exist for such an analysis, including

Author's Note: This chapter was first published in 1993 in the *American Journal of Criminal Justice*, 17(2),1-22. Reprinted with permission.

distance to crime research, demographical analysis, centrographic analysis, criminal geographic targeting, point pattern analysis, point spread analysis, crime site residential analysis, spatial-temporal ordering, and directional analysis (Rossmo, 1993).

Criminal geographic targeting appears to be a particularly useful technique for the needs of police investigators attempting to solve complex serial crimes. By examining the spatial data connected to a series of crime sites, the criminal geographic targeting (CHT) methodological model generates a three-dimensional choropleth probability map that indicates those areas most likely to be associated to the offender—home, work, social venue, or travel routes.

Based on the Brantingham and Brantingham model for crime site section (1981, chap. 1), and the routine activities approach, criminal geographic targeting goes beyond centrographic analysis. The model employs overlapping modified Pareto functions, variable buffer zones, and Manhattan distances. Parameters are empirically derived from specific serial crime geographic research. The methodology is also sensitive to the target/victim opportunity blackcloth, landscape issues, anisotropic spaces, and problems of spatial "outliers" that can significantly distort results.

Investigative Reponses

The nature of serial murder creates unique problems for law enforcement and requires special police tactics, strategies, and responses. Several investigative difficulties exist to complicate efforts to link and solve the murders, and to identify and apprehend the killer(s) (Egger, 1990, pp. 177-179; Holmes and DeBurger, 1988, pp. 112-121, 148-154; James, 1991, pp. 1-4). These problems include:

1. the lack of connections between the offender and the victims. Traditionally most homicides are cleared for the simple reason that there is usually some relationship between the victim and the offender. All stranger homicides, whether serial or not, are therefore very difficult to solve;

2. the difficulty in determining if a serial murderer is operating, and if so, in establishing what homicides are or are not connected (for a discussion of this problem in the Henry Lee Lucas investigation, see Egger, pp. 156-158);

3. the linkage blindness and cooperation problems, resulting from criminal investigations that cross jurisdiction boundaries that can exist between different police departments (Egger, pp. 169-175);

4. the intense public, media, and political scrutiny surrounding such cases (Holmes and DeBurger, pp. 114-116);

5. the learning process experienced by organized offenders as they become "practiced" at killing;

6. false confessions from unbalanced people attracted by the publicity;

7. the possibility of copy cat murders occurring;

8. the strain on resources resulting from too many suspects and too much information. In the still unsolved Green River Killer case, 18,000 suspect names have been collected, but as of February, 1992, the police have only had the time and resources to check out some 6,000 of these; 8,000 tangible items of evidence have been collected from the crime scene; and a single television special on the case generated 3,500 tips (Montgomery, 1992). The Yorkshire Ripper Case had, by the time it was solved, 268,000 names in the nominal index; 115,000 police actions were initiated and 31,000 statements were taken by police investigators; up to 1,000 letters were received by the police daily from the public; and 5.4 million vehicle registration numbers were recorded (Doney, 1990, pp. 101-102);

9. personal and coordination issues (especially when multiple agencies are involved). For example, in the Yorkshire Ripper case, 250 full-time detectives were involved for a period of over three years (Doney, p. 102);

10. the high cost involved in such extensive, long-term investigations. Green River Task Force costs are, to date, approximately $20 million (Montgomery), while the Yorkshire Ripper investigation involved over five million hours of police time at a cost of four million pounds (1981 figures) (Doney, p. 102).

To help address these problems, police agencies involved in serial murder cases have developed a variety of investigative responses. Egger provides a taxonomy of these responses (1990, pp. 180-198):

1. law enforcement conferences on specific series of solved or unsolved murders;

2. information clearinghouses that are established to provide information on an ongoing basis to police agencies involved in investigating serial murders;

3. task forces, which can be set up at the local level, or in cases of multi-jurisdictional crimes, at the regional level;

4. investigative consultant teams, composed of investigators with experience in similar cases, that provide advice and assistance to the agency responsible for the serial murder investigation (see Brooks, 1982; Brooks, Devine, Green, Hart, & Moore, 1988);

5. psychological profiling, also known as criminal personality profiling or criminal investigative analysis. Investigative support, research, and training in this area is provided by the Behavioral Science Unit at the Federal Bureau of Investigation (FBI) Academy; and

6. centralized investigative networks, such as the Violent Criminal Apprehension Program (VICAP), developed at the National Center for the Analysis of Violent Crime (NCAVC) in Quantico, Virginia. Some states have their own computerized investigative systems including the Homicide Assessment and Lead Tracking (HALT) system in New York State, the Homicide Investigation Tracking System (HITS) in Washington State, and the Indiana Criminal Apprehension Assistance Program (ICAAP) in Indiana. British Columbia, Canada, has, through the Royal Canadian Mounted Police (RCMP), the Major Crime Organizational System (MaCrOS). In Britain, Scotland Yard uses the Home Office Large Major Enquiry System (HOLMES) for managing large volumes of investigative case data (see Doney, 1990).

Egger (1990, pp. 196-198) also identifies other responses that have been used or are being developed and experimented with by police agencies that could assist in solving cases of serial murder. These include improved computerized analysis systems, geographical pattern analysis, and the paying of a serial murderer for evidence, as has only occurred in the Clifford Olson case in British Columbia, Canada (Bayless, 1982; Mulgrew, 1990). Geographical profiling, while developed from a different theoretical structure, is related to the early work in geoforensics begun by Newton and others (Newton and Newton, 1985; Newton and Swoope, 1987). Egger makes the statement that this research area is worthy of further development (p. 197).

Police departments have also used psychics to help search out clues, and special television programs designed to elicit tips, bring forward witnesses, and produce designed responses in the murderer. It is worthwhile stressing that normal investigative techniques, routine police patrol work, unsolicited suspect confession, and sheer luck have all played a significant role in the solving of serial murder cases.

Hunting Patterns

THE BRANTINGHAM MODEL

The locations where crimes occur are not completely random, but instead, often have a degree of underlying spatial structure. For a crime to occur there must be an intersection, in both time and place, between the offender and the victim. As chaotic as some crimes appear to be, there is often a rationality influencing the geography of their occurrence. Brantingham and Brantingham (1981, chap. 1) have developed a model for understanding the processes affecting the geography of crime.

Crimes tend to occur in space at those locations where suitable (in terms of profit and risk) victims or targets are found by offenders as they move throughout their activity spaces. As an offender travels between his home, workplace, and social activity sites, his or her activity space (composed of these locations and their connecting paths) describes an awareness space which forms part of a larger mental map—an "image of the city" built upon experience and knowledge.

Brantingham and Brantingham (1981, chap. 1) suggest that the process of criminal target selection is a dynamic one. Crimes occur in those locations where suitable targets are overlapped by the offender's awareness space. . . . Offenders may then move outward, following a distance decay function, in their search for more targets. Search pattern probabilities can be modeled by a Pareto function, originating from the locations and routes that comprise the activity space, and then decreasing with distance away from the activity space. There may also be a "buffer zone," centered around the criminal's home, within which the offender sees targets as being too risky to victimize because of their proximity to his or her residence (cf. The "coal-sack effect," Newton and Swoope, 1987).

Criminal profiling can assist in determining the relationship of offenders' activity spaces to their target patterns. Disorganized offenders, for example, will usually hunt closer to their activity spaces, staying well within their comfort zone. Organized offenders will be more likely to search for victims in areas located further away from their home or workplace. Their activity spaces, generally, will be larger and more complex than those of disorganized offenders.

TARGET BACKCLOTH

The locations of suitable victims may not be uniformly distributed within the killer's hunting areas. The target or victim backcloth is the form of the target or victim spatial distribution within a given area (Brantingham and Brantingham, 1991). For example, if a serial murderer is attacking prostitutes, the locations of the various "hooker strolls" will determine where the victims are hunted. Consequently, in such cases where the killer seeks out specific victim types (Holmes and DeBurger, 1988, pp. 51-52) that are not equally distributed throughout space, the attack locations will be influenced more by the victims' activity spaces than by the offender's. Victimology can therefore play a key role in target patterns.

LOCATION TYPES

There may be a variety of spatial sites involved in a serial murder (Newton and Swoope, 1987). Given the locations the killer might stalk the victim, abduct and hold him or her, and then transport the body, a single murder could potentially have different victim-offender encounter, attack, holding, murder, and body dump sites. Additionally, there may be vehicle and/or property dump sites, and witness sightings and evidence scenes that provide information on the travel routes between the various key locations.

Some possible crime location types that may exist in a serial murder case include:

1. victim's last known location
2. victim-offender encounter site (stalking sites)
3. attack
4. holding location (contact location)
5. body dump site
6. vehicle disposal site
7. property disposal sites
8. travel routes

In many cases, some of these locations could be the same (i.e., the attack location may be the murder scene and may also be the body dump site).

Prior to the apprehension of the killer, the only way these places become known to officials is through evidence recovery or by witness statement. Typically the police only know the body dump site (which may or may not be the murder scene) and the place where the victim was last seen. In some circumstances, they may only know the latter location.

Cases of minimal spatial location can hinder efforts to spatially analyze a series of crimes. The victims' last known locations may not be close to the sites of victim-offender encounters and thus would not provide much information about the murderer. Nonuniformed target backcloths can control the offender's selection of victim encounter sites. Multiple bodies may be dumped in a single location, providing only one geographic point for analysis. Thus the numbers of locations, their types, and the victim backcloth are all relevant variables in the construction of a geographic profile.

There may also be external influences on a criminal's hunting behavior that might have to be considered. Certain media disclosures and investigative strategies, including patrol saturation efforts, may create geographic and other forms of displacement (Gabor, 1978, p. 101; Repetto, 1976, p. 177). These influences can affect target patterns of serial offenders and, in some cases, hamper police investigative efforts.

Geographic Analysis

SPATIAL MEAN

The spatial mean, or mean center, is a univariate measure of the central tendency of a point pattern (Taylor, 1977, pp. 23-27). This geographic "center of gravity" minimized the sum of the squared distances from the spatial mean to the various points in the pattern. It provides a single summary location for a series of points and has a variety of geostatistical uses, sometimes classified together as centrography.

The spatial mean can serve as the basis for calculating the standard distance of a point pattern, a measure of spatial dispersion analogous to the standard deviation (Taylor, 1977, pp. 27-30). Changes over time in the location of the spatial mean also allow for the calculation of the geographic equivalents on concepts of velocity (rate of spatial change), acceleration (rate of change in velocity, and momentum (velocity multiplied by the number of points) (LeBeau, 1987, pp. 168-128).

Centrography has been used to examine the spatial mean for the crime of rape, and changes in its location over time, in the city of San Diego (LeBeau, 1987). It has also been used in a retrospective analysis to focus in on the residential area of Angelo Buono, one of the Hillside Stranglers (Newton and Swoope, 1987). Additionally, the FBI do some work in this area on serial arsons (Icove and Crisman, 1975). Centrography has thus been the primary form of spatial analysis used in geographic investigative support efforts.

Previous works in the field of distance to crime research, particularly those which are offense-specific studies, can help determine the most likely radius within which offenders search for their victims. Many criminals select targets that are located less than a mile or two from their residences (see, for example, McIver, 1981, pp. 24-25). Thus information is particularly useful when combined with centrographic analysis.

As valuable as this approach is, it suffers from three serious methodological difficulties: (1) centrographic analysis generally provides only a single piece of information; (2) it is susceptible to the influence of outliers; and (3) some theoretical models suggest that the locations of the confluences of the offender's activity space and the victim blackcloth may not be related to measures of central tendency. Additionally, the spatial mean might lack real world significance. LeBeau notes that "an important property about the mean center to remember is that it is a synthetic point or location representing the average location of a phenomenon, and not the average of the characteristics of the phenomenon at that location" (1987, pp. 126-127). In such cases, criminal geographic targeting, a more robust process that is less sensitive to outliers, might prove to be a more useful and valuable approach.

CRIMINAL GEOGRAPHIC TARGETING

Criminal geographic targeting, by analyzing the spatial information associated to a series of linked crimes, attempts to determine the most probable areas in which the offender might be located. The process can handle the effects of anisotrophic travel, variable buffer zones, and nonuniform target backcloths. The magnitude of the computations, however, requires the use of a special software program.

Borders for the map are first determined by adding to the northwest and east-west edges one-half of the average y and x inter-point distances respectively. Weighted circles, derived from modified Pareto functions that incorporate variable buffer zones calculated from the number of crimes and the zone of the hunting area, are centered on the various crime sites, and scores then assigned to each individual point in the field. These circles overlap, producing a three-dimensional map within which the neighborhood and color of the various zones represents the probability that those areas contain parts of the offender's activity space. . . . The higher the elevation, the greater that probability . . .

Parameters of the model can be empirically determined through the use of the gravity model. Derived in its classical form from Newton's Gravitational Law, the gravity model provides a mathematical formulation to address problems of scale and distance (Haynes and Fotheringham, 1984). It is widely used to analyze and forecast spatial interaction patterns in such diverse fields as transportation, development, planning, marketing, retailing, urban analysis, history, linguistics, anthropology, and archaeology. Its concern with destination, origin, and distance impacts can assist in the optimization of the criminal geographic targeting model for different types of offenders and under a variety of environmental conditions. An inversion of the model can even be used to help predict those areas in which the offender is most likely to next attack, though the confidence of such results is not overly strong.

CRIMINAL INVESTIGATIVE STRATEGIES

Such geographic information can be employed by police departments to help prioritize specific areas or suspects for investigative follow-up, and in the implementation of patrol saturation efforts. If a lengthy list of suspects has been developed, the geographic profile, in conjunction with the criminal offender profile, can help prioritize individuals for follow-up investigative work. The problem in many serial violent crime investigations is one of too many suspects rather than one of too few. Profiling can help prioritize lists of sometimes hundreds if not thousands of suspects, leads, and tips.

Areas that have been determined to most probably be associated with the offender can be used as a basis for directed or saturation police patrolling efforts. This strategy is particularly effective if the offender appears to be operating during certain time periods. Saturation efforts can then be focused in both space and time, increasing their chances for success.

New investigative leads can also be developed from the map areas, prioritized by probability, with the assistance of a variety of geographic data banks and computerized police dispatch and record systems (e.g., computer aided dispatch (CAD) systems, records management systems (RMS), and RCMP Police Information Retrieval System (PIRS), and the like). If a criminal or psychological profile has been prepared, the suggested offender information may assist in focusing the scope of such searches.

Data files from non-police sources are often geographically based. Information from parole and probation offices, social services agencies, mental health clinics, and other services located in the prioritized areas may be useful in specific cases. LeBeau (1992, p. 133) discusses the case of a serial rapist who emerged as a suspect after the police checked parolee records for sex offenders. In more complex and lengthy investigations, a computerized geographic information system (GIS) could help store, collate, and analyze voluminous quantities and various types of data from several different sources (Rogers, Craig, and Anderson, 1991).

The following is one example of a unique investigative approach based on the principles of geographic profiling. The postal codes for a city neighborhood within which a violent sexual offender was attacking children were prioritized by using the criminal geographic targeting model. First the relevant forward sorting areas (FSA)—the first three digits of the postal code—were identified. The criminal geographic targeting probability map was then superimposed over the letter carrier walks (LC) which could then be prioritized by probability. Planning and zoning maps were used to eliminate industrial, commercial, and other nonresidential areas. Socioeconomic and demographic census data were also consulted to reevaluate the priority of those neighborhoods that were inconsistent with the socioeconomic level of the offender as suggested by the psychological profile. Finally, the local distribution units (LDU)—the last three digits of the postal code—associated to the letter carrier walks were determined.

The complete postal codes, ranked by priority of probability, were then used to conduct an off-line computer search of the provincial motor vehicle department records which contain postal codes within the addresses connected to the vehicle registered owner and driver's license files.

Suspect vehicle information and an offender description had been developed by the detectives working on the case, and this was combined with the geographic data to effectively focus the off-line search. For example, a new station wagon driven by a tall white middle-aged male, with dark hair, may seem to be somewhat vague information. The description actually contains several parameters: vehicle style, vehicle color, vehicle year range, driver height range, driver race, driver hair color, and driver age range.

When combined with a prioritized list of postal or zip codes, representing the most probable one or two percent of a city's area, these parameters act as a form of linear program, or filter, to produce a surprisingly small set of records containing fields with all the appropriate data responses. Depending on the number of specifers, and the size of the ranges, thousands of cases can be narrowed down to a few dozen vehicles or drivers. Such a strategy can therefore produce significant results by focusing on limited areas that are a manageable size for most serious criminal police investigations.

Prioritized postal codes can also be employed to target areas for strategic household mail delivery, leaflet distributions, neighborhood canvassing efforts, area searches, information sign posting, and community cooperation and media campaigns. LeBeau (1992, p. 136) discusses the case of a serial rapist in San Diego who was arrested through canvassing efforts in an area determined from the locations of his crimes.

Conclusion

All violent offenses have crime scenes. The offender and the victim have to encounter each other at some point in time and space, and these points form spatial and temporal patterns (LeBeau, 1992, pp. 124-126). Whether these patterns have meaning, and whether that meaning is significant for law enforcement, depends on a variety of factors. Offender types, activity spaces, hunting styles, and target blackcloths are all relevant variables in an analysis of criminal target patterns.

Geographic profiling infers spatial characteristics of the offender from these target patterns. This method has qualitative and quantitative approaches, which attempt to understand the pattern from both a subjective and an objective perspective. Criminal geographic targeting is a specific statistical method that enhances the efforts of geographic profiling by delineating the most probable areas to which the offender might be associated.

This prioritization, which is at the postal code, block, or letter carrier walk level, allows for the focusing of police investigative efforts. Suspects can be prioritized and patrol saturation efforts directed. In cases of serial murder and other serial violent crimes, there are usually heavy pressures, both external and internal, to apprehend the offender(s). When traditional law enforcement strategies have not been successful, or when the number of suspects or volume of information is high, geographic profiling can help prioritize areas and focus investigative strategies. This can lead to a quicker case resolution, thereby reducing police costs and increasing community safety.

Geographic Profiling Requirements

The following is a standard list of geographic profiling information requirements. Any particular case may require additional details. The majority of the information will likely have already been collected during the course of the investigation. The absence of some of the requirements should not be seen as a barrier or reason to delay the analysis as alternative sources of information may be available. In such cases, consult with the geographic profiler.

1. CRIME DATA

   - Case summaries for all the crimes believed to be part of the series, including any details regarding locations, directions, movements, and other spatial data.
   - Information should include: crime type, modus operandi, weapon type, date, day of week, time, weather.

2. GEOGRAPHIC DATA

   - For all relevant sites (i.e., where victims last seen, first contact sites, crime sites, victim/body/property/vehicle dump sites, evidence recovered sites, etc.):

a. exact location (address and cross streets)
b. location type (residential, commercial, industrial, including relevant buildings)
c. neighborhood demographics and general area description (census demographic details including age and sex ratios, socieconomic character, overall crime rate, relevant area crime problems, and transiency levels)
d. maps (city or region, aerial routes, bus routes, crime scene, land use, zoning)
e. photos (crime scenes, general area, aerial)

3. VICTIMOLOGY

■ For all victims: sex, race, age, risk level assessment, residence, business, social, transportation, methods and routes.

4. CRIME/PSYCHOLOGICAL PROFILE

■ The criminal profile plays a very important role in determining the probable life and mind set of the offender and consequently is of great value when constructing a geographic profile, particularly in those cases where there is a minimum amount of spatial information (i.e., only a few relevant crime locations).

5. SUSPECT DATA

■ If available: sex, age, race, criminal record, previous police contacts, psychological/psychiatric history, location of present/past residences, present/past schools, and present/past occupations, social activities, transportation methods and routes, addresses of family members and friends.

Bibliography

Allen, H. E. (1990). "Serial Killer Captured." *The Trooper,* 28(1), pp. 2-6.
Bates, S. (1978). *Spatial and Temporal Analysis of Crime* (Research Bulletin). Chicago: Illinois. Criminal Justice Information Authority.
Baytless, A. (1982). "Paying a Murderer for Evidence." *Criminal Justice Ethics,* (Summer/Fall), pp. 47-55.

Benfer, R.A., Jr. Brent, Jr., E.E. and Furbee, L. (1990). "Expert Systems." *Sage University Paper Series and Quantitative Applications in the Social Sciences, 77.* Newbury Park, CA: Sage.

Boots, B.N. and Getis, A. (1988) "Point Pattern Analysis." *Sage University Paper Series on Scientific Geography,* 8. Newbury Park, CA: Sage.

Boyd, N. (1988). *The Last Dance: Murder in Canada.* Scarborough, NY: Prentice Hall.

Brantingham, P.J. and Brantingham, P. L. (Eds.). (1981). *Environmental Criminology.* Beverly Hills, CA: Sage.

Brantingham, P.J. and Brantingham, P.L. (1984). *Patterns in Crime.* New York: Macmillan.

Brantingham, P.J. and Brantingham, P.L. (1993). "Nodes, Paths, and Edges: Considerations on the Complexity of Crime and the Physical Environment." *Journal of Environmental Psychology,* 13, pp. 3-28.

Brooks, P.R. (1982). *The Investigative Consultant Team: A New Approach for Law Enforcement Cooperation.* Washington, DC: Police Executive Research Forum.

Brooks, P.R., Devine, M.J., Green, T.J., Hart, B.L., and Moore, M.D. (1987, June). "Serial Murder: A Criminal Justice Response." *The Police Chief,* pp. 40-44.

Brooks, P.R., Devine, M.J., Green, T.J., Hart, B.L., and Moore, M.D. (1988). *Multi-Agency Investigative Team Manual.* Washington, DC: National Institute of Justice.

Clark, W.A.V. (1986). "Human Migration." *Sage University Paper Series on Scientific Geography,* 7, Beverly Hills, CA: Sage.

Clark, K.C. (1990). *Analytical and Computer Cartography.* Englewood Cliffs, NJ: Prentice Hall.

Cornish, D.B., and Clark, R.V. (Eds.). (1980). *The Reasoning Criminal: Rational Choice Perspectives on Offending.* New York: Springer-Verlag.

Crokett, A. (Ed.). (1990). *Serial Murderers.* New York: Windsor Publishing.

Cryan, M.P. (1988). "Halt Program Joins VICAP in Hunting Serial Criminals." *Trooper Magazine,* (May/June), pp. 8-9.

Dietz, P.E. (1985). "Sex Offender Profiling by the FBI: A Preliminary Concept Model." In M. H. Ben-Aron, S.J. Hucker and C.D. Webster (Eds.), *Clinical Criminology: The Assessment and Treatment of Criminal Behavior* (pp. 207-219). Toronto: M&M Graphics.

Doney, R.H. (1990). "The Aftermath of the Yorkshire Ripper: The Response of the United Kingdom Police Service." In S.A. Egger (Ed.), *Serial Murder: An Elusive Phenomenon* (pp. 95-112). New York: Praeger.

Douglas, J.E., Ressler, R.K., Burgess, A.W., and Hartman, C.R. (1986). "Criminal Profiling from Crime Scene Analysis." *Behavioral Sciences and the Law,* 4, pp. 401-321.

Egger, S.A. (1984). "A Working Definition of Serial Murder and the Reduction of Linkage Blindness." *Journal of Police Science and Administration,* 12, 348-357.

Egger, S.A. (1985). "Serial Murder and the Law Enforcement Response." Unpublished doctoral dissertation, Sam Houston State University, Huntsville, TX.

Egger, S.A. (1989). "Serial Murder." In W.G. Bailey (Ed.), *The Encyclopedia of Police Science* (pp. 578-581). New York: Garland Publishing.

Egger, S.A. (1990). Serial Murder: An Elusive Phenomenon. New York: Praeger.

Engstad, P.A. (1975). "Environmental Opportunities and the Ecology of Crime." In R.A. Silverman and J.J. Teevan, Jr. (Eds.), *Crime in Canadian Society* (pp. 193-211). Toronto: Butterworth.

Figlio, R.M., Hakim, S. and Rengert, G.F. (Eds.). (1986). *Metropolitan Crime Patterns.* Monsey, NY: Willow Tree Press.

Ford, D.A. (1990). "Investigating Serial Murder: The Case of Indiana's Gay Murders." In S.A. Egger (Ed.), *Serial Murder: An Elusive Phenomenon* (pp. 113-133). New York: Praeger.

Fowler, K. (1990). "The Serial Killer." *RCMP Gazette,* 52(3), pp. 1-11.

Frank, G. (1966). *The Boston Strangler.* New York: Nal Penguin.

Gabor, T. (1978). "Crime Displacement: The Literature and Strategies for its Investigation." *Crime and Justice,* 6, pp. 100-106.

Gabor, T. and Gottheil, E. (1984). "Offender Characteristics and Spatial Mobility: An Empirical Study and Some Policy Implications." *Canadian Journal of Criminology,* 26, pp. 267-281.

Geberth, V.J. (1990). *Practical Homicide Investigation: Tactics, Procedures, and Forensic Techniques* (2nd ed.). New York: Elsevier.

Georges-Abeyie, D.E. and Harris, K.D. (Eds.). (1980). *Crime: A Spatial Perspective.* New York: Columbia University Press.

Goodchild, M.F., Kemp, K.K., and Poiker, T. (1990a). *Introduction to GIS* (NCGIA Core Curriculum). National Center for Geographic Information and Analysis.

Goodchild, M.F., Kemp, K.K., and Poiker, T. (1990b). *Technical Issues in GIS* (NCGIA Core Curriculum). National Center for Geographic Information and Analysis.

Gould, P. (1960). "On Mental Maps." *Michigan Inter-university Community of Mathematical Geographers Discussion Paper Series,* 9. Ann Arbor, MI: University of Michigan.

Gould, P. (1975). "Acquiring Spatial Information." *Economic Geography,* 51, pp. 87-99.

Gould, P. and White, R. (1974). *Mental Maps.* New York: Penguin.

Greenberg, D.F. (1979). *Mathematical Criminology.* New Brunswick, NJ: Rutgers.

Hakim, S. and Rangert, G.F. (Eds.). (1981). *Crime Spillover.* Beverly Hills, CA: Sage.

Harris, K. (1990). *Geographic Factors in Policing.* Washington, DC: Police Executive Research Forum.

Haynes, K.E., and Fotheringham, A.S. (1984). "Gravity and Spatial Interaction Models." *Sage University Paper Series on Scientific Geography*, 2. Beverly Hills: Sage.

Hazelwood, R.R. (1987) "Analyzing the Rape and Profiling the Offender." In R.R. Hazelwood and A.W. Burgess (Eds.), *Practical Aspects of Rape Investigation: A Multidisciplinary Approach* (pp. 169-199). New York: Elsevier.

Hazelwood, R.R. and Burgess, A.W. (Eds.). (1987). *Practical Aspects of Rape Investigation: A Multidisciplinary Approach.* New York: Elsevier.

Hazelwood, R.R., Dietz, P.E., and Warren, J. (1992). "The Criminal Sexual Sadist." *FBI Law Enforcement Bulletin*, 61(2), pp. 12-20.

Hazelwood, R.R., and Douglas, J. (1990). "The Criminal Behavior of the Serial Rapist." *FBI Law Enforcement Bulletin*, 59(2), pp. 11-16.

Hellman, D. A. (1981). "Criminal Mobility and Policy Recommendations." In S. Hakim and G.F. Rengert (Eds.), *Crime Spillover* (p. 148). Beverly Hills, CA: Sage.

Hickey, E.R. (1991). *Serial Murderers and Their Victims.* Pacific Grove, CA: Brooks/Cole Publishing.

Holmes, R.M. (1989). *Profiling Violent Crimes.* Newbury Park: Sage.

Holmes, R.M. and DeBurger, J. (1988). *Serial Murder.* Newbury Park: Sage.

Icove, D.J. (1986). "Automated Crime Profiling." *FBI Law Enforcement Bulletin*, 55(12), pp. 27-30.

Icove, D.J. (1975). "Application of Pattern Recognition in Arson Investigation." *Fire Technology*, 11(1), pp. 35-41.

Icove, D.J. and Horben, P.R. (1990, December). "Serial Arsonists: An Introduction." *The Police Chief*, pp. 46-48.

Jakle, J.A., Brunn, S., and Roseman, C.C. (1976). *Human Spatial Behavior: A Social Geography.* Prospect Heights, IL: Waveland Press.

James, E. (1991). *Catching Serial Killers.* Lansing, MI: International Forensic Services.

Jenkins, P. (1988). "Myth and Murder: The Serial Killer Panic of 1983-5." Sam Houston State University Criminal Justice Research Bulletin, 3(11).

Jenkins, P. (1988b). "Serial Murder in England 1940-1985." *Journal of Criminal Justice*, 16, pp. 1-15.

Jenkins, P. (1989a). "Serial Murder in the United States 1900-1940: A Historical Perspective." *Journal of Criminal Justice*, 17, pp. 377-392.

Jenkins, P. (1989b). "Sharing Murder: Understanding Group Serial Homicide." Paper presented at the meeting of the American Society of Criminology, Reno, NV.

Johnston, R.J. (1975). "Map Pattern and Friction of Distance Parameters: A Comment." *Regional Studies*, 9, pp. 281-283.

Keppel, R.D. (1989). *Serial Murder: Future Implications for Police Investigations.* Cincinnati: Anderson Publishing Co.

King, I.J. (1984). "Central Place Theory." *Sage University Paper Series on Scientific Geography, 1.* Beverly Hills: Sage.

Knoke, D. and Kuklinski, J.H. (1982). "Network Analysis." *Sage University Paper Series on Quantitative Applications in the Social Sciences,* 28. Beverly Hills, CA: Sage.

Lange, J.E.T. and DeWitt, Jr., K. (1990). *The Ripper Syndrome: A Perspective on Serial Murder.* Unpublished manuscript.

LeBeau, J.L. (1987). "The Journey to Rape: Geographic Distance and the Rapist's Method of Approaching the Victim." *Journal of Police Science and Administration,* 15, pp. 129-136.

LeBeau, J.L. (1987). "The Methods and Measures of Centrography and the Spatial Dynamics of Rape." *Journal of Quantitative Criminology,* 3, pp. 125-141.

LeBeau, J.L. (1992). "Four Case Studies Illustrating the Spatial-Temporal Analysis of Serial Rapists." *Police Studies,* 15, pp. 124-125.

Levin, J. and Fox, J. (1985). *Mass Murder.* New York: Plenum Press.

Leyton, E. (1986). *Hunting Humans.* Toronto: McClelland-Bantam.

Lowe, J.C. and Moryadas, S. (1975). *The Geography of Movement.* John Wiley and Sons.

Luce, R.D. (1959). *Individual Choice Behavior.* New York: John Wiley and Sons.

Lynch, K. (1960). *The Image of the City.* Cambridge, MA: MIT Press.

Malts, M.D., Gordon, A.C., and Friedman, W. (1991). *Mapping Crime in its Community Setting: Event Geography Analysis.* New York: Springer-Verlag.

McIver, J.P. (1981). "Criminal Mobility: A Review of Empirical Studies." In S. Hakim & G.F. Rengert (Eds.), *Crime Spillover* (pp. 20-47). Beverly Hills: Sage.

Montgomery, J.E. (1992, February). "Organizational Survival: Continuity of Crisis?" Paper presented at the Police Studies Series, Simon Fraser University, Vancouver, BC.

Morrill, R., Gaile, G.L. and Thrall, G.L. (1988). "Spatial Diffusion." *Sage University Paper Series on Scientific Geography.* Beverly Hills, CA: Sage.

Mulgrew, I. (1990). *Final Payoff: The True Price of Convicting Clifford Robert Olson.* Toronto: Seal Books.

Newton, M. (1990). *Hunting Humans: The Encyclopedia of Serial Killers: Vol. 1.* New York: Avon Books.

Newton, Jr., M.B. and Newton, D.C. (1985, October). "Geoforensic Identification of Localized Serial Crime: Unsolved Female Homicides, Forth Worth, Texas, 1983-85." Paper presented at the meeting of the Southwest Division, Association of American Geographers, Denton, TX.

Newton, Jr., M.B. and Swoope, E.A. (1987). *Geoforensic Analysis of Localized Serial Murder: The Hillside Stranglers Located.* Unpublished manuscript.

Norris, J. (1988). *Serial Killers.* New York: Doubleday.

Olson, C.R. (1992). *The Phenomena of Serial Murder—Ten Questions.* Unpublished manuscript.

Pinto, S., and Wilson, P.R. (1990). Serial Murder *(Trends and Issues in Crime and Criminal Justice, No. 25).* Canberra: Australian Institute of Criminology.

Ploughman, P.D. and Ould, P.J. (1990, November). "Toward a Self-Protective, Rational Calculus: The Nexus of Routine Activities and Rape Victimization Risk." Paper presented at the meeting of the American Society of Criminology, Baltimore, MD.

Pyle, G.F. (1974). *The Spatial Dynamics of Crime.* (Research Paper No. 159). Chicago: Department of Geography, University of Chicago.

Reber, A.S. (1985). *The Penguin Dictionary of Psychology.* Hammondsworth, Middlesex: Penguin.

Reboussin, R. and Cameron, J. (1989). "Expert Systems for Law Enforcement." *FBI Law Enforcement Bulletin,* 58(8), 12-16.

Rengert, G.F. and Wasilchick, J. (1985). *Suburban Burglary.* Springfield, IL: Charles C. Thomas.

Repetto, T.A. (1974). *Residential Crime.* Cambridge, MA: Ballinger Publishing.

Repetto, T.A. (1976). "Crime Prevention and the Displacement Phenomenon." *Crime and Delinquency,* 22, pp. 168-169.

Ressler, R.K., Burgess, A.W., and Douglas, J.E. (1988). *Sexual Homicide: Patterns and Motives.* Lexington, MA: Lexington Books.

Ressler, R.K., Burgess, A.W., Douglas, J.E., Hartment, C.R., and D'Agostino, R.B. (1986). "Sexual Killers and Their Victims: Identifying Patterns Through Crime Scene Analysis." *Journal of Interpersonal Violence,* 1, pp. 288-308.

Rhodes, W.M. and Conly, C. (1981). "Crime and Mobility: An Empirical Study." In P.J. Brantingham and P.L. Brantingham (Eds.), *Environmental Criminology* (pp. 167-188). Beverly Hills, CA: Sage.

Rogers, R., Craig, D. and Anderson, D. (1991, March). "Serial Murder Investigation and Geographic Information Systems." Paper presented at the conference of the Academy of Criminal Justice Sciences, Nashville, TN.

Rossmo, D.K. (1987). "Fugitive Migration Patterns." Unpublished master's thesis, Simon Fraser University, Burnaby, BC.

Rossmo, D.K. (1993). "Targeting Victims: Serial Killers and the Urban Environment." In T. O'Reilly-Fleming and S. Egger (Eds.), *Serial and Mass Murder: Theory, Research and Policy.* Toronto: University of Toronto Press.

Sherman, L.W., Gartin, P.R., and Buerger, M.E. (1989). "Hotspots of Predatory Crime: Routine Activities and the Criminology of Place." *Criminology,* 27, pp. 27-55.

Simmonetti, C. (1984). *Serial Murders: 1970-1983.* Unpublished master's thesis, State University of New York, Albany, NY.

Stea, D. (1969). "The Measurement of Mental Maps: An Experimental Model for Studying Conceptual Spaces." In K.R. Cox and R.G. Golledge (Eds.), *Behavioral Problems in Geography* (pp. 228-253). Evanston, IL: Northwestern University Press.

Stoufer, A. (1960). "Intervening Opportunities and Competing Migrants." *Journal of Regional Science*, 1, pp. 1-20.

Taylor, P. J. (1977). *Quantitative Methods in Geography.* Prospects Heights, IL: Waveland Press.

Tomlin, C.D. (1990). *Geographic Information Systems and Cartographic Modeling.* Englewood Cliffs, NJ: Prentice Hall.

Tversky, A. and Kahneman, D. (1983). "The Framing of Decisions and the Psychology of Choice." *Science*, 211, pp. 453-458.

Upwin, D. (1981). *Introductory Spatial Analysis.* London: Methuen.

Upton, G.J.G. and Fingleton, B. (1989). Spatial Data Analysis by Example: Vol. 3. *Categorical and Directional Data.* Chichester, NY: Wiley.

U.S. Department of Justice. (1990). *Annual Report 1990 (National Center for the Analysis of Violent Crime).* Washington, DC: U.S. Government Printing Office.

U.S. Department of Justice. (1991). *Serial/Mass Murder* (National Institute of Justice topical search TS 011664). Washington, DC: U.S. Government Printing Office.

Walker, J.T. (1991, March). "Hot Spots or Concentric Rings: Analysis of Human Ecology in Little Rock, Arkansas." Paper presented at the conference of the Academy of Criminal Justice Sciences, Nashville, TN.

Walmsley, D.J. and Lewis, G.J. (1984). *Human Geography: Behavioural Approaches.* London: Longman.

Webber, M.J. (1984). "Industrial Location." *Sage University Paper Series on Scientific Geography*, 3. Beverly Hills, CA: Sage.

Werner, C. (1985). "Spatial Transportation Modeling." *Sage University Paper Series on Scientific Geography*, 5. Beverly Hills, CA: Sage.

Wilson, A.G. (1967). "A Statistical Theory of Spatial Distribution Models." *Transportation Research*, 1, pp. 253-269.

Wilson, C. (1960). "My Search for Jack the Ripper." In R.G. Jones (Ed.), *Unsolved! Classic True Murder Cases* (pp. 13-32). New York: Peter Bedrick.

Wilson, C. and Seaman, D. (1990). *The Serial Killers: A Study in the Psychology of Violence.* London: W.H. Allen Publishing.

Young, M.L. (1992, June 19). "Dangerous Offender Warns of More Terror Unless He Gets Help." *The Vancouver Sun*, pp. B1, B4.

15

Serial Murder Investigation
Prospects for Police Networking

THOMAS O'REILLY-FLEMING

Introduction

In 1984, Steve Egger coined the term "linkage blindness" to describe the lack of coordination between investigation agencies in cases involving serial murder. Unfortunately in the decade since he drew our attention to this serious deficiency in police networking, little has changed in relation to information sharing in cases of unsolved homicide where a suspect(s) is not apparent within a reasonable period of time. Rather, a review of recent cases indicated that, at least at the local level, networking has not, despite the pivotal role it can play in crime solution, become a prerequisite of informed homicide investigation.

Serial Murder in Contemporary Society

Serial murder while not strictly a modern phenomenon (Jenkins, 1988; 1989; O'Reilly-Fleming, 1992) has only received significant law enforcement, public and academic attention since the mid 1980s as a distinct crime class. Ressler (1984) first used the term in the academic literature, and identified a specific form of career criminal. These mod-

Author's Note: This chapter was first published in 1992 in the *Journal of Contemporary Criminal Justice, 8,* 227-234. Reprinted with permission.

ern hunters of humans (Leyton, 1986) kill three or more victims over a period of hours, days, weeks or years usually selecting random strangers or slight acquaintances as victims. Their target selection ensures that law enforcement agencies have little evidence to work with in terms of motive, and often discover the remains of the victim after the perpetrator is far removed from the murder site. In many cases, as confessions long after their incarceration have demonstrated, the victims of serial killers remain undiscovered for many years. Ian Brady who along with Myra Hindkey collectively were known as the Moors Murders, were convicted of the murders of three children in Chester Castle in 1966. Twenty two years later they revealed the whereabouts of the body of Pauline Reade, a sixteen year old victim whom police had not discovered (Wilson and Seaman, 1989). Ted Bundy, during the period leading up to his execution in 1989 in Florida, "solved" several uncleared homicide cases in confessions to the F.B.I.

Females are the overwhelming victims of the serial killer (Hickey, 1991) although several cases involving male victims have received a great deal of media and academic attention. John Wayne Gacy, Jr. was convicted of the murders of 33 young males in Illinois. Dennis Nilsen of London, England picked up fifteen males, dismembering them and storing them under the floorboards of his flats. Jeffrey Dahmer killed thirteen young men in Milwaukee over a period of several years, dismembering them, cannibalizing the bodies, and decorating his apartment with their cleaned and painted skulls. Whether females or males, many serial killers tend to select victims who are marginal in some sense to the community in which they reside, and so are less likely to invoke aggressive action by law enforcement unless their numbers are overwhelming in a short period of time. Detroit's rash of eight murders in the Highland Park district in 1992 demonstrates this trend, as all of the victims are black females who have a history as prostitutes and crack addicts. Picking victims who are not upstanding citizens can effectively delay intense police efforts as the so-called Yorkshire Ripper case in England clearly demonstrates. Peter Sutcliffe was able to kill with little fanfare while he selected prostitutes as his victims but it was when he murdered a teenaged schoolgirl that police efforts dramatically intensified and the killings were publicly linked. On the other hand, serial murderers like Williams who recently confessed to four killings in Detroit, may be indiscriminate in their choice of victims, selecting them not in relation to their social status, but because of their perceived vulnerability. Serial murderers, like most felons who engage in progressive or serial forms of human violence, become extremely skilled at recognizing victimization potential in their targets. This involves perceptions of the victim's level of intoxication, their location in the physical environment, the likelihood of resistance, gullibility of the victim, potential for eyewitnesses in the location, age of the target and a range of other factors which have been identified in research with serial killers (Ressler, 1992; Hickey, 1991; Egger, 1990). The Williams case is another demonstration that there are severe difficulties that are inherent in attempting to link disappearances and murder victims to serial offenders.

The Dahmer case demonstrates another weakness in policing practice not at the level of interagency networking but in terms of preparing patrol officers for apprehension in the course of routine investigation. However, it also demonstrates and reinforces the view of serial offenders that police show bias and invest little in solving the homicides of marginals. The officers who responded to the "altercation" between Dahmer and 14 year old Konerak Sinthasomphone, a Laotian boy (Dvorchak and Holewa, 1991), categorized the assault as one between two consenting homosexuals. They found Konerak running down the street naked with blood running from his rectum, and were called back by concerned neighbors when nothing was done. Again letting bias against homosexuals color their response, the officers returned the boy to Dahmer who decapitated him soon after.

Female serial killers received little attention in the academic literature. Aileen Wuornos, 36, dubbed "the killer hooker" (Toronto Star, May 16, 1992) became the first female serial murderess sentenced to die in Florida's electric chair, although she is certainly not the first woman serial killer to be identified in research (Jenkins, 1988, 1989; Hickey, 1991). She confessed to the slaying of seven men over a period of time, 1989-1990, and made the fatal mistake of picking up a hitchhiker. Wuornos adopted a feminist perspective in speaking to her sentence in an hour-long statement when she argued that her death sentence was "sending a message that a woman who defends herself is likely to end up on Death Row. . . . They're saying that male dominance is okay, and woe be to the woman who takes action against a violent man" (Toronto Star, May 16, 1992). Wuornos' case demonstrates the inherent difficulties involved in the apprehension of serial killers who travel after committing a slaying through a variety of police jurisdictions making connection of the murderous events difficult, if not impossible, unless advanced police networking is in place.

Clifford Robert Olson: "The only reason they solved the thing was because I told them."

The case of Clifford Robert Olson is well known to the Canadian public where he is one of a handful of apprehended serial killers, and in terms of convictions, ranks as the most significant serial murderer in the nation's history. Olson has been the subject of two books (Ferry and Inwood, 1982; Mulgrew, 1991) and his case is well documented thus facilitating an analysis of police networking deficiencies which must be addressed in future practice.

Olson was a career criminal, prison informer (Mulgrew, 1991: 18) who had spent the majority of his life in prison before his final conviction as a serial murderer (Shantz, 1992). During his adult life, he spent "barely 50 months free from 24-hour supervision" (Mulgrew, 1991: xi). In 24 years, he had been convicted of 83 offenses, including armed robbery. In 1977, charges of sexual molestation against several children were dropped since Olson "was already serving time" (Mulgrew, 1991: 12). This was to be a consistent pattern of non-prosecution as the expense of a trial seemed too expensive when the accused was already incarcerated. In December 1980, the first of Olson's victims, all of whom were children, both males and females, was discovered in Richmond, British Columbia. Over the next eight months, a further ten victims would die until Olson was arraigned on August 21, 1981 in the murder of 18 year old Judy Kozma.

It had not been until July 31, 1981 that the Royal Canadian Mounted Police, who are responsible for both provincial (state) and local policing in the province of British Columbia, set up a task force on the Case of the Missing Lower Mainland Children. Police Investigators had found only three of the ten bodies of Olson's victims at this point. On July 27, 1981, police began surveillance on Olson at 4:45 p.m., about seven hours after he had already sexually assaulted and murdered Terri Lyn Carson, a fifteen year old girl (Ferry and Inwood, 1982: 88). On July 28, detective Dennis Tarr from Delta, British Columbia, met with Olson at 9:40 p.m. and Olson was taken into custody for a few hours on July 29 after he and two youths picked up two girls and plied them with alcohol. Police tails feared for the girls' safety. He was released after a few hours. On July 30,

Tarr, wearing a bodypack, again met with Olson in the company of Corporal Drozda and Corporal Fred Maille, of the Serious Crimes Unit. Their conversation included the offer of rewards for information on several murders in British Columbia. Olson left at 11:10 p.m. to cruise Highway 7, where he picked up Louise Marie Chartrand, a 17 year old who would be his last victim. Immediately after the murder, Olson stopped into a local police station where he had left some belongings a few months previously (Ferry and Inwood, 1982: 94-98).

By September 21, 1981, Olson faced ten murder counts since he had entered into a "cash for corpses" deal with the police and the government of Canada. Olson's wife received $100,000 in a trust fund, $10,000 for each of the bodies that Olson led the police to. Crown Prosecutor John Hall's comments on the payments underscored the difficulties inherent in police efforts to identify serial killers. "You are dealing with a crime involving people who are not related in any way by blood, or knowing each other. You do not have any link from an investigative point of view" (Ferry and Inwood, 1982: 136).

The Future of Serial Murder Investigation: Lessons and Prescriptions for Effectiveness from Britain, Canada, and the United States

The discussion presented to this juncture demonstrates some of the shortcomings of police efforts to isolate and capture serial killers. Many of these difficulties arise not from police incompetence but rather from the complex nature of serial murder, which is a crime which places severe strain on investigative personnel. This strain is two-fold, involving the pressure to solve heinous cases that are often unbelievably violent while at the same time enduring intense public pressure to find a culprit(s). The future of policing in serial murder cases must draw upon the accumulated failures and successes of previous investigations.

Egger, a former homicide detective and expert on the VICAP (Violent Criminal Apprehension Program) system (1990: 201-208), has summarized the six primary areas which must underlay future efforts at apprehension and which will promote "awareness and understanding." These are, (1) definitions of serial murder, (2) crime scene search and identification of physical evidence, (3) linkage blindness, (4) case law of serial murder cases on appeal, (5) serial murder solvability factors, and (6) psychological profiling. Serial murder investigations are often hampered in early, critical stages by both a lack of experience on the part of local homicide detectives with the phenomenon. This aggravates public tension as police agencies often resort to a denial of serial killings even when there is overwhelming evidence in support of this scenario. The ongoing investigation of the murder of eight black prostitutes in Detroit during 1992, all murdered in the same fashion and within the same geographical area (Highland Park) has been characterized by a flat denial of serial killing by official police sources. While one would not wish to unduly alarm the public, there is little reason to withhold this information if the determining factor is simply the avoidance of public pressure and scrutiny. That the public can provide crucial information is underscored by the Williams case in the same city, in which two observant citizens contacted police after the perpetrator was spotted attempting to strangle his victim in a graveyard. She was freed by the police from the trunk of Williams' car a few minutes later.

The British experience in tracking the Yorkshire Ripper (Doney, 1990: 95-112) is illustrative of the difficulties in apprehending serial killers when there is a lack of police interest in the investigation. Peter Sutcliffe murdered thirteen women in Britain between July 1975 and January 1981 when he was eventually arrested. It was not until Sutcliffe murdered a schoolgirl, rather than his usual victims, prostitutes, that police efforts intensified in the case. Before his arrest Sutcliffe had been interviewed nine times regarding the murders. Although serial murder is a relatively rare form of another atypical crime, murder, there is evidence to suggest that serial murder may be more common than frequently admitted by police authorities (Jenkins, 1993). The problems associated with finding a suspect in cases can lead us to reasonably speculate that there is a substantial "dark figure" for this crime, and to this one could add some of the thousands of individuals who annually go missing. The volume of work that can accumulate in an investigation of this type was illustrated by the move of documents to a new building when their sheer weight (24 tons) threatened to collapse the structure (Doney, 1990: 1023). The British police developed a retrospective critique of their own work in the case and recommended changes for future police practice which could be of use to all jurisdictions. They recommended the following: (1) standardization of procedures; (2) computerization of records; (3) training of senior investigating officers; (4) appointment of an advisory team; and (5) use of specialist and scientific support. The HOLMES (Home Office Large Major Enquiry System) was finally developed after several computer systems were experimented with which address the substantive problems encountered in serial murder or serial rape cases. Most pointedly, it ensures that investigating officers have updated information when they interview suspects, a deficiency that was noted in the Sutcliffe case (Doney, 1990: 100-105).

Computerization of information seems to be a key for the direction of future police efforts for it allows entry of relevant data on unsolved homicides across the country that can be instantly accessed by homicide investigators, facilitates comparative analysis, and permits the inputting of new case materials. In the United States, the VICAP located in the Behavioral Science Unit of the FBI National Academy at Quantico, Virginia is the central site for the collection of national data on unsolved violent crimes. VICAP, as Egger notes, (1990: 193) "collects, collates, and analyzes all aspects of the investigation of similar pattern, multiple murders, on a nationwide basis, regardless of the location or number of police agencies involved." The success of VICAP is largely dependent upon the voluntary participation of local law enforcement personnel who must complete a long and very detailed sixteen page form. While VICAP is certainly a highly useful tool, and the development of a national database on multiple murder is central to future police efforts, some lack of cooperation on the local level can be attributed to the view that VICAP requires an immense amount of manpower investment but often gives little in return (Keppel, 1989). At the local level police agencies must develop the ability to do simple cross-referencing and aggregate data retrieval to allow for easily comparable information that can be accessed in a timely fashion. Automated fingerprint systems which have the ability to process thousands of prints in a matter of minutes will also provide a key, though obviously costly portion of future interactive data systems.

The evidence is that police priorities will have to shift somewhat if multiple murderers are to be more readily apprehended, treating, for example, missing persons reports more seriously and expeditiously, as it has been recognized that missing persons may appear later as victims of a serial criminal. This is true in the Gacy, Williams (1992) and Lucas cases to name a few. The Canadian experience, where the murder rate has remained relatively constant since 1900, and where the average number of known homicides a year is approximately 650 is in the development stages of a VICAP type system although lack of financial support has hindered its completion and widespread implementation (MacKay, 1992).

The central priority which will determine the success or failure of efforts in police investigation of serial murders will reside in their ability to effectively interact and share information with other law enforcement agencies. Egger (1990: 208) has astutely summarized the core of this problem when he states that police agencies must "put professional competition, jealousies, turf-protecting, case-based investigative assignments, and jurisdictional myopia behind them." To do less will allow the serial killer to benefit from these self-imposed limitations. Roy Hazelwood (1992) in a recent lecture on the sadistic serial killer reported that such murderers study true crime magazines, law enforcement bulletins, and academic journals to learn how to avoid detection. Given this, the future of serial murder investigation must not only rectify the mistakes of the past, but build upon the many advances made in the apprehension of these heinous perpetrators. The lesson of the future for serial killers must be that law enforcement agencies can, and do, share information effectively across not only state, but national and international boundaries.

References

Doney, R. H. (1984). "The Aftermath of the Yorkshire Ripper: The Response of the United Kingdom Police Service." In S. Egger, Serial Murder: An Elusive Phenomenon. New York: Praeger, 95-113.

Dvorchak, R. and L. Holewa. (1991). Milwaukee Massacre. New York: Dell.

Egger, S. (1984). "A Working Definition of Serial Murder and the Reduction of Linkage Blindness." Journal of Police Science and Administration. Vol. 12, No. 3, 348-357.

Egger, S. (1990). Serial Murder: An Elusive Phenomenon. New York: Praeger.

Ferry, J. and D. Inwood. (1982). The Olson Murders. Langley: Cameo.

Hazelwood, R. (1992). "Sadistic Serial Murder." Paper presented to Serial and Mass Murder: Theory, Research and Policy. The First International Conference. University of Windsor, April 4.

Hickey, E. (1991). Serial Murderers and their Victims. Pacific Grove: Brooks/ Cole.

Jenkins, P. (1988). "Serial Murder in England, 1940-1985." Journal of Criminal Justice, Vol. 16, 1-15.

Jenkins, P. (1989). "Serial Murder in the United States, 1900-1940: A Historical Perspective." Journal of Criminal Justice, Vol. 17, 377-392.

Jenkins, P. (1993). "New Perspectives on Serial Murder in England." Forthcoming in T. O'Reilly-Fleming and S. Egger (eds.) Serial Murder: Theory, Policy, and Research. Toronto: University of Toronto Press, May.

Keppel, R. (1989). Serial Murder: Future implications for police investigations. Cincinnati: Anderson.

Levin, J. and J. Fox. (1985). Mass Murder: America's Growing Menace. New York: Plenum. (Paperback edition, 1992).

Leyton, E. (1986). Hunting Humans: The Rise of the Modern Multiple Murderer, Toronto: Seal.

MacKay, R. (1992). "VICAP and Police Networking." Roundtable Discussant. Serial and Mass Murder: Theory, Policy and Research. The First International Conference. University of Windsor, April 5, 1992.

Mulgrew, I. (1991). Final Payoff. Toronto: Seal.

O'Reilly-Fleming, Thomas. (1992). "Serial Murder: Towards Integrated Theorizing." The Critical Criminologist. Forthcoming.

Ressler, R. (1984). "Serial Murder: A New Phenomenon of Homicide." Paper presented at the annual meeting of The International Association of Forensic Sciences, Oxford, England.

Ressler, R. (1992). Those Who Hunt Monsters. New York: St. Martin's.

Shantz, R. (1992). Lecture on Clifford Olson delivered at The University of British Columbia. (Courtesy of R.S. Ratner). The Toronto Star, May 16, 1992.

Wilson C. and D. Seaman. (1989). Encyclopedia of Modern Murder. London: Pan.

16

Selected Problems in Serial Murder Investigations

RONALD M. HOLMES
STEPHEN T. HOLMES

It seems that there are few weeks that pass that some jurisdiction is not involved in a serial murder investigation. Some investigations gather national attention, whereas others gather meager media exposure.

The Ted Bundy investigation is an example of the former. When Ted escaped from jail in Colorado, there was a national search for him. The FBI immediately placed him on their Ten Most Wanted list, and he was captured not by the FBI but again by accident, in Pensacola, Florida. People breathed a little easier knowing that he had been apprehended, and they could sleep better at night, especially young women who were of the age that Bundy preferred. The Bundy murder case involved many victims (Michaud & Aynesworth, 1983; Rule, 1980), and it alerted law enforcement to the uniqueness of a serial murder investigation.

There are problems in serial murder cases that may be the same as in "typical" homicides, but there are others that are unique. This is the focus of this chapter—the special problems that may be unique to a serial murder investigation.

Special Problems in the Investigation of Serial Murder

There are several problematic areas present in a serial murder case that are not extant in other, more traditional homicide investigations.

The order discussed may not necessarily be indicative of the importance in any one particular serial murder investigation; not all are present in any one investigation. Additionally, one item in a specific case may be more important than the others. In another case, an item may be completely missing and unimportant. What we have decided here is to list several problematic areas in an attempt to address what may be obvious concerns.

DETERMINING A SERIAL MURDER CASE

This is perhaps the most difficult and the most obvious of all the special and unique problems in a serial murder investigation. Unless the serial killer leaves a distinct or unique signature at the crime scene, the police may not recognize the similarity of the killings.

Seeing a common element in several reports of missing or murdered people in one large city is difficult enough. Seeing it across city or state lines magnifies the problem. Some killers are able to kill on the move so that they are already hundreds of miles away before police discover the crime (Levin & Fox, 1985, p. 182).

Levin and Fox (1985) state that serial killers may be hiding in the anonymity of large urban centers or are nomadic in their cruising for victims. Holmes and Holmes (1996) take issue with the "cruising for victims" portion of this statement. It may be true that the transient serial killer may be aware of the information sharing that, in effect, aids in his apprehension. In either case, the exact number of serial killers is unknown, and therefore the number of serial murder cases is also unknown. The determination of a case as a serial murder episode is impeded unless a direct connection is made and the murders are thus recognized as related.

The problem here is that the basic discovery of a murder victim or victims may not be enough to alert the police that there is, indeed, a serial murder case. For example, in the Ted Bundy case, several victims were found before the police were convinced that there was a serial murderer in their midst. The parents of one victim had to almost plead with the police to convince them that the murders were connected (Rule, 1980).

PROTECTING ONE'S TURF AND INFORMATION SHARING

In the investigation of serial murder cases, the ugly head of turf protection becomes apparent. If a case is a high-profile one, its successful resolution would result in a major coup for the police department. Witness the O.J. Simpson case, where this highly suspected defendant was found not guilty of a double homicide. The district attorney's office, as well as the police department, received major criticisms for "losing" this case. The next high-profile case involving this same department will be handled differently. For example, in the next celebrated murder case, the media may be restricted in terms of information granted to them. This was already seen in the civil case against Simpson, where television cameras and information were controlled by the court.

Politics often restrict information sharing. This may become critical when the chief law enforcement officer is an elected official, or when some other high-ranking public official who has some control over the police agency is also close to reelection. If this case is not handled properly, or it is unresolved, some political and law enforcement careers may be severely impaired.

Turf protection may result in a lower number of victims than when one counts cases and victims only by looking at the media. This is one reason we are convinced that there are more serial killers than some believe. We also believe there are more victims, but certainly not as many as 5,000, as some suspect (Bernick & Spangler, 1985). Lindsey (1984), although not offering a definite number, did say that there was an unknown number of serial killers quietly killing across the country and inferred that the number of victims may number in the hundreds.

DECIDING THE TYPE OF SERIAL KILLER

One problem that may result is not determining the type of serial murderer currently under investigation. As has already been seen in previous readings, certain types of serial predators will vary in their methods of murder. The visionary serial killer will kill in a chaotic fashion, and the crime scene and the kill site are both the same site. Moreover, the kill site is filled with physical evidence. This type of serial killer is more apt to live and work close to the place where the body was found. The power/control serial killer, on the other hand, is more apt to be a transient person, and he may already be gone from the area. He is a "five-stage" killer (Holmes, 1988).

The professional and educated investigator should be alerted to the various types of serial killers and the manner in which they will not only kill and dispose of the victims, but also the manner in which they select their victims and other such pertinent items. To gain such information, investigators can attend workshops and seminars conducted by various groups and organizations around the country. Additionally, law enforcement professionals should keep up with the latest research concerning serial homicide and the traits and characteristics of serial killers.

DEDICATION OF THE AGENCY TOWARD
A SUCCESSFUL RESOLUTION

The investigation of a serial murder case is an expensive venture. The number of personnel involved increases with the dedication of the department. Additionally, there are other expenses that will increase with the size of the task force: telephone and other communication expenses; personnel allotment; administrative and secretarial support; supplies; and other incidental expenses, including outside expert help in the investigation itself.

Various serial homicide investigations have resulted in huge amounts of monies spent. It is one thing to validate financial expenditures when a case is solved (e.g., the Hillside Stranglers case, the Hollywood Strip Murder case, and the Bobby Joe Long case in Tampa). It is quite another scenario when the case remains unresolved (e.g., the Green River case, in which millions of dollars have been spent and the slayer of more than 40 women is still at large).

TRAINING AND EDUCATION OF HOMICIDE DETECTIVES

The investigation of a serial murder case is different from the traditional murder case. The education of an investigator must include all the natural elements of a traditional homicide investigation, but it must also include those factors that are unique to the serial murder investigation and the serial killer.

Serial murder investigations could take some hints from homicide officers who investigate sex crimes that result in murder. Often, there are evident methods of operation and signatures. The serial killer who is sexually motivated does not significantly differ from the sexually motivated killer. The possession of an ideal victim type with fetishes and partialisms and the method of fatal dispatchment would resemble the sexual killer who often kills not a single time but is compelled by his compulsion to repeat his sexual predations. These items, and others, are common educational components in homicide investigation seminars.

EXISTENCE AND EXTENT OF LINKAGE BLINDNESS

One of the major obstacles to the successful resolution of serial murder investigations is linkage blindness (Egger, 1984). Linkage blindness is the lack of information sharing, as well as turf issues.

There is a lack of networking among the professional investigators and the various agencies on the local, state, and federal levels. This networking is an important manifest function of a task force. It is not only to bring investigators together to share the information discovered in the case but also to create cooperative relationships among the individuals in this case and in future cases. There may be a reluctance among many departments on the local and state levels to share information with some federal agencies because of the lack of information that is returned to the initiating agency.

Linkage blindness has been apparent in several celebrated serial murder cases. For example, in the Ted Bundy case, the killings in Seattle and in neighboring counties around King County had not been connected by the various police agencies until the murder of Susan Elaine Rancourt (Michaud & Aynesworth, 1983). Ted killed in various jurisdictions, and he told Ronald Holmes in an interview that he could have killed young women in his own neighborhood but decided to roam in his selection of victims because he knew from his experiences within the crime commission in Seattle that police departments and agencies do not share information.

Ted continued to kill after he moved from Washington State to Utah to attend his second law school, the University of Utah. He roamed the neighboring communities, Murray, Provo, and others, and ventured into Colorado to kill several other young women. After he was captured and sent to prison not for murder but for kidnapping, and then later extradited to Colorado to stand trial for the murder of Caryn Campbell, he then escaped from jail to run to Florida. Don Patchen, of the Tallahassee Police Department, was in contact with Mike Fisher, an investigator from Colorado Springs. They shared information about the murders in their states (the murders in Colorado and the Chi-Omega murder cases in Florida) and suggested that Bundy might be responsible for the murders in Florida because the attacks resembled the method of operation that Bundy used on his victims in the western part of the United States. Linkage blindness was reduced in the Bundy case by the personal communication by these two law enforcement professionals. In addition, Jerry Thompson, former deputy sheriff from Salt Lake City, was also in communication with Patchen and Fisher about the murders in Utah (D. Patchen, M. Fisher, and J. Thompson, personal communication, 1986). Fisher, Thompson, and Patchen are excellent examples of officers who put aside politics and turf issues to use their power for the common good of bringing a serial killer to justice.

IDENTIFICATION OF MISSING PERSONS AS VICTIMS OF SERIAL MURDER

Of the many missing persons who vanish each year, many are presumed runaways, and others are thought to have vanished of their own volition. Some are victims of a friend, relative, or other affiliative killer, and some are victims of serial killers. National organizations have been formed to help resolve such concerns. For example, The Fallen Wall was formed recently to help in the fight against serial killers and other murderers, and to locate victims. The organization crosses state lines and hopes soon to have an international audience. (The web address site at the time of this writing is http://www.netzone.com/holmes/wall/index.html.) The Chicago Police Department has also gone high tech in locating missing persons. It, too, has a web page that is devoted to asking for citizen aid in locating possible victims of homicide. The Texas Department of Public Safety has developed a web page that asks for help in identifying deceased victims. Some are victims of fatal violence, and some are bodies found that may have been the victims of a vehicular accidents. Other states have followed suit, including Hawaii, Colorado, California, Florida, and Minnesota.

Regardless of the present state of the empirical science, there is no valid way to ascertain the exact number of missing adults or children. The National Center for Missing and Exploited Children, for example, has constructed a large bureaucracy for the determination of the missing children problem. How many are actually victims of killers and serial killers is unknown. How many missing adults also fall prey to serial killers is unknown. Despite this, some authors have decided that almost 25% of the missing and unresolved murder cases involve serial killers (Bernick & Spangler, 1985). This is not only preposterous to assume, it also causes undue alarm. When confronted on national TV, author Ann Rule was hesitant to recant her earlier estimate of a large number of victims of serial killers by saying that she would rather err on the side of caution ("Murder by Number," 1993).

In essence, there is no easy or responsible way to determine that someone has fallen victim to a serial killer if the victim is still missing. Of course, there is an exception to this scenario. If the killer confesses to such a murder, one may accept his confession as evidence. Bundy did this with several cases the day before his execution. Bundy confessed to the murder of one high school student in Utah, Debbie Smith. The only body part the police were able to retrieve was a kneecap. This was almost 15 years after her murder! (Holmes, 1998)

Conclusion

This chapter has concerned itself with some of the problems in the investigation of a serial murder case. The problems exist to some degree in most, if not all, law enforcement agencies that have a serial murder investigation underway. These problems are exacerbated by the enormous task presented by the acts of a serial killer as well as the personal, domestic, occupational, and health problems presented to the homicide investigator.

Departments that are forced to investigate a serial murder case are met with problems that are not ordinarily present in some cases. Some of these problems have been discussed, and perhaps only a few will be present in any one serial murder investigation. However, if only a few are there, the investigation is hampered by the special and unique problems.

What is so very important is that the investigator become aware of the special mindset of the serialist and how the crimes of the serial killer are different from other types of homicides. The serialist is often seen as a murderer who kills for no apparent reason. But there is a reason, and the investigator must learn the reason or motivation for this murder. This becomes a part of the nonphysical evidence that must be considered in the investigation. There are hazards, too, and these special hazards or concerns must be addressed if the homicide investigation is to be resolved successfully.

References

Bernick, B., & Spangler, J. (1985, September 16). Rovers kill up to 5,000 each year, experts say. *Deseret News*, p. A2.

Egger, S. (1984). A working definition of serial murder and the reduction of linkage blindness. *Journal of Police Science and Administration, 12*(3), 348-357.

Holmes, R. (1988). A model of personal violence. *Kentucky Research Bulletin, 2,* 1-5.

Holmes, R., & Holmes, S. (1996). *Profiling violent crimes: An investigative tool* (2nd ed.). Thousand Oaks, CA: Sage.

Holmes, R. & Holmes, S. (1998). *Serial Murder, 2nd ed.* Thousand Oaks, CA: Sage.

Levin, J., & Fox, J. (1985). *Mass murder: America's growing menace.* New York: Plenum.

Lindsey, R. (1984, January 21). Officials cite a rise in killers who roam U.S. for victims. *New York Times*, pp. 1, 7.

Michaud, S., & Aynesworth, H. (1983). *The only living witness.* New York: Signet.

Murder by number. (1993). CNN documentary.

Rule, A. (1980). *The stranger beside me.* New York: Signet.

Index

About the Editors

Ronald M. Holmes is Professor of Justice Administration at the University of Louisville. He is the author of several books, including *Sex Crimes, Profiling Violent Crimes, Murder in America, Serial Murder,* and *Criminology: Theory, Research, and Policy.* Dr. Holmes is also the author of more than 50 articles in journals and periodicals. He is a psychological profiler and has profiled more than 375 murder and rape cases for police departments across the United States. He has lectured in the United States and Europe on sex crimes and homicide investigation. Dr. Holmes is also the vice president of the National Center for the Study of Unresolved Homicides, Inc., and of the American Institute of Criminal Justice. He received his doctorate from Indiana University.

Stephen T. Holmes is an assistant professor at the University of Central Florida. Prior to this position, he was a social systems analyst for the National Institute of Justice in Washington, DC. He co-authored, with Ronald Holmes, *Profiling Violent Crimes* and *Murder in America.* Dr. Holmes received his PhD from the University of Cincinnati.

About the Contributors

Andrew Bolin is a research assistant at the University of Tampa. His interests lie in the creation and enforcement of the law and is criminal behavior. Mr. Bolin is a doctoral student in criminal justice.

Al C. Carlisle was the psychologist for the Utah State Prison until he recently retired. He was at one time the psychologist for such inmates as Gary Gilmore, Ted Bundy, and Arthur Bishop. He has also interviewed serial killers such as Westly Dodd and others. Carlisle at the present time is devoting his time counseling violent juvenile offenders and writing.

Joseph A. Davis is the Executive Director for the Center for Applied Forensic-Behavioral Sciences, and an adjunct professor of Forensic Studies and Crime Analysis at California State University at Fullerton and at San Diego State University. For the last decade, he has taught and specialized in investigative-forensic psychology and applied criminology. His professional and research interests focus on mental illness and violent crime, forensic-behavioral sciences, the criminal investigative analysis process (profiling), questionable/equivocal death investigation, stalking, sex crimes, serial, mass and spree homicide, and paraphilias.

James E. DeBurger is professor emeritus of sociology at the University of Louisville. While a professor of sociology at Louisville, DeBurger had a research interest in religion and family studies and published widely in sociological journals dealing with such topics. He retired five years ago, but he has still pursued his interest in religion and has visited multiple historical religious locations in his research.

Robert Hale is an assistant professor of criminal justice at Southeastern Louisiana State University. He has published numerous articles dealing with violence and serial crimes in various journals including *The American Journal of Criminal Justice, The Journal of Contemporary Criminal Justice* and *Sociological Spectrum*. He is also the author of a book on juveniles and the death penalty.

Eric Hickey is probably best known as the author of *Serial Killers and Their Victims*. Dr. Hickey is well-known and well-respected as an expert on serial murder. He has conducted interviews with several serial killers in his research. He is published widely in this area. Because of his expertise, Dr. Hickey is widely sought after for his knowledge of serial crimes by the media including national and international television productions. He is presently an associate professor of criminal justice at California State University at Fresno. Prior to coming to his present teaching position, Dr. Hickey was in the criminology department at Ball State University.

Philip Jenkins is the author of *Using Homicide: The Social Construction of Murder*. Dr. Jenkins is a professor at The Pennsylvania State University. Dr. Jenkins has authored widely on homicide and serial murder and is widely respected as a scholar on criminal justice topics. His publications include *A History of Wales 1536-1900* and *Intimate Enemies: Moral Panics in Contemporary Great Britain* as well as numerous articles in historical and criminal justice/criminological journals.

Thomas O'Reilly-Fleming is Professor of Sociology at the University of Windsor, Ontario. He is a widely pulished and recognized expert in serial murder, mass murder, and homicide theory.

Sgt. David W. Rivers is the commanding officer of the Cold Case Unit for the Metro-Date (Florida) Sheriff's Office. A twenty-five year veteran of the police department, Sgt. Rivers has been a patrol officer and a homicide officer, and was instrumental in developing one of America's finest Cold Case Units. A consultant to various police departments across the United States and several foreign countries, he has lectured on homicide investigation throughout our country as well as Canada, England, and The Netherlands. He is also a consultant to MGM Studio on unresolved homicides, and he is also the President of the National Center for the Study of Unresolved Homicides, Inc.

Kim Rossmo is a Detective Inspector in charge of the Vancouver Police Department's Geographic Profiling Unit. Almost a 20 year veteran, he has worked various assignments including patrol, emergency response, crime prevention, organized crime intelligence, and offender profiling. He holds a Ph.D. in criminology from Simon Friseur University where he teaches courses on profiling, serial murder, environment criminology, and problem-oriented policing. He is currently Executive Vice-President of the Canadian Police Association.